WONDER
WOMAN

INTRODUCTION BY **GLORIA STEINEM**

INTERPRETIVE ESSAY BY **PHYLLIS CHESLER**

DESIGNED BY **BEA FEITLER**

A ***Ms.*** BOOK

PUBLISHED BY

HOLT, RINEHART AND WINSTON

AND WARNER BOOKS

NEW YORK

CHICAGO SAN FRANCISCO

A Ms. Book Published by Holt, Rinehart and Winston, Inc. and Warner Books, Inc.

Published simultaneously
in Canada by Holt, Rinehart and Winston of Canada, Limited.
ISBN: 0-03-005376-5
Library of Congress Catalog Card Number: 72-89654
First Edition
Printed in the United States of America

CONTENTS

AN INTRODUCTION BY

GLORIA STEINEM

COMIC BOOKS WERE NOT QUITE RESPECTABLE, WHICH WAS A LARGE PART OF THE REASON I READ THEM: UNDER THE COVERS WITH A FLASHLIGHT, IN THE CAR WHILE MY PARENTS TOLD ME I WAS RUINING MY EYES, IN A TREE OR SOME OTHER INACCESSIBLE SPOT; ANY PLACE THAT PROVIDED SWEET PRIVACY AND INDEPENDENCE. ALONG WITH CEREAL BOXES AND KETCHUP LABELS, THEY WERE THE PRIMERS THAT TAUGHT ME HOW TO READ. THEY WERE EVEN CHEAP ENOUGH TO BE THE FIRST ITEMS I COULD BUY ON MY OWN; A CUSTOMER WHOSE HEAD DIDN'T QUITE REACH THE COUNTER BUT WHOSE DIGNITY WAS GREATLY ENHANCED BY MAKING A SELECTION (USUALLY AFTER MUCH AGONIZING) AND OFFERING UP MONEY OF HER OWN.

IF AS I HAVE ALWAYS SUSPECTED CHILDREN ARE SIMPLY SHORT PEOPLE—ANCIENT SPIRITS WHO HAPPEN TO BE LOCKED UP IN BODIES THAT AREN'T BIG ENOUGH OR SKILLFUL ENOUGH TO COPE WITH THE WORLD—THEN THE SUPERHUMAN FEATS IN COMIC BOOKS AND FAIRY TALES BECOME LOGICAL AND NECESSARY. IT'S SATISFYING FOR ANYONE TO HAVE HEROES WHO CAN SEE THROUGH WALLS OR LEAP OVER SKYSCRAPERS IN A SINGLE BOUND. BUT IT'S ESPECIALLY SATISFYING IF OUR WORLDVIEW CONSISTS MOSTLY OF KNEES, AND TYING OUR SHOES IS STILL AN EXERCISE IN FRUSTRATION.

THE TROUBLE IS THAT THE COMIC BOOK PERFORMERS OF SUCH SUPERHUMAN FEATS—AND EVEN OF ONLY DIMLY COMPETENT ONES—ARE ALMOST ALWAYS HEROES. LITERALLY. THE FEMALE CHILD IS LEFT TO BELIEVE THAT, EVEN WHEN HER BODY IS AS GROWN-UP AS HER SPIRIT, SHE WILL STILL BE IN THE CHILDLIKE ROLE OF HELPING WITH MINOR TASKS, APPRECIATING MEN'S ACCOMPLISHMENTS, AND BEING SO INCOMPETENT AND PASSIVE THAT SHE CAN ONLY HOPE SOME MAN CAN COME TO HER RESCUE. OF COURSE, RESCUE AND PROTECTION ARE COMFORTING, EVEN EXHILARATING EXPERIENCES THAT SHOULD BE AND OFTEN ARE SHARED BY MEN AND BOYS. EVEN IN COMIC BOOKS, THE HERO IS FREQUENTLY CALLED ON TO PROTECT HIS OWN KIND IN ADDITION TO HELPLESS WOMEN. BUT DEPENDENCY AND ZERO ACCOMPLISHMENTS GET VERY DULL AS A STEADY DIET. THE ONLY OPTION FOR A GIRL READER IS TO IDENTIFY WITH THE MALE CHARACTERS—PRETTY DIFFICULT, EVEN IN THE ANDROGYNOUS YEARS OF CHILDHOOD. IF SHE CAN'T DO THAT, SHE FACES LIMITED PROSPECTS: AN "IDEAL" LIFE OF SITTING AROUND LIKE A TECHNICOLOR CLOTHES HORSE, GETTING INTO JAMS WITH VILLAINS, AND SAYING THINGS LIKE "OH, SUPERMAN! I'LL ALWAYS BE GRATEFUL TO YOU," EVEN AS HER HERO GOES OFF TO BIGGER AND BETTER ADVENTURES. IT HARDLY SEEMS WORTH LEARNING TO TIE OUR SHOES.

I'M HAPPY TO SAY THAT I WAS RESCUED FROM THIS PLIGHT AT ABOUT THE AGE OF SEVEN OR EIGHT; RESCUED (GREAT HERA!) BY A WOMAN. NOT ONLY WAS SHE AS WISE AS ATHENA AND AS LOVELY AS APHRODITE, SHE HAD THE SPEED OF MERCURY AND THE STRENGTH OF HERCULES. OF COURSE, BEING AN AMAZON, SHE HAD A HEAD START ON SUCH ACCOMPLISHMENTS, BUT SHE HAD EARNED THEM IN A HUMAN WAY BY TRAINING IN GREEK-STYLE CONTESTS OF DEXTERITY AND SPEED WITH HER AMAZON SISTERS. (SOMEHOW IT ALWAYS SEEMED BORING TO ME THAT SUPERMAN WAS A CREATURE FROM ANOTHER PLANET, AND THEREFORE HAD BULLET-PROOF SKIN, X-RAY VISION, AND THE POWER TO FLY. WHERE WAS THE CONTEST?) THIS BEAUTIFUL AMAZON DID HAVE SOME FANTASTIC GADGETS TO HELP HER: AN INVISIBLE PLANE THAT CARRIED HER THROUGH DIMENSIONS OF TIME AND SPACE, A GOLDEN MAGIC LASSO, AND BULLET-PROOF BRACELETS. BUT SHE STILL HAD TO GET TO THE PLANE, THROW THE LASSO WITH ACCURACY, AND BE AGILE ENOUGH TO CATCH BULLETS ON THE STEEL-ENCLOSED WRISTS.

HER CREATOR HAD ALSO SEEN STRAIGHT INTO MY HEART AND UNDERSTOOD THE SECRET FEARS OF VIOLENCE HIDDEN THERE. NO LONGER DID I HAVE TO PRETEND TO LIKE THE "POW!" AND "CRUNCH!" STYLE OF CAPTAIN MARVEL OR THE GREEN HORNET. NO LONGER DID I HAVE NIGHTMARES AFTER READING GHOULISH COMICS FILLED WITH TORTURE AND MAYHEM, COMICS MADE ALL THE MORE HORRIFYING BY THEIR REAL-LIFE SETTING IN WORLD WAR II. (IT WAS A TIME WHEN LEATHER-CLAD NAZIS WERE MARCHING IN THE NEWS-

DIANA PRINCE

REELS *AND* IN THE COMICS, AND THE BLOOD ON THE PAGES SEEMED FRIGHTENINGLY REAL.) HERE WAS A HEROIC PERSON WHO MIGHT CONQUER WITH FORCE, BUT ONLY A FORCE THAT WAS TEMPERED BY LOVE AND JUSTICE. SHE CONVERTED HER ENEMIES MORE OFTEN THAN NOT. AND IF THEY WERE DESTROYED, THEY DID IT TO THEMSELVES, USUALLY IN SOME UNBLOODY ACCIDENT.

SHE WAS BEAUTIFUL, BRAVE, AND EXPLICITLY OUT TO CHANGE "A WORLD TORN BY THE HATREDS AND WARS OF MEN."

SHE WAS WONDER WOMAN.

LOOKING BACK NOW AT THESE WONDER WOMAN STORIES FROM THE '40'S, I AM AMAZED BY THE STRENGTH OF THEIR FEMINIST MESSAGE. ONE TYPICAL STORY CENTERS ON PRUDENCE, A YOUNG PIONEER IN THE DAYS OF THE AMERICAN FRONTIER. (WONDER WOMAN IS TRANSPORTED THERE BY HER INVISIBLE PLANE, OF COURSE, WHICH ALSO SERVED AS A TIME MACHINE.) RESCUED BY WONDER WOMAN, PRUDENCE REALIZES HER OWN WORTH AND THE WORTH OF ALL WOMEN: "I'VE LEARNED MY LESSON," SHE SAYS PROUDLY IN THE FINAL SCENE. "FROM NOW ON, I'LL RELY ON MYSELF, NOT ON A MAN." IN YET ANOTHER EPISODE, WONDER WOMAN HERSELF SAYS, "I CAN NEVER LOVE A DOMINANT MAN WHO IS STRONGER THAN I AM." AND THROUGHOUT THE STRIPS, IT IS ONLY THE DESTRUCTIVE, CRIMINAL WOMAN–THE WOMAN WHO HAS BOUGHT THE WHOLE IDEA THAT MALE MEANS AGGRESSION AND FEMALE MEANS SUBMITTING–WHO SAYS "GIRLS WANT SUPERIOR MEN TO BOSS THEM AROUND."

MANY OF THE PLOTS REVOLVE AROUND EVIL MEN WHO TREAT WOMEN AS INFERIOR BEINGS. IN THE END, ALL ARE BROUGHT TO THEIR KNEES AND MADE TO RECOGNIZE WOMEN'S STRENGTH AND VALUE. SOME OF THE STORIES FOCUS ON WEAK WOMEN WHO ARE DESTRUCTIVE AND CONFUSED. THESE MISLED FEMALES ARE CONVERTED TO SELF-RELIANCE AND SELF-RESPECT THROUGH THE EXAMPLE OF WONDER WOMAN. THE MESSAGE OF THE STRIPS IS SOMETIMES INCONSISTENT AND ALWAYS OVERSIMPLIFIED (THESE ARE, AFTER ALL, COMICS), BUT IT IS STILL A PASSABLE VERSION OF THE TRUISMS THAT WOMEN ARE REDISCOVERING TODAY: THAT WOMEN ARE FULL HUMAN BEINGS; THAT WE CANNOT LOVE OTHERS UNTIL WE LOVE OURSELVES; THAT LOVE AND RESPECT CAN ONLY EXIST BETWEEN EQUALS.

WONDER WOMAN'S FAMILY OF AMAZONS ON PARADISE ISLAND, HER BAND OF COLLEGE GIRLS IN AMERICA, AND HER EFFORTS TO SAVE INDIVIDUAL WOMEN ARE ALL WELCOME EXAMPLES OF WOMEN WORKING TOGETHER AND CARING ABOUT EACH OTHER'S WELFARE. THE IDEA OF SUCH COOPERATION MAY NOT SEEM PARTICULARLY REVOLUTIONARY TO THE MALE READER: MEN ARE ROUTINELY DEPICTED AS WORKING WELL TOGETHER. BUT WOMEN KNOW HOW RARE AND THEREFORE EXHILARATING THE IDEA OF SISTERHOOD REALLY IS.

WONDER WOMAN'S MOTHER, QUEEN HIPPOLYTE, OFFERS YET ANOTHER WELCOME EXAMPLE TO YOUNG GIRLS IN SEARCH OF A STRONG IDENTITY. QUEEN HIPPOLYTE FOUNDS NATIONS, WAGES WAR TO PROTECT PARADISE ISLAND, AND SENDS HER DAUGHTER OFF TO FIGHT THE FORCES OF EVIL IN THE WORLD. PERHAPS MOST IMPRESSIVE IN AN AGE FRAUGHT WITH FREUDIAN SHIBBOLETHS, SHE ALSO MARSHALS HER QUEENLY STRENGTH TO PROTECT HER DAUGHTER IN BAD TIMES. HOW MANY GIRL CHILDREN GREW TO ADULTHOOD WITH NO EXPERIENCE OF A COURAGEOUS AND WORLDLY MOTHER, EXCEPT IN THESE SLENDER STORIES? HOW MANY ADULT WOMEN DISDAIN THE BIRTH OF A FEMALE CHILD, BELIEVE IT IS "BETTER" TO BEAR MALE CHILDREN, AND FEAR THE COMPETITION AND JEALOUSY THEY HAVE BEEN CONDITIONED TO BELIEVE IS "NATURAL" TO A MOTHER AND DAUGHTER? FEMINISM IS JUST BEGINNING TO UNCOVER THE SENSE OF ANGER AND LOSS IN GIRLS WHOSE MOTHERS HAD NO POWER TO PROTECT THEM IN THE WORLD, AND SO TRAINED THEM TO BE VICTIMS, OR LEFT THEM TO IDENTIFY WITH THEIR FATHERS IF THEY HAD ANY AMBITIONS OUTSIDE THE TRADITIONAL FEMALE ROLE.

WONDER WOMAN SYMBOLIZES MANY OF THE VALUES OF THE WOMEN'S CULTURE THAT FEMINISTS ARE

A QUICK CHANGE

NOW TRYING TO INTRODUCE INTO THE MAINSTREAM: STRENGTH AND SELF-RELIANCE FOR WOMEN; SISTERHOOD AND MUTUAL SUPPORT AMONG WOMEN; PEACEFULNESS AND ESTEEM FOR HUMAN LIFE; A DIMINISHMENT BOTH OF "MASCULINE" AGGRESSION AND OF THE BELIEF THAT VIOLENCE IS THE ONLY WAY OF SOLVING CONFLICTS.

OF COURSE, THE WONDER WOMAN STORIES ARE NOT ADMIRABLE IN ALL WAYS. MANY FEMINIST PRINCIPLES ARE DISTORTED OR IGNORED. THUS, WOMEN ARE CONVERTED AND SAVED. MAD SCIENTISTS, FOREIGN SPIES, CRIMINALS, AND OTHER MALE VILLAINS ARE REGULARLY BROUGHT TO THE POINT OF RENOUNCING VIOLENCE AND, MORE OFTEN, OF SAYING, "YOU'RE RIGHT, WONDER WOMAN. I'LL NEVER MAKE THE MISTAKE OF THINKING WOMEN ARE INFERIOR AGAIN." IS THE READER SUPPOSED TO CONCLUDE WOMEN ARE SUPERIOR? THE WONDER WOMAN STORIES NOT ONLY DEPICT WOMEN AS CULTURALLY DIFFERENT (IN WAYS THAT ARE SOMETIMES CONSTRUCTIVE AND SOMETIMES NOT), THEY ALSO HINT THAT WOMEN ARE BIOLOGICALLY, AND THEREFORE IMMUTABLY, SUPERIOR TO MEN.

FEW MODERN FEMINISTS WOULD AGREE. THERE ARE AS YET NO PERFECTLY CULTURE-FREE TESTS TO PROVE TO US WHICH TRAITS COME FROM CONDITIONING AND WHICH DO NOT, BUT THE CONSENSUS SEEMS TO BE THAT SOCIETY, NOT BIOLOGY, ASSIGNS SOME HUMAN TRAITS TO MALES AND OTHERS TO FEMALES. WOMEN HAVE SUFFERED FROM BEING TAUGHT TO DEVELOP WHAT SOCIETY CONSIDERS THE LESS-VALUED TRAITS OF HUMANITY, BUT THIS DOESN'T MEAN WE WANT TO SWITCH TO A SOLE CLAIM ON THE "MORE VALUABLE" ONES EITHER. THAT MIGHT ACCOMPLISH NOTHING MORE THAN CHANGING PLACES WITH MEN IN THE HIERARCHY. MOST FEMINIST PHILOSOPHY SUPPOSES THAT THE HIERARCHY ITSELF MUST BE ELIMINATED; THAT INDIVIDUALS WHO ARE FREE OF ROLES ASSIGNED BECAUSE OF SEX OR RACE WILL ALSO BE FREE TO DEVELOP THE FULL RANGE OF HUMAN QUALITIES. IT'S THE MULTITUDINOUS DIFFERENCES IN INDIVIDUALS THAT COUNT, NOT THE LOCALIZED DIFFERENCES OF SEX OR RACE.

FOR PSYCHOLOGIST WILLIAM MOULTON MARSTON—WHO, UNDER THE PEN NAME OF "CHARLES MOULTON," CREATED WONDER WOMAN—FEMALES WERE SOMETIMES ROMANTICIZED AS BIOLOGICALLY AND UNCHANGEABLY SUPERIOR. "WOMEN," HE WROTE, "REPRESENT LOVE; MEN REPRESENT FORCE. MAN'S USE OF FORCE WITHOUT LOVE BRINGS EVIL AND UNHAPPINESS. WONDER WOMAN PROVES THAT WOMEN ARE SUPERIOR TO MEN BECAUSE THEY HAVE LOVE IN ADDITION TO FORCE." IF THAT'S THE CASE, THEN WE'RE STUCK WITH YET ANOTHER SOCIAL ORDER BASED ON BIRTH.

FOR THE PURPOSES OF MOST WONDER WOMAN STORIES, HOWEVER, THE CLASSIC ARGUMENT OF NATURE VERSUS NURTURE IS A MERE INTELLECTUAL QUIBBLE. JUST HELPING WOMEN TO RESPECT THEMSELVES, TO USE THEIR STRENGTH AND REFUSE DOMINATION BY MEN IS TIME-CONSUMING ENOUGH: WONDER WOMAN RARELY HAS THE LEISURE TO HINT AT WHAT THE FUTURE SOCIAL ORDER OUGHT TO BE. AS FOR MEN, WE DO GET THE IDEA THAT THEY HAVE SOME HOPE—EVEN IF VAGUE—OF COLLECTIVE REDEMPTION. "THIS MAN'S WORLD OF YOURS," EXPLAINS WONDER WOMAN, "WILL NEVER BE WITHOUT PAIN AND SUFFERING UNTIL IT LEARNS RESPECT FOR HUMAN RIGHTS." PUT IN MORE POSITIVE TERMS, THIS DOES SEEM TO INDICATE THAT HUMANIZED MEN WILL HAVE FULL MEMBERSHIP IN THE NEW SOCIETY.

SOME OF THE WONDER WOMAN STORIES PREACH PATRIOTISM IN A FALSE WAY, BUT MUCH OF THE BLAME RESTS WITH HISTORY. WONDER WOMAN WAS BORN IN 1941, JUST ABOUT THE TIME THAT WORLD WAR II BECAME A REALITY FOR MOST AMERICANS, AND SHE THEREFORE HAD TO SPEND MUCH OF HER TIME PROTECTING THIS COUNTRY FROM FOREIGN THREATS. USUALLY, THAT TASK BOILED DOWN TO PROVING THAT WOMEN COULD BE JUST AS BRAVE AND LOYAL AS MEN IN THE SERVICE OF THEIR COUNTRY. EVEN WHEN HER ADVENTURES TOOK PLACE IN OTHER COUNTRIES OR AT OTHER TIMES, THEY STILL INVARIABLY ENDED WITH SIMPLISTIC COMMERCIALS ABOUT DEMOCRACY. ALTHOUGH WONDER WOMAN WAS SHOCKED BY AMERICA'S UN-

THE INVISIBLE PLANE

JUST PATRIARCHAL SYSTEM—A SHOCK SHE RECORDED ON HER ARRIVAL HERE FROM PARADISE ISLAND—SHE NEVER HAD MUCH OPPORTUNITY TO FOLLOW UP ON IT; A NATION MOBILIZED FOR WAR IS NOT A NATION PREPARED TO ACCEPT CRITICISM. IN FACT, HER COSTUME WAS PATTERNED AFTER THE AMERICAN FLAG, AND HER WARTIME ADVENTURES SOMETIMES HAD HIGHLY JINGOISTIC AND EVEN RACIST OVERTONES, ESPECIALLY WHEN SHE WAS DEALING WITH JAPANESE AND GERMANS.

COMPARED TO THE OTHER COMIC BOOK CHARACTERS OF THE PERIOD, HOWEVER, WONDER WOMAN IS STILL A RELIEF. MARSTON INVENTED HER AS A COUNTER TO THE VIOLENCE AND "BLOODCURDLING MASCULINITY" THAT PERVADED MOST COMIC BOOKS, AND HE REMAINED TRUE TO HIS PURPOSE. WONDER WOMAN AND HER SISTERS WERE ALLOWED TO USE VIOLENCE, BUT ONLY IN SELF-DEFENSE AND ONLY IF IT STOPPED SHORT OF ACTUALLY KILLING SOMEONE. MOST GROUP CONFLICTS BETWEEN MEN AND WOMEN WERE SET NOT IN AMERICA, BUT IN A MYTHOLOGICAL PAST. THUS MARS, THE GOD OF WAR, PERIODICALLY ENDANGERED THE AMAZON COMMUNITY AND SOMETIMES TRIED TO DISARM QUEEN HIPPOLYTE THROUGH THE RUSES OF LOVE. MARS, OF COURSE, WAS THE "HEAVY." HE PREACHED THAT WOMEN "ARE THE NATURAL SPOILS OF WAR" AND MUST REMAIN AT HOME, THE HELPLESS SLAVES OF THE MALE VICTORS. MARSTON USED MARS AS THE SYMBOL OF EVERYTHING WONDER WOMAN MUST FIGHT AGAINST, BUT HE ALSO GAVE THE GOD OF WAR A RATIONALE FOR HIS BELIEFS THAT WAS REALLY THE FEMALE SUPERIORITY ARGUMENT ALL OVER AGAIN: IF WOMEN WERE ALLOWED TO BECOME WARRIORS LIKE THE AMAZONS, THEY WOULD GROW STRONGER THAN MEN, AND PUT AN END TO WAR. WHAT FUTURE FOR AN UNEMPLOYED GOD?

THE INCONSISTENCIES IN WONDER WOMAN'S PHILOSOPHY ARE ESPECIALLY APPARENT IN HER LOVE LIFE. IT IS CONFUSED, TO SAY THE LEAST. SOMETIMES HER ADVENTURES WITH STEVE, THE PILOT SHE IS SUPPOSEDLY "IN LOVE" WITH, BEAR A FEMINIST MESSAGE. AND SOMETIMES THEY SIMPER AND GO CONVENTIONAL IN A WAY THAT CONTRADICTS EVERYTHING THAT HAS GONE BEFORE. IN HER AMERICAN DISGUISE AS MILD-MANNERED DIANA PRINCE (A CLEAR STEAL FROM SUPERMAN), SHE PLAYS THE CLASSIC FEMININE ROLE: SECRETARY, NURSE, AND WORSHIPFUL, UNREQUITED SIDEKICK TO STEVE. THE IMPLICIT MORAL IS THAT, AT LEAST AS WONDER WOMAN, SHE CAN LOVE ONLY AN EQUAL. BUT AN EQUAL NEVER TURNS UP, AND SOMETIMES SHE LOSES HER GRIP ON HERSELF AND FALLS FOR THE MASCULINE NOTION THAT THERE MUST BE A PERMANENT WINNER AND A PERMANENT LOSER, A CONQUEROR AND A CONQUERED. "SOME GIRLS LOVE TO HAVE A MAN STRONGER THAN THEY ARE TO MAKE THEM DO THINGS," SHE MUSES ALOUD. "DO I LIKE IT? I DON'T KNOW, IT'S SORT OF THRILLING. BUT ISN'T IT MORE FUN TO MAKE A MAN OBEY?"

I REMEMBER BEING WORRIED BY THESE CONTRADICTIONS. HOW COULD WONDER WOMAN BE INTERESTED IN STEVE, WHO SEEMED SO WEAK AND SO BORING? DID WOMEN REALLY HAVE TO LIVE IN A COMMUNITY BY THEMSELVES—A SEPARATE COUNTRY LIKE PARADISE ISLAND—IN ORDER TO BE BOTH HAPPY AND COURAGEOUS? THE VERY FACT THAT THE IDEAL WAS AN ISLAND—INSULAR, ISOLATED, SELF-CONTAINED, CUT-OFF—BOTH PLEASED AND BOTHERED ME. AND WHY, WHEN SHE CHOSE AN EARTHLY DISGUISE, DID WONDER WOMAN HAVE TO PICK SUCH A LOSER? HOW COULD SHE BEAR TO BE LIKE DIANA PRINCE? DID THAT MEAN THAT ALL WOMEN REALLY HAD TO DISGUISE THEIR TRUE SELVES IN WEAK FEMININE STEREOTYPES IN ORDER TO SURVIVE?

BUT ALL THESE DOUBTS PALED BESIDE THE RELIEF, THE SWEET VENGEANCE, THE TOE-WRIGGLING PLEASURE OF READING ABOUT A WOMAN WHO WAS STRONG, BEAUTIFUL, COURAGEOUS, AND A FIGHTER FOR SOCIAL JUSTICE. A WOMAN WHO STRODE FORTH, STOPPING WARS AND KILLING WITH ONE HAND, DISTRIBUTING LARGESSE AND COMPASSIONATE AID WITH THE OTHER. A WONDER WOMAN.

IN 1947, WILLIAM MARSTON DIED, LEAVING HIS HEROINE IN THE HANDS OF WRITERS WHO DIDN'T REALLY

WONDER WOMAN & STEVE

UNDERSTAND HER SPIRIT. GRADUALLY, HER FEMINIST ORIENTATION BEGAN TO WANE. SHE BECAME SIMULTANEOUSLY MORE SUBMISSIVE TO MEN. I DON'T REMEMBER THE TRANSITION VERY WELL, POSSIBLY BECAUSE I MYSELF WAS ON THE VERGE OF ADOLESCENCE AND WAS THEREFORE PUTTING COMIC BOOKS BEHIND ME. OR POSSIBLY BECAUSE THE COMPARATIVELY FREE YEARS OF MY CHILDHOOD WERE AT AN END. LIKE WONDER WOMAN, THE FULL IMPACT OF THE FEMININE ROLE WAS BEGINNING TO CLOSE AROUND ME. NOW I WAS THIRTEEN AND MADE TO SEE THAT THE IDEA OF ACCOMPLISHING ANYTHING ON MY OWN WAS AT BEST ECCENTRIC AND AT WORST IMPOSSIBLE. RECOGNITION AND STATUS THROUGH MEN WAS THE BEST POSSIBILITY; IT WAS ALSO SOCIALLY REWARDED AND SOCIALLY ENFORCED. BOTH WONDER WOMAN AND I FELL INTO SOME VERY HARD TIMES IN THE '50'S.

LOOKING AT HER MOST RECENT ADVENTURES IS EVEN MORE DISCOURAGING. BY 1968, SHE HAD GIVEN UP HER MAGIC LASSO, HER BRACELETS, HER INVISIBLE PLANE, AND ALL HER SUPERHUMAN AMAZONIAN POWERS. SHE HAD BECOME DIANA PRINCE, A MERE MORTAL WHO WALKED ABOUT IN BOUTIQUE CLOTHES AND TOOK THE ADVICE OF A MALE MASTERMIND NAMED "I CHING." SHE STILL HAD ADVENTURES AND SHE HAD LEARNED SOMETHING ABOUT KARATE, BUT ANY ATTRACTIVE MAN COULD DISARM HER. SHE WAS A FEMALE JAMES BOND—BUT FAR MORE BORING SINCE SHE WAS DENIED HIS SEXUAL FREEDOM. SHE HAD BECOME A SIMPLEMINDED "GOOD GIRL."

IN 1973, WONDER WOMAN COMICS WILL BE BORN AGAIN; I HOPE WITH THE FEMINISM AND STRENGTH OF THE ORIGINAL WONDER WOMAN—*MY* WONDER WOMAN—RESTORED. BUT REGARDLESS OF HER FUTURE, THESE SELECTIONS FROM THE ORIGINAL ADVENTURES OF THE GOLDEN FORTIES WILL REMAIN CLASSICS FOR CHILDREN, BOYS AS WELL AS GIRLS. AND PERHAPS FOR MANY HEROINE-STARVED AND NOSTALGIC GROWN-UPS AS WELL. IF WE HAD ALL READ MORE ABOUT WONDER WOMAN AND LESS ABOUT DICK AND JANE, THE NEW WAVE OF THE FEMINIST REVOLUTON MIGHT HAVE HAPPENED LESS PAINFULLY AND SOONER.

WONDER WOMAN IS A COMIC BOOK CHARACTER. SHE AND HER AMAZON SISTERS ARE FICTIONAL CREATIONS. INDEED, AMAZONS HAVE GENERALLY BEEN CONSIDERED FIGMENTS OF THE IMAGINATION, PERHAPS THE MYTHOLOGICAL EVIDENCE OF MAN'S FEAR OF WOMAN. YET THERE IS A TENTATIVE BUT GROWING BODY OF ANTHROPOLOGICAL AND ARCHEOLOGICAL EVIDENCE TO SUPPORT THE THEORY THAT AMAZON SOCIETIES WERE REAL; THEY DID EXIST. GERMAN AND BRAZILIAN SCIENTISTS EXPLORING THE JUNGLES OF BRAZIL, FOR INSTANCE, RECENTLY CAME UPON THE CAVES OF WHAT APPEARS TO HAVE BEEN AN ALL-FEMALE SOCIETY. THE CAVES ARE STRIKINGLY DEVOID OF THE USUAL PHALLIC DESIGN AND THEME; THEY FEATURE, INSTEAD, THE TRIANGULAR FEMALE SYMBOL. (THE ONLY CAVE THAT DOES BEAR MALE DESIGNS IS BELIEVED TO HAVE BEEN THE COPULATORIUM.)

THOUGH THE BRAZILIAN RESEARCH IS STILL TOO INDEFINITE FOR CONCLUSIONS, THERE ARE MANY EVIDENCES OF THE EXISTENCE OF AMAZON SOCIETIES IN ALL PARTS OF THE WORLD. DR. PHYLLIS CHESLER DETAILS THEM IN THIS BOOK TO MIND-BLOWING EFFECT AND WITH GREAT SCHOLARSHIP. BEING A WRITER, NOT A SCIENTIST TIED TO PROVEN FACT, I HAVE FUSED THE SOMETIMES CONTRADICTORY VERSIONS OF AMAZONIA INTO ONE AMALGAM; INTO A STORY THAT SOUNDS RIGHT TO ME IN THE WAY THAT A DREAM INTERPRETATION OR A RACE-MEMORY SEEMS SUDDENLY, THUDDINGLY RIGHT AS IT STRIKES OFF OUR SUBCONSCIOUS. MUCH OF IT HAS BEEN PROVED, BUT I TELL IT AS A STORY.

ONCE UPON A TIME, THE MANY CULTURES OF THIS WORLD WERE ALL PART OF THE GYNOCRATIC AGE. PATERNITY HAD NOT YET BEEN DISCOVERED, AND IT WAS THOUGHT (AS IT STILL IS IN SOME TRIBAL CULTURES) THAT WOMEN BORE FRUIT LIKE TREES—WHEN THEY WERE RIPE. CHILDBIRTH WAS MYSTERIOUS. IT WAS VITAL. AND IT WAS ENVIED. WOMEN WERE WORSHIPPED BECAUSE OF IT, WERE CONSIDERED SUPERIOR BECAUSE OF IT. MEN PRAYED TO FEMALE GODS AND, IN THEIR RELIGIOUS

CEREMONIES, IMITATED THE ACT OF BIRTH (AS MANY TRIBESMEN STILL DO). IN SUCH A WORLD, THE ONLY CLEAR GROUPING WAS THAT OF MOTHERS AND CHILDREN. MEN WERE ON THE PERIPHERY—AN INTERCHANGEABLE BODY OF WORKERS FOR, AND WORSHIPPERS OF, THE FEMALE CENTER, THE PRINCIPLE OF LIFE.

THE DISCOVERY OF PATERNITY, OF SEXUAL CAUSE AND CHILDBIRTH EFFECT, WAS AS CATACLYSMIC FOR SOCIETY AS, SAY, THE DISCOVERY OF FIRE OR THE SHATTERING OF THE ATOM. GRADUALLY, THE IDEA OF MALE OWNERSHIP OF CHILDREN TOOK HOLD; WITH IT CAME THE IDEA OF PRIVATE PROPERTY THAT COULD BE PASSED DOWN TO CHILDREN. IF PATERNITY WAS TO BE UNQUESTIONED, THEN WOMEN HAD TO BE SEXUALLY RESTRICTED. THAT WAS THE ORIGIN OF MARRIAGE.

GYNOCRACY ALSO SUFFERED FROM THE PERIODIC INVASIONS OF NOMADIC TRIBES. GYNOCRACIES WERE PROBABLY STABLE AND PEACEFUL AGRICULTURAL SOCIETIES SINCE AGRICULTURE WAS SOMEWHAT MORE—THOUGH NOT TOTALLY—A FEMALE OCCUPATION. NOMADIC TRIBES SURVIVED BY HUNTING, WHICH WAS SOMEWHAT MORE—THOUGH NOT TOTALLY—A MALE OCCUPATION. THE CONFLICT BETWEEN THE HUNTERS AND THE GROWERS WAS REALLY THE CONFLICT BETWEEN MALE-DOMINATED AND FEMALE-DOMINATED CULTURES.

RESTRICTED BY NEW SYSTEMS OF MARRIAGE AS WELL AS BY OCCASIONAL PREGNANCIES, WOMEN GRADUALLY LOST THEIR FREEDOM, MYSTERY, AND SUPERIOR POSITION. FOR FIVE THOUSAND YEARS OR MORE, THE GYNOCRATIC AGE HAD FLOWERED IN PEACE AND PRODUCTIVITY. SLOWLY, IN VARYING STAGES AND IN DIFFERENT PARTS OF THE WORLD, THE SOCIAL ORDER WAS PAINFULLY REVERSED. WOMEN BECAME THE UNDERCLASS, MARKED BY THEIR VISIBLE DIFFERENCES REGARDLESS OF WHETHER THEY HAD CHILDREN. OFTEN, THE PATRIARCHAL TAKE-OVER OF FEMALE-DOMINATED SOCIETIES WAS ACCOMPLISHED VIOLENTLY. EVERYWHERE, FEAR OF GODDESSES, OF WOMEN'S MAGICAL PROCREATIVE POWERS, AND OF THE OLD RELIGIONS CAUSED MEN TO SUPPRESS THE OLD SOCIAL ORDER VERY CRUELLY INDEED.

SOME WOMEN RESISTED THE PATRIARCHAL AGE. THEY BANDED TOGETHER TO PROTECT THEIR FEMALE-CENTERED CULTURE AND RELIGIONS FROM A MORE VIOLENT, TRANSIENT, AND MALE-CENTERED WAY OF LIFE. MEN WERE DANGEROUS, TO BE TOLERATED ONLY DURING PERIODIC MATING CEREMONIES. THE WOMEN THEMSELVES BECAME ADEPT AT SELF-DEFENSE.

THESE WERE BACKLASH CULTURES, DOOMED BY THEIR OWN IMBALANCE. BUT THEY DID SURVIVE IN VARIOUS GROUPINGS ON EVERY CONTINENT FOR MANY THOUSANDS OF YEARS. WHY DON'T THEY TURN UP IN HISTORY? FOR ONE REASON, MOST OF THEIR EXISTENCE WAS LIVED IN THOSE THOUSANDS OF YEARS DISMISSED AS *PRE*HISTORY—THAT IS, PRELITERATE. THE FEW RECORDS THAT ARE AVAILABLE TO US WERE WRITTEN UNDER THE PATRIARCHAL ASSUMPTIONS OF A MUCH LATER AGE. EVEN ARCHEOLOGY AND ANTHROPOLOGY HAVE SUFFERED FROM THE FUNDAMENTAL, ALMOST SUBCONSCIOUS ASSUMPTION THAT MALE AND FEMALE ROLES AS WE SEE THEM IN THE PATRIARCHAL AGE ARE "NATURAL"; THEREFORE, THEY MUST HAVE BEEN THE SAME IN THE PREHISTORIC PAST. ONLY LATELY HAVE WE BEGUN TO QUESTION AND CHECK OUT THOSE ASSUMPTIONS. LARGE, STRONG, AND PRESUMABLY MALE SKELETONS FROM PREHISTORIC SITES, FOR INSTANCE, HAVE TURNED OUT ON CLOSER EXAMINATION TO BE FEMALE AFTER ALL.

PERHAPS THE MYSTERY STORY DR. CHESLER TRACES THROUGH HISTORY AND MYTHOLOGY IS SOON TO BE SOLVED. AFTER ALL, MYTHOLOGY IS A COLLECTIVE HUMAN MEMORY THAT HAS, ON OTHER OCCASIONS, TURNED OUT TO BE ACCURATE ABOUT INVASIONS, GREAT FLOODS, THE COLLISION OF STARS. THE AMAZON CULTURES MAY ALSO ONE DAY BE PROVEN AS FACT. MEANWHILE, THE FASCINATION THAT BRINGS THEM UP AS FANTASY AGAIN AND AGAIN MAY ITSELF BE SOME PSYCHIC EVIDENCE OF THEIR EXISTENCE.

IF SO, WONDER WOMAN BECOMES JUST ONE SMALL, ISOLATED OUTCROPPING OF A LARGER HUMAN MEMORY. AND THE GIRL CHILDREN WHO LOVE HER ARE RESPONDING TO ONE SMALL ECHO OF DREAMS AND CAPABILITIES IN THEIR OWN FORGOTTEN PAST.

THE AMAZON LEGACY

AN INTERPRETIVE ESSAY BY

PHYLLIS CHESLER

HELEN DINER: "Were there actually nations of fabulous women—mounted demons, a man-hating army with clanging weapons and awesome customs?"

INTERVIEWER: "Are you referring to successful female versions of patriarchy? Because a good many experts believe civilization was originally based on the mother-child relationship and that culture was, in that sense, a female invention—that the earliest cultures were matriarchal."

HELEN DINER: "No! I'm talking about physically powerful women, women who feared, used, exiled, and suppressed men—much as men have done to women. Amazons were as different from the earthy, fertile, chaste, and spiritual Great Mother figures as patriarchs. Amazon culture was neither serenely tolerant nor biologically based. Amazons conceded no separate existence to the active or male principle; they absorbed it and developed it in an androgynous fashion. And they reared only female children to full-fledged membership in the Amazon community."

INTERVIEWER: "You mean they were female chauvinists. I can't accept that women would ever, *could* ever do anything that violent, that unnatural, that unsatisfying. Women aren't physically strong enough. And men would never stand for it. But even if women could do it, they wouldn't want to. They'd be denying their own maternal instincts, their own need for love and security. And they'd be no better than men: They'd wage war, they'd worship their own bodies, they'd be sexually promiscuous, they'd be homosexuals. They'd be glorifying a perennial adolescence of adventure and selfishness."

PHYLLIS CHESLER: "Maybe so, but just as men have made quite an ideal out of adolescence and have insisted on redefining or rejecting maturity, so women might if forced to or given a chance. But that's not the real point: Amazons didn't reject motherhood or female control of security and sexuality any more than matriarchs did. They wanted to protect such female rights and add others—like adventure and leisure and poetry."

INTERVIEWER: "It doesn't matter anyway. Amazons never existed. They're just myths. We have no proof."

HELEN DINER: "Many of the most important discoveries of ancient cities and cultures—female-dominated Minoan Crete, for example—only came about because scholars took legends and myths seriously."

PHYLLIS CHESLER: "Myths are themselves a very important kind of proof. Myths preserve the history of human thought—dreams, nightmares, and memories—as well as the history of human deeds. And tangible proof aside, the legendary Amazons have been an almost universal male nightmare. Men have believed in them. Psychologically speaking, we don't fear something that doesn't exist, something that never happened, something that never could happen—any more than people forbid or regulate something no one wants to do anyway."

INTERVIEWER: "That may all be true, but I'd prefer having hard facts, especially now, when feminists are trying to resurrect culture heroines or role models where none have existed. Objectivity is essential when the atmosphere is so emotional, so angry, so—well, forgive me, so hysterical. If Amazons, or even matriarchs, really existed, why has objective science so little to say about them?"

JOHANN BACHOFEN: "When it seems impossible to explain a phenomenon, the only way out is to doubt and, ultimately, deny its existence. The critics speak of improbability, but probabilities change with the times. What is out of tune with the spirit of one culture stage is in harmony with that of the next; what seems improbable in one becomes probable in the other."

INTERVIEWER: "Then there's no such thing as objective truth?"

PHYLLIS CHESLER: "The truth does seem to change according to who is looking for it—and why."

INTERVIEWER: "And now women are looking for some lost Golden Age and will seize on a bunch of female John Waynes as real in order to justify or glorify their own desires for revenge."

A re-created conversation drawn from Helen Diner's *Mothers and Amazons* and Johann Bachofen's *Mother-Right* and from many conversations between the author and her contemporaries.

PHYLLIS CHESLER: "Not revenge: self-defense, pride, self-determination."

INTERVIEWER: "Isn't it really all motivated by romantic notions? Women are, after all, very romantic, and the vision of powerful women captures the imagination. Just think of 100,000 women massed on a battlefield or of 50,000 women maintaining global peace. It's romantic on a really grand scale."

JOHANN BACHOFEN: "Romantic is hardly the word. Every change in the relation between the sexes is attended by bloody events. Wherever an intensification of female power occurs, it presupposes a previous degradation of women."

INTERVIEWER: "Then you're saying that first women dominate and oppress men and then men take revenge and oppress women—who, in turn, take revenge and oppress men once more. When does it end?"

PHYLLIS CHESLER: "What you've just said about human history may be so, but you make it sound like a conspiracy or a battle fought by the same rotten married couple since time began: Mr. Good against Mrs. Evil, Mrs. Love against Mr. War. The pendulum swings of history—if there were any—were probably more impersonal and complicated than that."

INTERVIEWER: "All right. Let's get to some impersonal facts. How large was that Amazon army? Where did Amazons live and how did they fight? What did they do for sex—who took care of the children? When did they live? And what happened to all those Great Mother cultures?"

AMAZONS: THE UNIVERSAL MALE NIGHTMARE

Men have written about and believed in Amazons just as they have believed in the existence of an earthly Paradise: as something marvelous and incredible, as an unbelievable and yet remembered phenomenon. From century to century and on all continents, men have described Amazons and Amazon customs with enough fear, guilt, and confusion to render them "legendary." Amazons are a universal male nightmare, exorcised by ridicule or disbelief. Or by subtle transformation: Behind each of these fiercely heroic and man-like warriors, behind each of these original "Belle Dames Sans Merci," is the most wondrous Mother of them all, the most powerful of Goddess-saviours, more beautiful and more compassionate than any male divinity. Precisely in their moments of greatest fear or murderousness, men crave grace, demanding to be rescued from evil by women, by the biological "other."

Many ancient Greek and Roman (male) historians, geographers, statesmen, philosophers, and poets described Amazons in Africa, in the European Caucasus, and in Greece itself. French, Portuguese, and Spanish explorers in the sixteenth and seventeenth centuries returned from North and South America, from Eastern Europe, Russia, and Africa with "astonishing" tales of female warriors, queens, and priestesses and with the insistent reports, given by natives, of a legendary Amazon state—often just beyond the next river or mountain; more often, in a region that the guide-informant was afraid to explore.

We have no tangible written record of the deeds and thoughts of legendary Amazon societies. Either such records never existed or they were completely destroyed. Perhaps they have yet to be unearthed. What we know about Amazons come to us only through men—and men who wrote, traveled, fought, and painted in fiercely patriarchal cultures. As such, it is remarkable that any "proof" of Amazons exists at all. What proof does exist must be viewed as a combination of phobic male denials and hasty guilty admissions, as a somewhat distorted and suppressed record of both fact and feeling, and as an inevitably romantic confusion of matriarchal and Amazon themes—a justifiable confusion, perhaps. Thus, for example, the mythical or magical prowess attributed to Amazon archers (especially by the Greeks) may have been a way of minimizing military defeats that resulted from the initially superior Asiatic weaponry Amazons and other "eastern" groups, such as the Hittites and Scythians, introduced into Greece. In attributing magical powers (of horse-handling, courage, height, and strength) to Amazons, the Greeks may have been rationalizing their defeat by *women* and, conversely, maximizing the importance of victories over "mere" women. Then too, the ambivalence and guilt probably felt by early patriarchs in violating the Great Mother Goddess and Her cultures could be resolved and exorcised by repeatedly slaying Her in Her most terrible (her man-hating and man-killing) aspect, all the while justifying such destruction by distinguishing between the Terrible Woman (Amazons) and the Good Woman (the real mothers and sisters)—a deceptive distinction since it was with the latter that sons and brothers were historically and psychologically waging a war in earnest.

Reports about Amazons from (male) Christian Europeans present still other problems. The ancients were closer—historically, geographically, and psychologically—to such matriarchal phenomena as female ownership and inheritance of land and crops, female "ownership" of children, and female control of reproduction and religion. Ancients would not so quickly take such phenomena as proof of a supernatural or Amazon culture. Such phenomena, however, would indeed be "astonishing" to Christian Europeans. For example: Celtic and Gothic ("barbarian") women leading and joining their men in battle and in all political decisions; Indian women of North and South America fighting and trading with Columbus and Pizarro; Eastern European, Mediterranean, Central Asian, and African women alone, without men, in their nomadic camps, or in mountain and island "villages," who could and did defend their homes against attack—such women would have appeared to constitute an all-female state, to be in effect, Amazons. In such a scheme of things, men must have seemed as oppressed and debased as women in fact were in Judeo-Christian Europe. In much the same way, from the fifteenth to the nineteenth centuries, European male explorers "saw" Amazons in many a peaceful Indian village in the Americas.

And yet many South American and African informants who were presumably out of touch with Greek mythology and history—insisted on the existence of "legendary" or classical Amazons in their own countries. Central European explorers in the seventeenth century heard reports of Amazons in the Black Sea and Caucasus regions and offered all sorts of "proof" that they really existed: armor, weapons, clothing, grave-sites, temple celebrations, the observed prowess of women warriors, queens, priestesses, and politicians, and a multitude of Amazon-like customs. Such proofs are highly controversial and can be explained in many ways, but the geographical universality and historical longevity of the belief in legendary Amazonism is almost more important proof of their ancient existence than are various artifacts. Strong beliefs—legends that won't die—are always some sort of race-memory. The lasting belief in Amazons embodies a universal history of male-female conflict, and the Amazon myths presuppose the existence of the Great Mother cultures as well as the revolt of both daughters (Amazons) and sons (patriarchs).

AMAZONS: A PSYCHO-HISTORICAL PERSPECTIVE

"Isocrates and Aristeides praise the Greek victory over the Amazons as more important than that over the Persians or any other deed in history; the wars between the Greeks and Persians were wars between two male-dominated societies. In the Amazon war, the issue was which of the two forms of life was to shape European civilization in its image. . . . Persians and other enemies had merely been driven from the country, but the Amazons had been driven from human nature."

—Helen Diner

"Amazonism is a universal phenomenon. It is not based on the special physical or historical circumstances of any particular people but on conditions that are characteristic of all human existence. Amazonian phenomena are interwoven with the origins of all peoples. They may be found from Central Asia to the Occident, from the Scythian north to West Africa."—J. J. Bachofen

At one time, legendary Amazons existed on every continent. They eventually died out—mysteriously, accidentally, inevitably—their customs either absorbed or banished by later societies. Perhaps Amazons (daughters) were defeated by patriarchs (sons) in wars of sibling rivalry. Perhaps just when daughters could afford to question a certain lack of passion, boldness, and freedom in early matriarchal culture, sons found it possible to rebel against female rule—despite its "civilizing" features and in a way that would have been unthinkable to the most rebellious of daughters.

Some theorists view Amazonism as an extreme form of matriarchy (and, within their perspective, it is either "degraded" or advanced): to such thinkers, it is an excess of female power, which ultimately precipitates a male, or patriarchal, revolt. Other theorists see Amazonism as the female attempt to restore matriarchy or gynocracy just as men, seeking either to "progress" to another form of society or to "regress" to an earlier cultural stage, were in the process of abolishing female rule.* Still other theorists feel that Amazonism was necessary in order to force men—and women—to progress away from the early chaos of hetaerism to the later order of matriarchy. Certain theorists suggest that "outbursts" of legendary Amazonism occur in male-dominated cultures each time that *some* women perceive the cults of "femininity"—the worship of Aphrodite or Dionysius—for what they really represent: a bogus "sexual revolution" that sacrifices women to allow men civilization—and access to "natural" infantile, disorderly, or bestial behaviors. The female revolt against such a sexual revolution and the male definitions of "civilization" that accompany it have often been derided as Amazonism or Puritanism. The patriarchal victories over such female revolts have just as often been called "male backlash" or patriarchal excesses.

*The various myths and epic poems about the Amazon presence at the Battle of Troy are most important for what they reveal about the historic confrontation of matriarchy, Amazonism, and patriarchy. Presumably, Troy was a more matriarchal civilization than Athens, and, psycho-historically, the Amazons were defending matriarchy against patriarchal encroachments. In the *Oresteia*, Aeschylus gives a clear depiction of the forces at play in this contest. Agamemnon, leader of the Greek forces, sacrifices his daughter Iphigenia, as an offering to the gods for his troops. His wife, Clytemnestra—a matriarchal figure who is thus naturally closer to her daughter than to her husband—kills him. Her son, Orestes—a patriarchal hero—murders her to avenge the death of his father. To a matriarchal society, there is no more extreme crime than matricide; to a patriarchal society, patricide or husband-killing are the extreme crimes. Orestes' crime is pardoned, mainly through the intercession of Athena—a goddess unthinkable in a matriarchal society, a goddess who has no mother and protects only male heroes.

According to many theorists, the first stage of human culture was "hetaeric": chaotic, disorganized, pre-agricultural, and sexually abusive to women—who probably were more exhausted (as a result of being continually pregnant) than "offended" by male or female sexual "promiscuity" or by male sexual violence. Matriarchal culture represented the female desire for a more securely ordered, fruitful, lawful, ethical, and spiritual way of life. "Great Mothers" invented a culture based on biological motherhood, on marriage, agriculture, religion, and on *female* control of production and reproduction. And such female rule may have been kinder to both men and women than male rule has been to either of the sexes. Such female rule may indeed have accepted, developed, and valued both male and female biology as well as the special alliance with the inner and spiritual world that women seem to have—an alliance long shunned by our excessively male culture.

The mother-daughter relationship was at the heart of matriarchal culture. Men, as husbands, were essentially peripheral to their wives' and daughters' family-grouping; as sons and brothers they were, in a spiritual sense, their mothers' and sisters' "servants."* If men were to gain more power, or to redefine civilization, they would have somehow to gain control of the family. To gain political and spiritual power, men would have to pit the *concept* of Fatherhood against the *fact* of Motherhood. And they would have to overthrow the Great Mother Goddess—that bountiful giver of life, that terrible thief of life. The Great Mother Goddesses (their mothers and sisters) were too powerful, too all-encompassing, too set in their ways. Men had to find a way to keep the Good Mother (Nature) "good," while somehow destroying or minimizing the "bad" aspects: death, disease, and female control of the means of production (agriculture) and reproduction. Through a violent and unnatural act of will, Fathers, not Mothers, would be the starting point of culture and knowledge. Had Amazonism triumphed, perhaps a similar "unnatural will" not solely based on reproductive maternity would have been at the basis

*It must be kept in mind that "matriarchs" did not hate men—or even, in their culture's terms, "suppress" men.

of modern culture—but, of course, it did not.

The Amazon or daughter rebellion was more complicated and difficult. Amazons had both less and more cause to deny certain matriarchal principles: less cause if their own power base was being threatened by males; more cause if such a power base bequeathed them the luxury of wanting more, or of "seeing" new things.* For women to revolt against a female-dominated past would take enormous energy, supreme self-denial, and great visionary ardor. Amazons were interested in founding a culture that incorporated many matriarchal values and customs—but it was a culture that would not be based simply on biological and spiritual "givens." Unlike patriarchs, heroic Amazons had to deal with not one but two "enemies": their own ties to female biology, spirituality, and matriarchal culture, and the male revolt against any kind of female rule.

Amazonism, like patriarchy, must essentially have been a valiant, heroic, and dangerous rebellion against Nature and Tradition. Nature and Biology were no longer experienced as inherently just, reasonable, inevitable, or sacred. Nature could be controlled and used for new ends. Perhaps even Amazons could not conceive of how self-destructively harsh, how dangerously narrow and unrelenting men would be toward both Nature and Spirituality after patriarchal "victory." Matriarchs, and even their passionately individualistic Amazon daughters, might not have foreseen their sons' and brothers' need to debase so totally all that was previously sacred (Nature and Women), in order to experience themselves as divine, in order to found a civilization based on their own sacredness.

ETYMOLOGY

To ancient Greek mythographers and historians, as well as in later South American, Indian, and Eastern European accounts, "Amazon" usually meant belligerent or physically powerful women united in self-governing politics and showing an aversion to any kind of permanent matrimonial tie, although this aversion varied in gradation from group to group. The word "Amazon," possibly Scythian in origin, could have many meanings and derivations. The Cherkassian *Emetchi* simply means "those who count by the mother," and would indicate matriarchal kinship and inheritance practices. In the Kalmuck language, a healthy, strong, heroic woman is called *Aemetzaine*. Europeans in the Caucasus region told an eighteenth-century traveler that their people had once been at war with the *Emmetsh*—a female tribe full of warlike spirit that welcomed any woman who cared to share its wanderings and join its heroic guild. Another eighteenth-century traveler was told about the *Emazuhn* in the mountains of Great Tartary; these women were accomplished hunters and warriors and kept their husbands in a subservient position. And, in the sixteenth and seventeenth centuries, South American informants referred to manlike women or women without husbands as "Amazons."

If the term "Amazon" was derived from *Amazosas*, it means "opposed to man." Homer called the Amazons *antianeirai*—"mannish" or "man-hating." (The difference is, of course, crucial.) If "Amazon" is derived from *Amastos* or *A-Mazo*, it means "those without a breast." Many writers describe the Amazon practice of burning off the right lacteal gland in childhood, presumably in order to become better archers or more strongly muscled in the right arm. Perhaps this rite can also be interpreted as a way of cutting off the "right" (or "male") side* and absorbing it androgynously. Amazon could also be related to *Azona*, which means "chastity belt"; in Amazon life, this was the symbol of an autonomous, unmarried state rather than of a virginal or sexually innocent condition. When Greek patriarchal adventurers (such as Hercules and Theseus) came to rob the Amazon Queen of her "belt," they were attempting to usurp her power, to plunder her geographical territory and independence, as well as her biological (child-bearing) "territory."

*Regardless of the circumstances, for women to fight, or to *need* to fight, with men is already a major departure from the spirit of matriarchy.

*"Left" is traditionally the female side and, in our culture, usually has negative meanings. "Left" is mysterious, sinister, radical, wrong; right is "right."

Whatever the derivation of the word, the point is that it was used in widely scattered geographical regions to signify a particular kind of culture or type of woman. Its usage may signify the existence of one original culture (or type of woman) or of many independently originated cultures. Or it may indicate the geographical migration either of such cultures or of the myths about them. Whatever the case, the wide use and recognition the term has had suggests some kind of historical justification for the mythmakers.

THE LEGENDARY AMAZONS

Classical or legendary Amazon societies were either all-female or female-dominated. In matriarchal fashion, the women controlled the means of production and reproduction and were also physically bold and politically autonomous. Commonly, such societies are depicted as having two queens—one for military affairs, the other for domestic.

Amazons were related to men and maternity in a variety of ways. Perhaps not every Amazon had to reproduce herself; perhaps only once was enough. Amazon societies engaged in annual rituals of "indiscriminate" sexual intercourse with certain male neighbors. They usually kept the female offspring and returned the male infants to their fathers. More radical Amazon societies killed all male infants, or crippled them in various ways and kept them as servants. Among the African Amazons, only the Gorgons maintained a pure, man-hating, Amazon state.* Other African Amazons maintained some men in their military camps. According to Helen Diner:

The Libyan Amazons, who removed their right breasts, had compulsory military service for all girls for a number of years, during which time they had to refrain from marriage. After that, they became a part of the reserves and were allowed to take a mate and reproduce their kind. The women monopolized government and other influential positions. In contrast to the later Thermondontines, however, they lived in a permanent relationship with their sex partners, even though the men led a retiring life, could not hold public office, and had no right to interfere in the government of the state or society.

According to the ancient Greeks and Romans, legendary Amazons arose in two main geographical regions and at two different times. The earliest group originated in northwestern Africa at the foot of the Atlas Mountains—areas then known as "Libya" and "Numidia," which now correspond to Morocco, Tunisia, and Algeria. The second major Amazon culture occurred somewhat later and arose in the Black Sea region—either on its European or Asiatic side. They were "Thermodon" Amazons.*

It was the Thermodon Amazons, led by Queen Penthesilea, whom certain Greek poets and artists often placed at the battle of Troy, which may have occurred any time from 1270 B.C. to 1134 B.C.† Thus, these later Amazons may have flourished at the time of the female-dominated Minoan culture (1600 B.C.), the Bronze Age in Greece, and the seventeenth and eighteenth dynasties in Egypt, which would place them after or partly co-existent with the Babylonian Dynasty in Mesopotamia.

The North African-based Amazons presumably arose independently during a much earlier period. They wore red leather armor and snakeskin shoes and carried python-skin shields. Legend has it they founded a city near Lake Triton, where they practiced animal husbandry but had no agriculture, living almost exclusively on meat and milk. A great part of Libya and Numidia was under their domination. Herodotus, writing as late as the fifth century B.C., described many Amazon-like customs in the Lake Triton area, such as girls, still wearing red leather clothes, engaging in military practice com-

*Medusa was one of their queens: It is little wonder that she has come down to us through male eyes as a horrible monster, one who could turn men to stone and who was, of course, defeated by a patriarchal hero, Perseus.

*Homer and Strabo place the Thermodon Amazons in countries that now correspond to Turkey, Yugoslavia, and Hungary—then called Scythia, Hercanium, Caspia, Thrace, etc. Hesiod places them on the Asiatic side of the Euxine (Black Sea). Diodorus Siculus places the African Amazons on the island of Hisperia, or "Tritonia," somewhere near the modern Canary Islands. One legend has it that Tritonia—like Atlantis—was submerged in the sea, and the Amazons with it.

†According to Philostrates, Hiera fought at Troy as a leader of the Mycian women's troops but Homer did not mention her in *The Iliad* because she would have "outshone his heroine, Helen."

bat with each other. Much later, Strabo commented on the tradition in Africa of many generations of "belligerent women" who wore helmets and dressed in clothing made from animal skins. Strabo also described a supposed battle between the African Gorgon Amazons and another Amazon group, led by Queen Myrine. Myrine was victorious and, after the Gorgon war, conquered large areas in Egypt and Arabia: Syria, Phrygia, and all the lands along the Caicus River seacoast. She began building cities—often the same cities that the later Thermodon Amazons re-conquered or occupied. Islands such as Samos, Lesbos, Parthenos, and Samothrace may also have been conquered by Myrine.

The Thermodon (Caucasus-based) Amazons were the women Greeks meant when they wrote about, drew, and sculpted Amazons. Amazons depicted in classical Greek art are often shown in Asiatic (Oriental or Scythian) costumes: long, narrow, checkered trousers, or leggings; soft, high, and often fur-topped boots; Phrygian caps or mantles; and long belted tunics, often with stars on them. Amazon weapons included axes, usually the famous double-edged variety, an androgynous symbol of many female-dominated nations, sabres, bows and arrows, spears, and moon-shaped shields (sometimes decorated with animals such as panthers, lions, and dogs). These Amazons are also shown wearing greaves and Attic or Thracian helmets. Sometimes they are shown barefoot, or wearing supporting ankle-straps; sometimes they are wearing short chitons and are depicted as wounded.

Amazons were often depicted on horseback or driving chariots, and the horse was long considered as one of their "magical symbols."* And, in fact Amazons were said to have invented cavalry and cavalry battle techniques. Hippocrates described the Scythian women of his time as excellent horsewomen who used bow and arrow even when riding at full speed.†

*Many Greek transliterations of Amazon (Scythian) names contained the Greek word *hippos*, meaning horse: Alcippa, Melanippa, Hippolyte, Dioxippa, Lysippe, Hippomache, and Hippothoe.

†Herodotus, Hippocrates, and Pliny the Elder similarly described Amazon or Amazon-like women in the Black Sea area variously called Scythia and Sauromatia. Herodotus, in his day, commented that "the women of this region still ride horseback with their husbands, still take the field in war, and dress like men." Similar Amazon customs are described in the same region in the sixteenth, seventeenth, and eighteenth centuries.

The Ionian tradition refers to the Thermodon Amazons as the founders of cities and sanctuaries: Smyrna, Sinope, Cýme, Gryne, Ephesus, Pitania, Magnesia, Clete, Pygela, Latoreia and Amastris all boasted Amazons as godmothers and founders.

THE GREEK AMAZON MYTHS

At the psychological heart of every major Greek Amazon myth are two important themes. First, there is the theme of women sacrificing and killing men: in battle, because they are "enemies"; in religious ceremonies, to appease or honor female divinities; in infancy, because they, like infant girls in patriarchal cultures, are less important or too burdensome to raise; or in the slower and less "violent" death of lifelong domesticity and political subservience. The other theme is that of the ultimate male triumph over such female acts: by slaughtering and defeating the Amazons in battle, or by converting them to Aphrodite or Dionysius male-worship. Sometimes the Amazons "fall in love" with their male opponents, put down their arms, and desert their comrades to become wives and mothers. It is important to note, however, that Greek *men* do not "fall in love" with Amazons until *after* the women are wounded and dying. Achilles, for example, who fought with Queen Penthesilea at the Battle of Troy, was suddenly and romantically overcome by her valor and beauty—as she lay dying before him.

Like all myths, these themes shape, re-create, and explain both human and individual history. Thus, for example, female children must still give up or minimize supposedly "male" activities, must "naturally" desert preadolescent or adolescent female comrades if they are to please boys, get married, and become mothers. And male children certainly never fall in love with or marry "Amazons"—at least, not until such women are safely disarmed.

The most famous Greek Amazon myths concern the territorial exploits of Bellerophon, Hercules, and Theseus against the Amazons, and the subsequent Amazon invasion of Athens, their retreat, and their later presence at the Battle of Troy. Another type of Greek Amazon myth concerns female revolt against fathers and husbands—as typified by the Danaïds and the women of Lemnos.

In the first instance, the ninth labor of Hercules was to steal the Amazon Queen Hippolyte's girdle—a "magic" belt given to her by her father Mars (Ares), the God of War. Hercules (or Hercules and Theseus, in some accounts), trick or force the relatively peaceful Amazons into battle. Hippolyte is vanquished, and Theseus abducts her sister Antiope, taking her with him to Athens. Some versions of the myth have Antiope falling in love with Theseus and later fighting by his side in Athens against the Amazons, who kill her. Oreithyia, the third sister and the Amazon military queen, has been away. Too late, she rushes back with her army, but the marauding Greeks have already left. She decides to march on Athens. The Amazons invade the city, besiege the Acropolis, and occupy the Areopagus. The fighting is intense, and both sides suffer heavy losses, Finally, a compromise is reached. The Amazons depart—some say broken-heartedly—without achieving the avenging destruction of Athens (or of patriarchy). During their march back to the Thermodon region, Oreithyia and/or Hippolyte die of grief and shame. The presence of Amazon troops at the Battle of Troy is attributed to the resulting long-lasting Amazon hatred of everything Greek.

The second instance of Greek Amazon myth—the revolt of the women of Lemnos—concerns the female desertion of Aphrodite-worship.* Aphrodite punishes the women by making them sexually unattractive to their men. The men promptly enslave some Thracian girls for sexual and domestic purposes—and are as promptly slain by the Lemnian women. The Lemnian revolt represents the militant reaction of outraged matriarchs whose men had begun to "adventure" abroad. Pillaging and raping, these men were violating the marriage bond and, in their treatment of wife and slave-girl alike, debasing the female sex.

*Lemnos was, historically, a matriarchal culture.

Various Greek (male) poets have presented the Lemnian women as "regretful" and "lonely" afterward, as eager for new marriages—even with such patriarchs as Jason. It is Jason who has a love affair with the Lemnian Queen Hypsiplye. Of course, Jason leaves her, just as he leaves Medea, just as Odysseus leaves Penelope and Aeneus leaves Dido, Queen of Carthage, because in order to continue his heroic pilgrimage—in this case, the search for the Golden Fleece—he *must*. In patriarchy, men must always leave their mothers, their sisters, and, of course, their wives and mistresses, for adventures and "advancement" outside the family.

The myth of the Danaïds—the fifty daughters of Danaus—belong to a whole cycle of blood weddings in which the bridegrooms are killed. The Danaïds are forced, against their will, into marriage. Their revolt is a murderous and remorseless one. Of course, there is one nonmurderer: Hypermnestra. Originally, this nonmurdering Danaïd was the contemptible exception; in later versions, she became the only heroine. These later versions also condemn the other forty-nine Danaïds to Hades, where they must forever pour water into a jar with holes in it.

THE HISTORICITY OF THE GREEK AMAZON MYTHS

Specific "proof" of Amazon exploits has understandably become a very controversial matter. Plutarch, in his *Life of Theseus*, apologizes for indulging in mythical history, but, in John Forsdyke's words, "when he [Plutarch] comes to the Amazonian attack on Athens, he writes as a serious historian." Plutarch notes that the enterprise was no "slight or womanish" endeavor. He says:

The Athenians were routed, and gave way before the women, as far as to the temple of the Furies, but, fresh supplies coming in from the Palladium, Ardettus, and the Lyceum, [the Athenians] charged their right wing, and beat them back to their tents, in which action a great number of the Amazons were slain. At length, after four months, a peace was concluded between them by mediation. . . . That this war, however, was ended by a treaty is evident . . . from the ancient sacrifice which used to be celebrated to the Amazons the day before the Feast of Theseus. The Megarians also show a spot in their city where some Amazons were buried. . . . It appears further that the passage of the Amazons through Thessaly was not without opposition, for there are yet shown many tombs of them near Scotussa and Cynoscephalae.

Herodotus did not doubt the reality of Amazons, but thought they were extinct, having crossed the Black Sea from the Thermodon to the Tanaïs (Don) and become the progenitors of the Sarmatians. The Sarmatians of his day were a Scythian people living east of the Crimea. Their women were still Amazon-like, "frequently hunting on horseback with their husbands, sometimes even unaccompanied; in war taking the field and wearing the same dress as the men."* Some stories of Ionian cities sacked or founded by the Amazons may have come from such experiences. The dress and weapons that the Greeks assigned to Amazons were the same as those of the Scythians in Xerxes' army, whom Herodotus described as "wearing trousers and having on their heads tall stiff caps rising to a point."

Pausanias believed in the existence of the legendary Amazons. He stated that the Megarians of his day (the second century A.D.) still believed that the tomb of Queen Oreithyia and/or Hippolyte was located in Megara; and he had no reason to doubt their belief. Pausanias also tells us that, according to Pindar, the temple of Artemis at Ephesus was founded by those Amazons involved in the siege at Athens. The Roman historian Tacitus also connected the origins of the Temple of Ephesus with Amazons. But, in Pausanias' own opinion, the temple was much older, and its Amazon associations were derived from Amazons who simply took refuge there.

*Herodotus also claimed that some Amazons plundered the temple of Aphrodite (Astarte) at Ascalon and were consequently afflicted by that goddess with a "sexual aberration," from which their descendants in Scythia still "suffered." (Lesbianism and homosexuality.)

Strabo also accepted the reality of Amazons, relating that in the Ilian plain there was a hill dedicated to the Amazon Queen Myrine, supposedly for her feats of horsewomanship. Earlier, Homer had placed the grave of an Amazon Queen named Myrine in Troad.

Greek writers probably suppressed certain proofs of Amazon existence. Some denied it entirely. Still others "explained" these proofs as some other kind of phenomena: for example, as nothing more than the Persian and Eastern invasions of the Greek world, which, although undertaken primarily by men, sometimes included women.

Certainly, the sight of women who were physically fit and militarily capable was not startling to ancient Greek and Roman writers. The playwright Euripides, for example, describes the daughters of Sparta as "shameful"; "they are never home, they mingle with the young men in wrestling matches, their clothes cast off, their hips all naked." And Herodotus describes an African-based culture that honors its goddess by staging battles between women. "The girls are divided in two groups and fight with one another. . . . Maidens who die of their wounds are considered impure. The girls who conduct themselves with the greatest bravery are decorated with a Corinthian helmet, put on a chariot, and led all the way around the lake." Virgil, in *The Aeneid* describes Thracian, Tyrian, and Spartan girls as swift runners and excellent horsewomen who dress as huntresses, wearing animal skins or simple tunics and carrying bows and arrows.

Such women would not be mistaken by the ancients as Amazons. But sixteenth- and seventeenth-century missionaries and explorers would be less well equipped to make the distinction. Still, Father Cristobal D'Acuña, a sixteenth-century missionary, described a group of Brazilian Indians as Amazons,

Women of great valor who had always preserved themselves without the ordinary intercourse with men; and even when men, by agreement, come every year to their land, they receive them with arms in their hands such as bows and arrows, which they brandish about for a time, until they are satisfied that the Indians come with peaceful intentions . . . the Indians return to their own country, repeating their visits every year at the same season.

Few, however, could offer eye-witness accounts. Sir Walter Raleigh, for example, was *told* "about an all-female state in the province of Topago"; in legendary fashion, the women supposedly engaged in "promiscuous" ritual intercourse for procreative purposes, returning the sons to their fathers and keeping only the daughters. Between the sixteenth and eighteenth centuries some Spanish and English explorers actually set out to find legendary Amazons in South America, but again, their evidence was hearsay. Hernando de Ribera, in Peru, Anthony Knivet and Charles Marie de La Condamine, in Brazil, and Father Gili, in Guiana, were all *told* about warrior women who lived alone, were excellent arrow-makers and archers, mated only ritually, and had knowledge of "magical" herbs. Some cut off their right breasts, and some possessed great mineral wealth.

Two sixteenth-century missionaries working independently of each other in Abyssinia—Fathers Alvarez and Bermudez—heard about a group of women in the province of Damute who were "much addicted to war and hunting and much more daring than the men of their country." The women were described as searing off their right breasts, rarely marrying, and sending male children back to their fathers. Their queen, worshipped as a Goddess, remained a virgin.

Withal, not all reports were second-hand. A temporary Amazon state may once have existed in Africa in the region of the Congo. A priest, one Father Cavazzi, told of a period in African Jaga history during which young girls were trained militarily and were prohibited from making permanent marriages, while their queen killed each of her lovers after a brief dalliance, eventually ordering the sacrifice of infant males. And according to various sixteenth-century Portuguese observers, a group of female warriors existed in the Congo region and they were very adept militarily; their king assigned certain districts to them in which they reared female children exclusively.

Although matriarchal and female-dominated states existed throughout India, the only unmistakable account of Indian Amazons is contained in the poem *The Mahabharata*, probably rewritten many times by Brahmin patriarchs. The poem depicts the encounter of its male hero, Arjuna, with a militarily and economically powerful all-female state. The young girls are described as dazzlingly lovely "warrior-maidens"; the older women received and entertained men but killed them if they remained for longer than a month. They did not rear male infants.

A number of writers have described a temporary but legendary-style Amazon state in European Bohemia (a Thermodon Amazon region), during the reigns of Queens Libussa and Dlasta (or Valesca). Libussa, born in approximately 680 A.D., instituted a political-religious "council of virgins," raising many women to high public office. Upon Libussa's death in 738 A.D. Dlasta, her chief confidante, headed a temporarily successful "woman's revolt." Dlasta ordered that only women be militarily trained, and she attempted to render male infants and adolescents unfit for warfare by blinding them in one eye. Dlasta is said to have reigned for seven years, after which time the Bohemian nation resumed "its normal course." For years, ruins of Mount Vidovole, known as *Divin-Hrad* (the Virgin's City), were pointed out as Dlasta's headquarters.

MATRIARCHAL AND GYNOCRATIC SOCIETIES

To understand the meaning of Amazonism, it is essential to view its relationship to other kinds of female-dominated societies. There is no question that matriarchies and gynocracies existed—in early history as well as in more complicated and powerful forms in later history—or that matriarchal "themes" and customs have been present in both male- and female-dominated societies and on all continents.* Various matriarchal and gynocratic societies were to be found

*Even in patriarchal Greece and Rome, women retained many matriarchal practices. For example, they worshipped female divinities, and served as oracles, seers, and priestesses. Matriarchy in Egypt may have applied mainly to its royal caste rather than to the general population. And Egyptian dynastic (royal) history presents a long record of the decline of matriarchy and the rise of patriarchy.

at one time in Lycia, Athens, Crete, Lemnos, Locris, Elis, Mantinea, Lesbos, Catabria, Egypt, Tibet, Central Asia, and India. Despite enormous variations, an essential spirit of matriarchy was everywhere widely retained: a superior female alliance with both the material-natural universe and the supersensory or spiritual universe. Within this context, both women and men could be sexually chaste or sexually "insatiable" at certain times of their lives, at certain times in the year, or during their entire lives. Within this context, women and men could be warriors, agriculturalists, and hunters—or not; child-rearers—or not; military and political decision-makers—or not. Divinities and their worldly representatives in the religious and political realm, however, were essentially female. Male priests served priestesses and female deities; royal kings received their power only through their mothers and sisters, whom they sometimes married, as in Egypt. Some matriarchies —in India, Africa, and South America—had only queens, never kings.

In matriarchal or somewhat matriarchal societies, it was not uncommon for women and men to live separately for long periods of time, or for men to visit their wives' homes as "guests," usually for specific sexual or family purposes. What, in our terms, would be seen as role reversals were, in matriarchal societies, not exceptional.* Women were priestesses and goddesses, warriors and military leaders, hunters and politicians in various matriarchal cultures. Men were sometimes—but perhaps more rarely than we would like to suppose—the cooks, childbearers, and "sex-objects." In matriarchal societies, sons and brothers respected and worshipped their mothers and sisters—who, in turn did not "hate" men. Brothers had sacred responsibilities to sisters; sons were "protected" by their mothers in many ways. Only the husband-wife relationship was relatively less important. Eventually, men were valued by women for their procreative, hunting, and warrior functions, none of which they were forced to do without female participation. In matriarchies, women did not despise the conception and rearing of children, making of pottery, chores of agriculture, food-gathering, and cooking. These activities sustained the family and the group. More than hunting and warfare, these activities were what the group was about.

Such matriarchal themes were retained in many later and more patriarchal cultures. Certain customs common to some matriarchal and all Amazon cultures were also continued—specifically, the custom of having a queen and the custom of women warriors.

QUEENS

Queens have existed on every continent, in matriarchal, patriarchal, "transitional," and Amazon cultures. They have existed in class and caste societies, in societies that kept slaves and prostitutes, that built cities, fought wars, and produced art and scientific knowledge.

We know about the rule of queens mainly from men. Herodotus credits the engineering marvels of ancient Babylon to two queens, Semiramis and Nitocris. The earliest and perhaps the most powerful queens known to us were African: Queen Hatshepsut of Egypt lived 1500 years before the birth of Christ. She reigned for twenty-one years despite her half-brother's continued attempts to dethrone her. One of the best-known female rulers was Makeda, the Queen of Sheba, who has been mentioned—and underestimated—in the Old Testament and the Koran, as well as in Greek accounts of the period. Many queens ruled Ethiopia and all were known as Candace (or Candice). Their cumulative reign lasted nearly eight centuries. In an attempt to circumvent the spread of Greek and Roman imperialism, "Candace" opposed Alexander the Great, Caesar Augustus, the Roman general Petro, Nero, and others. Strabo, writing in 7 B.C., described the Candace of his time "as a masculine sort of woman, blind in one eye." This queen "personally

*Herodotus, for example, writing in the fifth century B.C., reports that, in Egypt of his day, "the women attend to the mercantile business, conducting trade and providing for the family, while the men sit at home at the loom." He also adds, "In Egypt, sons need not support their parents but daughters must." And Strabo noted: "In North Africa, the women were not in the army any more but they ruled the country politically, while the men were still without significance in the state, occupying themselves largely with body care and hair-do [and] greedy for golden jewelry."

led 10,000 troops in battle against the Roman governor of Egypt, Publius Patronious. "Candace" is also mentioned by Pliny the Elder and Seneca.

Perhaps the most famous of the Egyptian queens was Cleopatra, born approximately in 69 B.C. An astute politician, Cleopatra's various matrimonial alliances—with her brothers, with Julius Caesar, and with Mark Antony—ensured Egypt's status as a preferred Roman protectorate (rather than colony) and were quite in keeping with royal Egyptian matrilineal codes. Yet another famous African ruler was Queen Dahia-Al-Kahina. A Jew, she fought both the Moslem and the Roman-Christian invaders of Africa, capturing Carthage from the Moslems in 698 A.D. Many African Bantu kingdoms were also ruled by queens. Angola, led by Queen Nzinga Ngola of Jega origin, valiantly resisted Portuguese invasions. A Dutch officer in the seventeenth century described her as "a cunning and prudent virago, so much addicted to arms that she hardly used other exercises." Queens ruled among the Fanti on the Gold Coast, and as "chieftains" of numerous smaller tribes—including the Biblical Israelites.

European queens and female chieftains also existed before the influence of Christianity diminished their ranks. According to Herodotus, the Celtic Queen Tomyris directed an army against Cyrus the Great, King of Persia, who had murdered her son. She personally engaged him in battle and killed him.* Tacitus wrote about two supposedly mythical Celtic queens, Boadicea and Cartismandua. Boadicea led an army that routed the Romans, killing 70,000 of them. Tacitus quotes her as telling her people that "in this battle we must conquer or die. This is a woman's resolve. *As for men, they may live and be slaves.*" Ultimately faced with capture despite impressive victories, Boadicea followed through on her words, killing herself in 62 A.D. Cartismandua, Queen of the Brigantes (the British Celts) was described by Tacitus and later writers as an outstanding politician and ruler.

Modern Irish historians treat Queen Eire as a real historical personage; she is is said to have killed Scota, Queen of the Milesians (an early Scottish ruler), in battle. And the British Celtic Queen, Martia Proba, is credited with formulating a legal code in the third century B.C. that is the source for modern English common law.

Concurrent with the rise and triumph of European imperialism, queens reigned in India, China, Africa, and islands of the South Seas. In North America, a form of female rule—if not actual queenship—was commented on by an eighteenth-century traveler to the continent. Father Lafitau, observing the five great tribes of the Iroquois, noted that:

> *All the real authority rests in the women of the country. The fields and all harvest belong to them. They are the soul of the councils, the arbiters of war and peace, and the guardians of the public. . . . It is through them that the prisoners are delivered, they arrange for the weddings, govern the children and determine the laws of inheritance according to their blood.**

In Christian Europe, royal caste has always superseded sexual caste—despite virulent anti-female attitudes—and Europe has had many queens. Few exercised real and total power. One of the most notable queens—Elizabeth of England—remained husbandless and childless, and this may have underlain her power. Most European queens were forced into unwanted marriages and pregnancies, were denied sex and freedom, and were killed, imprisoned, or dominated by consorts, uncles, and brothers in ways kings never were.

WOMEN WARRIORS

Like queens, female warriors and military leaders have existed on every continent and in every type of society. It was Christianity that suppressed this female tradition in Europe—as well as our knowledge of it elsewhere. Female warriors fought for both kings and queens; in matriarchal, Amazon, patriarchal, and transitional

*Elizabeth G. Davis notes that, although Herodotus' account of how Cyrus died was given only a few years after it happened, most modern sources insist they do not know the circumstances of his death.

*Of course, with the coming of white Christian Europeans, the power and importance of Indians in general and Indian women in particular was forced into a decline. White men would not easily "make deals" with women.

societies. They led both female and male troops, and they served as military strategists and tacticians for all-female and all-male armies. There are traditions of particularly "fierce" fighting women among the Tartars and Mongols, the Germans, Scandinavians, British, and Irish, as well as among certain African and South American peoples.

Herodotus, Tacitus, Strabo, and a great number of later writers describe female generals and warriors from Asia and India. Some of these reports may be ascribed to culture shock, as, for example, that of the thirteenth-century envoy to the Mongol courts of Asia, the Franciscan Friar William of Rubrouck, who observed that Mongol women "sit on horseback bestriding their horses like men. Moreover their women's garments differ not from their men's saving that they are somewhat longer. When a great company of such gentlewomen ride together and are beheld afar off, they seem to be soldiers with helmets on their heads carrying their lances upright." Others must be taken more literally, as for example, Herodotus, describing Artemisia of Halicarnassus, a great admiral in the Persian wars, said she was "superior to any on the Persian side except that of the Phoenicians . . . and she likewise gave Xerxes sounder counsel than any of his other allies."

Among the European "barbarians," Celtic women comprised the joint chiefs of staff of their army. According to Julius Caesar, "it was for the matrons to decide—when troops should attack and when withdraw." Irish Celtic women, like their British counterparts, always fought together with their men, and only Christianity forced them to cease such practices.

In his history of the Roman Empire, Edward Gibbon describes a triumphant procession, ordered by the Emperor Aurelius, in which ten captured Gothic warrior women were exhibited to the Roman populace as "Amazons." The Roman historian Appianus writes of a female contingent in the army of King Mithridates and tells how, after the battle, the Romans "found several women among the prisoners and hostages whose wounds were as great and as dangerous as those of the men." Roman reports describe the women as fiercer than their men, often killing their children and committing suicide rather than be captured.

Reports of female warriors in the European Caucasus abound. In the seventeenth century, Father Angelo Lamberti reported that Prince Dadian of Mingrelia, a principality in the Caucasus, told of finding "a number of women among the dead" after one battle. Although he never saw a "live Amazon," his messengers brought him the weapons and clothes of these female warriors: helmets, breast plates, short skirts of a woolen material dyed a bright red, and soft, high ornamented boots. The women carried swords, bows, and arrows, the latter seeming to be of ancient Scythian and Asiatic origin. Another seventeenth-century traveler, Sir John Chardin, reported that, while in Gheorgistan, he was told tales of an Amazon state. He never saw it for himself, but he was shown some female warrior costumes said to belong to the Amazons. In the same century, yet another traveler, John Cartwright, reported "warlike" women in Armenia and he described them as "very skillful and active in shooting and managing any sort of weapon."

If these travelers had difficulty actually finding a "live Amazon," it is nonetheless true that many sixteenth- and seventeenth-century explorers fought against women warriors in Brazil, Guiana, Peru, and the region of the Orinoco River. Even Columbus reported being attacked by female archers, and the priests and militarists who accompanied de Orellana, Pizarro, and de Bastides were all to describe battles in which women fought beside their men. They were excellent archers, some even using the long dart and poison-tipped arrows. South America even had its Joan of Arc—Maria Candalaria, who, at twenty, organized an army to drive out the Europeans. Although her revolt was eventually suppressed, she never fell into Spanish hands.

Many American Indian tribes had female warriors and, as Robert Briffault notes, as late as 1854, women warriors among the Klamath Indians fought against U.S. troops. But female warriors were not confined to Europe and the Americas. Briffault also observed that in New Guinea, Malaya, and in many parts of the Pacific, including New Zealand and Hawaii, "women were accustomed to fight along with the men, and in the Ladrones they fought under female leaders."

In North Africa, the situation was complicated by the coming of Islam—much as Christianity changed women's warrior roles in Europe. (There are however many accounts of Moslem women who defended Damascus against the Greeks.) Briffault, among others, characterizes pre-Islamic women as "noble and free"—whether they were warriors, judges, queens, or subjects. "Many an Arab woman personally led the men to battle. As late as the time of Rhashid, Arab maidens fought on horseback and commanded troops. Royal princesses clad in mail fought under Mansour against the Byzantines."

Sub-Saharan Africa also had its female warriors. Herodotus described various African tribes with warrior women—among them the Zavecians, "whose wives drove their chariots into battle." And Portuguese accounts of the Congo in the sixteenth and seventeenth centuries describe legions of fighting women. Such African monarchs as the King of Dahomey kept an all-female bodyguard. (So did the Nizan of Hyderabad.) Sir Richard Burton observed and talked to the King of Dahomey's "Amazon" bodyguard, quoting one as boasting that "she was not a woman, but a man." Traditionally, the bodyguard did not marry and preferred death to the slavery, prostitution, or marriage that might come with defeat. Burton also noted that the King of Behr, on the Upper Nile, was guarded by spearwomen.

At times of great urgency, and not as a matter of institutionalized course, women in almost all cultures have participated militarily: during the French and American Revolutions and, more recently, the Russian and Chinese, as well as in wars and insurgencies fought by Israelis, Arabs, Cubans, and Vietnamese. With the exception of Joan of Arc, however, modern women have rarely been military leaders and strategists, and just as rarely have they been trained to fight "like men." Most twentieth-century countries that induct women into armies generally train them for "light" military and "heavy" nursing and secretarial responsibilities.

WONDER WOMAN

In a sense, Amazonism—as a bold and extreme expression of female human power—is perhaps a phenomenon more of the technological future than of the biological past. Certainly, this is how it appears in the Wonder Woman comic strips of the 1940's. In these, women are seen as natural leaders who could rule the world. As embodied in the comic strip, woman—or the female principle—is inherently just, peaceful, compassionate, and altruistic. The Amazons are raised to be powerful but humane; independent, yet fiercely cooperative and loyal; submissive to female authority, but heroically self-sufficient. Amazon rule is based on the "inspiring of affections," on the love of excellence, and on kindness.

Amazons wear bracelets as reminders of the slavery in store for women if they submit to men. Wonder Woman herself is the embodiment of the use of force for love, while men, wonderful or otherwise, represent the use of force for hate or evil. The stories stress the need for women to be "strong"—physically, morally, and scientifically—in order to counteract and subdue the "evil" use of force by men. Wonder Woman was conceived as a counter to the bloody "masculinity" of most American comic books, and the strip's use of force is tempered accordingly. As Wonder Woman says: "The better you can fight, *the less you'll have to.*"

There are faults. Most of Wonder Woman's patron deities (Diana is the exception) are patriarchal rather than Amazon divinities. And Amazons obviously never dressed in "sexy" costumes covered with United States emblems. Still, many genuine Amazon and matriarchal themes are portrayed. The Amazon matriarchal code is an altruistic and humane one: They are loyal to each other and committed to aid those in need. The traditionally superior spiritual and altruistic powers of women are depicted in Wonder Woman's "telepathic" abilities. Modern science is never presented in its too "narrow" or purely rational form, but is instead correctly shown as an adjunct or guide to the "supernatural" or the "invisible" universe! Wonder Woman travels in an invisible airplane at 3,000 miles-per-hour; she wields a "magic lasso" that nonviolently compels obedience; she uses science for medical healing. Such devices, while oriented toward the future, are also reminiscent of the spirit of historically practiced female "magic."

The comic strip presents a prosperous, advanced,

ordered, compassionate, and basically androgynous all-female society. Diana Prince, or Wonder Woman, is *sculpted* by her mother, and life is breathed into her by the Goddess Aphrodite. Reproduction—or rather, life—is portrayed as a spiritual and entirely female affair. We may note that in terms of modern science, parthenogenesis ("virgin" births or self-duplication) through cloning is, like extra-uterine reproduction, an eventual—and, to many, a "frightening"—possibility.

As futuristic as the comic strip is, it is nonetheless grounded in reality. It clearly portrays the fact that women have to be better and stronger than men to be given a chance in a man's world: Often Wonder Woman is called at the midnight hour, when men, feeling the odds are impossible, have deserted the task. The comic also underlines the importance of successful female role models in teaching women strength and confidence. And, as a corollary, the comic depicts as "natural" the love of a strong woman for a man who, in *macho* terms, is "weaker" than herself. In all these ways, Wonder Woman was ahead of her time.

Well,

she's long about her coming, who must be
more merciless to herself than history.
Her mind full to the wind, I see her plunge
breasted and glancing through the currents,
taking the light upon her
at least as beautiful as any boy
or helicopter,
poised, still coming,
her fine blades making the air wince
but her cargo
no promise then:
delivered
palpable
ours.

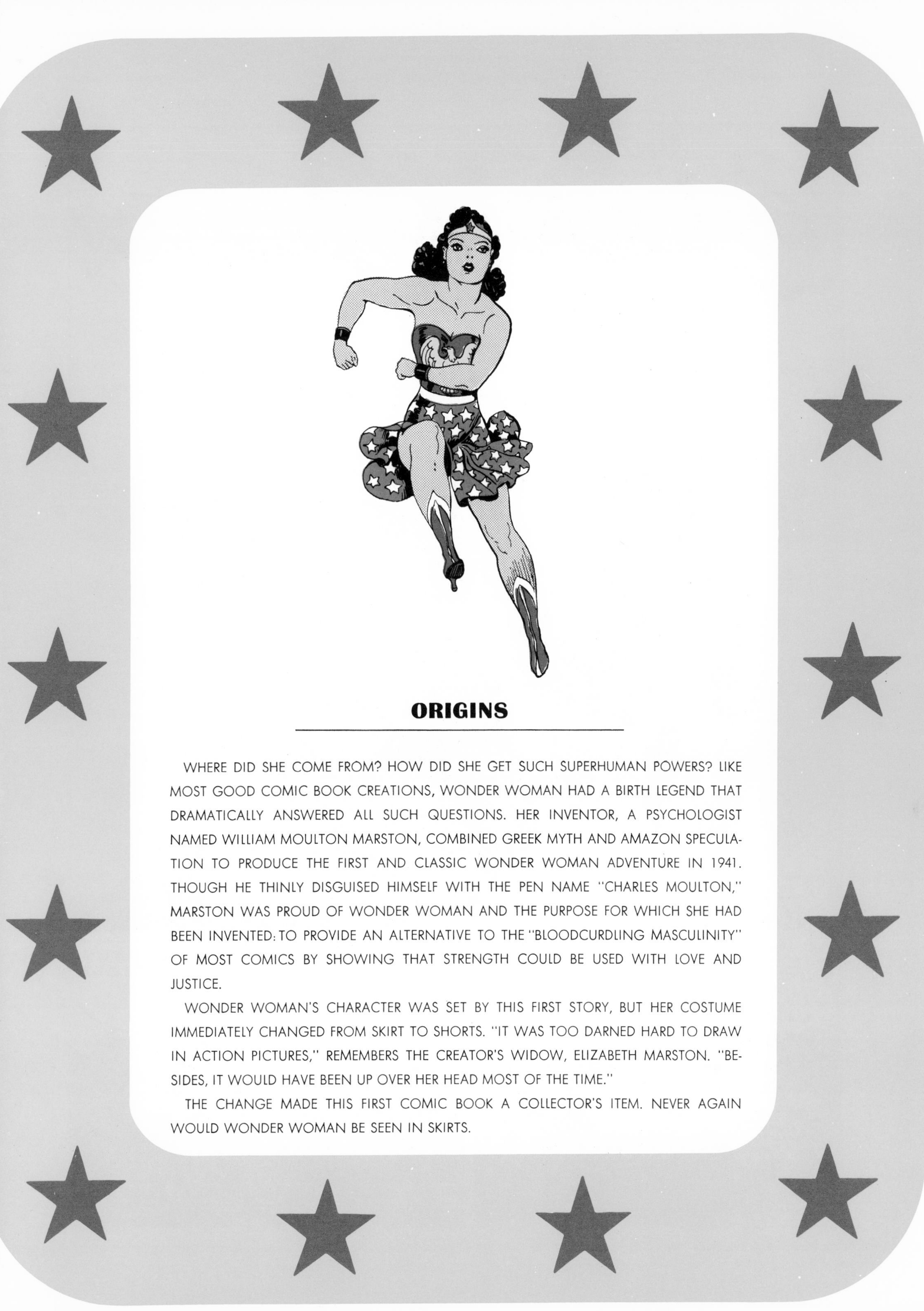

ORIGINS

WHERE DID SHE COME FROM? HOW DID SHE GET SUCH SUPERHUMAN POWERS? LIKE MOST GOOD COMIC BOOK CREATIONS, WONDER WOMAN HAD A BIRTH LEGEND THAT DRAMATICALLY ANSWERED ALL SUCH QUESTIONS. HER INVENTOR, A PSYCHOLOGIST NAMED WILLIAM MOULTON MARSTON, COMBINED GREEK MYTH AND AMAZON SPECULATION TO PRODUCE THE FIRST AND CLASSIC WONDER WOMAN ADVENTURE IN 1941. THOUGH HE THINLY DISGUISED HIMSELF WITH THE PEN NAME "CHARLES MOULTON," MARSTON WAS PROUD OF WONDER WOMAN AND THE PURPOSE FOR WHICH SHE HAD BEEN INVENTED: TO PROVIDE AN ALTERNATIVE TO THE "BLOODCURDLING MASCULINITY" OF MOST COMICS BY SHOWING THAT STRENGTH COULD BE USED WITH LOVE AND JUSTICE.

WONDER WOMAN'S CHARACTER WAS SET BY THIS FIRST STORY, BUT HER COSTUME IMMEDIATELY CHANGED FROM SKIRT TO SHORTS. "IT WAS TOO DARNED HARD TO DRAW IN ACTION PICTURES," REMEMBERS THE CREATOR'S WIDOW, ELIZABETH MARSTON. "BESIDES, IT WOULD HAVE BEEN UP OVER HER HEAD MOST OF THE TIME."

THE CHANGE MADE THIS FIRST COMIC BOOK A COLLECTOR'S ITEM. NEVER AGAIN WOULD WONDER WOMAN BE SEEN IN SKIRTS.

Introducing
Wonder Woman
AT LAST, IN A WORLD TORN BY THE HATREDS AND WARS OF MEN, APPEARS A WOMAN TO WHOM THE PROBLEMS AND FEATS OF MEN ARE MERE CHILD'S PLAY- A WOMAN WHOSE IDENTITY IS KNOWN TO NONE, BUT WHOSE SENSATIONAL FEATS ARE OUTSTANDING IN A FAST-MOVING WORLD! WITH A HUNDRED TIMES THE AGILITY AND STRENGTH OF OUR BEST MALE ATHLETES AND STRONGEST WRESTLERS, SHE APPEARS AS THOUGH FROM NOWHERE TO AVENGE AN INJUSTICE OR RIGHT A WRONG! AS LOVELY AS APHRODITE—AS WISE AS ATHENA—WITH THE SPEED OF MERCURY AND THE STRENGTH OF HERCULES—SHE IS KNOWN ONLY AS WONDER WOMAN, BUT WHO SHE IS, OR WHENCE SHE CAME, NOBODY KNOWS!
by
CHARLES MOULTON
TO BEGIN THE STRANGE HISTORY OF "WONDER WOMAN," LET US GO OUT OVER THE SEA AND FOLLOW IN THE WAKE OF A PLANE, ENTIRELY OUT OF GASOLINE! AS WE WATCH, IT FLOUNDERS HELPLESSLY IN THE SKY, AND FINALLY CRASHES ON THE SHORES OF AN UNCHARTED ISLE SET IN THE MIDST OF A VAST EXPANSE OF OCEAN....
BURSTING FROM THE SURROUNDING FOLIAGE, TWO BEAUTIFUL FIGURES RACE TOWARD THE WRECKED PLANE...
LOOK, PRINCESS, A STRANGE PLANE!
WELL, WHAT ARE WE WAITING FOR? COME ON, LET'S SEE IF ANYONE IS HURT!
PRINCESS, IT'S—IT'S—
A MAN! A MAN ON PARADISE ISLAND! QUICK! LET'S GET HIM TO THE HOSPITAL.
1

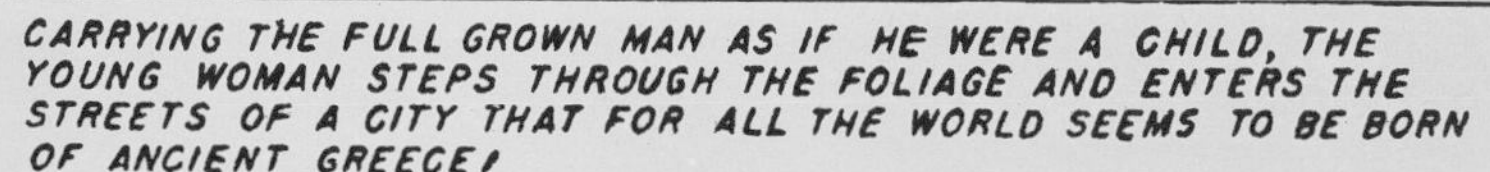
WONDER WOMAN

CARRYING THE FULL GROWN MAN AS IF HE WERE A CHILD, THE YOUNG WOMAN STEPS THROUGH THE FOLIAGE AND ENTERS THE STREETS OF A CITY THAT FOR ALL THE WORLD SEEMS TO BE BORN OF ANCIENT GREECE!
A MAN!
HOW DID HE GET HERE?
SOMEONE TELL THE QUEEN THERE'S A MAN ON PARADISE ISLAND!

AT THE HOSPITAL —
IS HE ALL RIGHT? WILL HE LIVE?
I DON'T KNOW... HE'S HAD A CONCUSSION. WE WON'T KNOW ANYTHING FOR DAYS. I WONDER WHAT THE QUEEN WILL DO WITH HIM. HE CAN'T BE MOVED.

SUDDENLY, HIPPOLYTE, THE QUEEN, ENTERS THE HOSPITAL ROOM...
MOTHER!
THE QUEEN!
I HEARD THAT THERE WAS A MAN HERE, BUT I COULDN'T BELIEVE IT. WHO IS HE?

HIS PLANE CRASHED ON THE BEACH OF THE ISLAND THIS MORNING. THE PRINCESS AND MALA BROUGHT HIM HERE. I FOUND THESE PAPERS IN HIS POCKET.
"CAPT. STEVEN TREVOR, U.S. ARMY INTELLIGENCE SERVICE." HMM. WE CAN'T LET HIM DIE. SEE THAT HE GETS THE BEST OF ATTENTION. KEEP HIS EYES COVERED SO THAT, IF HE SHOULD AWAKE, HE WILL SEE NOTHING! HAVE HIS PLANE REPAIRED, FOR HE MUST LEAVE AS SOON AS HE IS WELL! KEEP ME INFORMED OF HIS PROGRESS!

IN THE ENSUING DAYS, THE PRINCESS, THE QUEEN'S ONLY DAUGHTER, IS CONSTANTLY AT THE BEDSIDE OF THE UNCONSCIOUS MAN, HELPING — WATCHING —
YOU OUGHT TO GET SOME SLEEP, PRINCESS. YOU HAVE BEEN ON THE JOB NOW FOR FOURTEEN HOURS.
NEVER MIND ME. WE - WE MUST MAKE HIM WELL.

LEAVING THE PRINCESS TO WATCH OVER THE INJURED PILOT, THE DOCTOR SEEKS AUDIENCE WITH THE QUEEN....
WHAT HAS HAPPENED THAT YOU DISTURB ME AT THIS HOUR? IS THE MAN—
NO, HE IS ALIVE. IT IS THE PRINCESS I AM WORRIED ABOUT. I DON'T THINK SHE OUGHT TO BE ALLOWED IN THE HOSPITAL ANY MORE. SHE ACTS RATHER STRANGELY ABOUT THAT MAN.

SO SHE IS IN LOVE! I WAS AFRAID OF THAT! YOU ARE QUITE RIGHT, DOCTOR. I SHALL TAKE STEPS IMMEDIATELY.
THAT WOULD BE WISE. IT'S FOR THE CHILD'S OWN GOOD.

AND SO THE PRINCESS, FORBIDDEN THE PLEASURE OF NURSING THE ONLY MAN SHE CAN RECALL EVER HAVING SEEN IN HER LIFE, GOES TO HER MOTHER, HIPPOLYTE, THE QUEEN OF THE AMAZONS!
BUT MOTHER — I DON'T UNDERSTAND— I MUST SEE HIM! I MUST KNOW WHO HE IS, HOW HE GOT HERE! AND WHY HE MUST LEAVE? I-I LOVE HIM!
I WAS AFRAID, DAUGHTER, THAT THE TIME WOULD SOME DAY ARRIVE THAT I WOULD HAVE TO SATISFY YOUR CURIOSITY. COME— I WILL TELL YOU EVERYTHING!

AND THIS IS THE STARTLING STORY UNFOLDED BY HIPPOLYTE, QUEEN OF THE AMAZONS, TO THE PRINCESS, HER DAUGHTER!

In the days of Ancient Greece, many centuries ago, we Amazons were the foremost nation in the world. In Amazonia, women ruled and all was well. Then one day, Hercules, the strongest man in the world, stung by taunts that he couldn't conquer the Amazon women, selected his strongest and fiercest warriors and landed on our shores. I challenged him to personal combat—because I knew that with my MAGIC GIRDLE, given me by Aphrodite, Goddess of Love, I could not lose.

And win I did! But Hercules, by deceit and trickery, managed to secure my MAGIC GIRDLE—and soon we Amazons were taken into slavery. And Aphrodite, angry at me for having succumbed to the wiles of men, would do naught to help us!

Finally our submission to men became unbearable—we could stand it no longer—and I appealed to the Goddess Aphrodite again. This time not in vain, for she relented and with her help, I secured the MAGIC GIRDLE from Hercules.

With the MAGIC GIRDLE in my possession, it didn't take us long to overcome our masters, the MEN—and taking from them their entire fleet, we set sail for another shore, for it was Aphrodite's condition that we leave the man-made world and establish a new world of our own! Aphrodite also decreed that we must always wear these bracelets fashioned by our captors, as a reminder that we must always keep aloof from men.

And so, after sailing the seas many days and many nights, we found Paradise Island and settled here to build a new World! With its fertile soil, its marvelous vegetation—its varied natural resources—here is no want, no illness, no hatreds, no wars, and as long as we remain on Paradise Island and I retain the MAGIC GIRDLE, we have the power of Eternal Life—so long as we do not permit ourselves to be again beguiled by men! We are indeed a race of Wonder Women!

That was the promise of Aphrodite—and we must keep our promise to her if we are to remain here safe and in peace!

That is why this American must go and as soon as possible!

Come, let me show you the Magic Sphere you've heard me talk about. It was given to me by Athena, the Goddess of Wisdom, just after we conquered the Herculeans and set sail for Paradise Island! It is through this Magic Sphere that I have been able to know what has gone on and is going on in the other world, and even, at times, forecast the future!

That is why we Amazons have been able to far surpass the inventions of the so-called man-made civilization! We are not only stronger and wiser than men—but our weapons are better—our flying machines are further advanced! And it is through the knowledge that I have gained from this Magic Sphere that I have taught you, my daughter, all the arts and sciences and languages of modern as well as ancient times!

But let us see where your American captain came from and how he got here. Watch closely—

The Magic Sphere reveals that Captain Trevor had been pursuing a Nazi spy ring when his fighter plane ran out of fuel, causing him to crash land on Paradise Island. Learning this, Princess Diana entreats her mother to help the officer return to America. Hippolyta dismisses her daughter in order to hold private council with the Amazon's Olympian benefactors.

IN THE QUEEN'S SOLITUDE, THE SPIRITS OF APHRODITE AND ATHENA, THE GUIDING GODDESSES OF THE AMAZONS, APPEAR AS THOUGH IN A MIST...

HIPPOLYTE, WE HAVE COME TO GIVE YOU WARNING. DANGER AGAIN THREATENS THE ENTIRE WORLD. THE GODS HAVE DECREED THAT THIS AMERICAN ARMY OFFICER CRASH ON PARADISE ISLAND. YOU MUST DELIVER HIM BACK TO AMERICA — TO HELP FIGHT THE FORCES OF HATE AND OPPRESSION.

YES, HIPPOLYTE, AMERICAN LIBERTY AND FREEDOM MUST BE PRESERVED! YOU MUST SEND WITH HIM YOUR STRONGEST AND WISEST AMAZON — THE FINEST OF YOUR WONDER WOMEN! — FOR AMERICA, THE LAST CITADEL OF DEMOCRACY, AND OF EQUAL RIGHTS FOR WOMEN, NEEDS YOUR HELP!

YES, APHRODITE, YES, ATHENA. I HEED YOUR CALL. I SHALL FIND THE STRONGEST AND WISEST OF THE AMAZONS. SHE SHALL GO FORTH TO FIGHT FOR LIBERTY AND FREEDOM AND ALL WOMANKIND!

AND SO THE AMAZON QUEEN PREPARES A TOURNAMENT TO DECIDE WHICH IS THE MOST CAPABLE OF HER SUBJECTS...

BUT MOTHER, WHY CAN'T I ENTER INTO THIS TOURNAMENT? SURELY, I HAVE AS MUCH RIGHT —

NO, DAUGHTER, NO! I FORBID YOU TO ENTER THE CONTEST! THE WINNER MUST TAKE THIS MAN BACK TO AMERICA AND NEVER RETURN, AND I COULDN'T BEAR TO HAVE YOU LEAVE ME FOREVER!

THE GREAT DAY ARRIVES! FROM ALL PARTS OF PARADISE ISLAND COME THE AMAZON CONTESTANTS! BUT ONE YOUNG CONTESTANT INSISTS ON WEARING A MASK...

IF YOU ARE ALL READY, LET THE TOURNAMENT BEGIN — AND MAY THE BEST MAIDEN WIN!
PROCLAMATION
12
7
49
4

THE TESTS BEGIN! FIRST...THE FOOT RACE! A TRAINED DEER SETS THE PACE! AS THE DEER EASILY OUTRUNS THE PACK, SUDDENLY THE SLIM MASKED FIGURE DARTS FORWARD, HER LEGS CHURNING MADLY...

AND NOT ONLY CATCHES UP WITH THE DEER — BUT PASSES IT!

AS THE TESTS OF STRENGTH AND AGILITY GO ON THROUGHOUT THE DAY, MORE AND MORE CONTESTANTS DROP OUT WEARILY, UNTIL NUMBER 7, THE MASKED MAIDEN, AND MALA — NUMBER 12 — KEEP WINNING EVENT AFTER EVENT... UNTIL EACH HAS WON TEN OF THE GRUELLING CONTESTS!

AND NOW A DEADLY HUSH BLANKETS THE AUDIENCE. THE QUEEN HAS RISEN...

BULLETS AND BRACELETS!
BULLETS AND BRACELETS!
CONTESTANTS 7 AND 12, YOU ARE THE ONLY SURVIVORS OF THE TOURNAMENT! NOW YOU MUST GET READY FOR THE 21ST, THE FINAL AND GREATEST TEST OF ALL — BULLETS AND BRACELETS!
BULLETS AND BRACELETS!
BULLETS AND BRACELETS!
12
7
10
8
42
19

EACH OF YOU WILL SHOOT FIVE TIMES. YOUR OPPONENT MUST CATCH THE BULLETS ON HER BRACELET - OR ELSE EXPECT TO BE WOUNDED! NOW TAKE YOUR PLACES NUMBER 12 WILL SHOOT FIRST.

THE COMMAND... AND THE GIRL FIRES POINT-BLANK AT NUMBER 7, THE MASKED MAIDEN!

THE ULTIMATE TEST OF SPEED OF BOTH EYE AND MOVEMENT! NO.7'S BRACELETS BECOME SILVER FLASHES OF STREAKING LIGHT AS THEY PARRY THE DEATH-THRUSTS OF THE HURTLING BULLETS!

NO.7 PASSES THE TEST UNSCATHED! NOW IT IS HER TURN TO FIRE. HER OPPONENT'S FAST— BUT NOT FAST ENOUGH!

THE WINNER... CONTESTANT NO.7 — THE MASKED MAIDEN!

I KNEW IT— I FELT IT! I THOUGHT PERHAPS - WELL, IT'S TOO LATE NOW! YOU'VE WON AND I'M PROUD OF YOU! IN AMERICA YOU'LL INDEED BE A "WONDER WOMAN," FOR I HAVE TAUGHT YOU WELL! AND LET YOURSELF BE KNOWN AS DIANA, AFTER YOUR GODMOTHER, THE GODDESS OF THE MOON! AND HERE IS A COSTUME I HAVE DESIGNED TO BE USED BY THE WINNER, TO WEAR IN AMERICA.

WHY MOTHER, IT'S LOVELY!

AND SO DIANA, THE WONDER WOMAN, GIVING UP HER HERITAGE, AND HER RIGHT TO ETERNAL LIFE, LEAVES PARADISE ISLAND TO TAKE THE MAN SHE LOVES BACK TO AMERICA—THE LAND SHE LEARNS TO LOVE AND PROTECT, AND ADOPTS AS HER OWN!

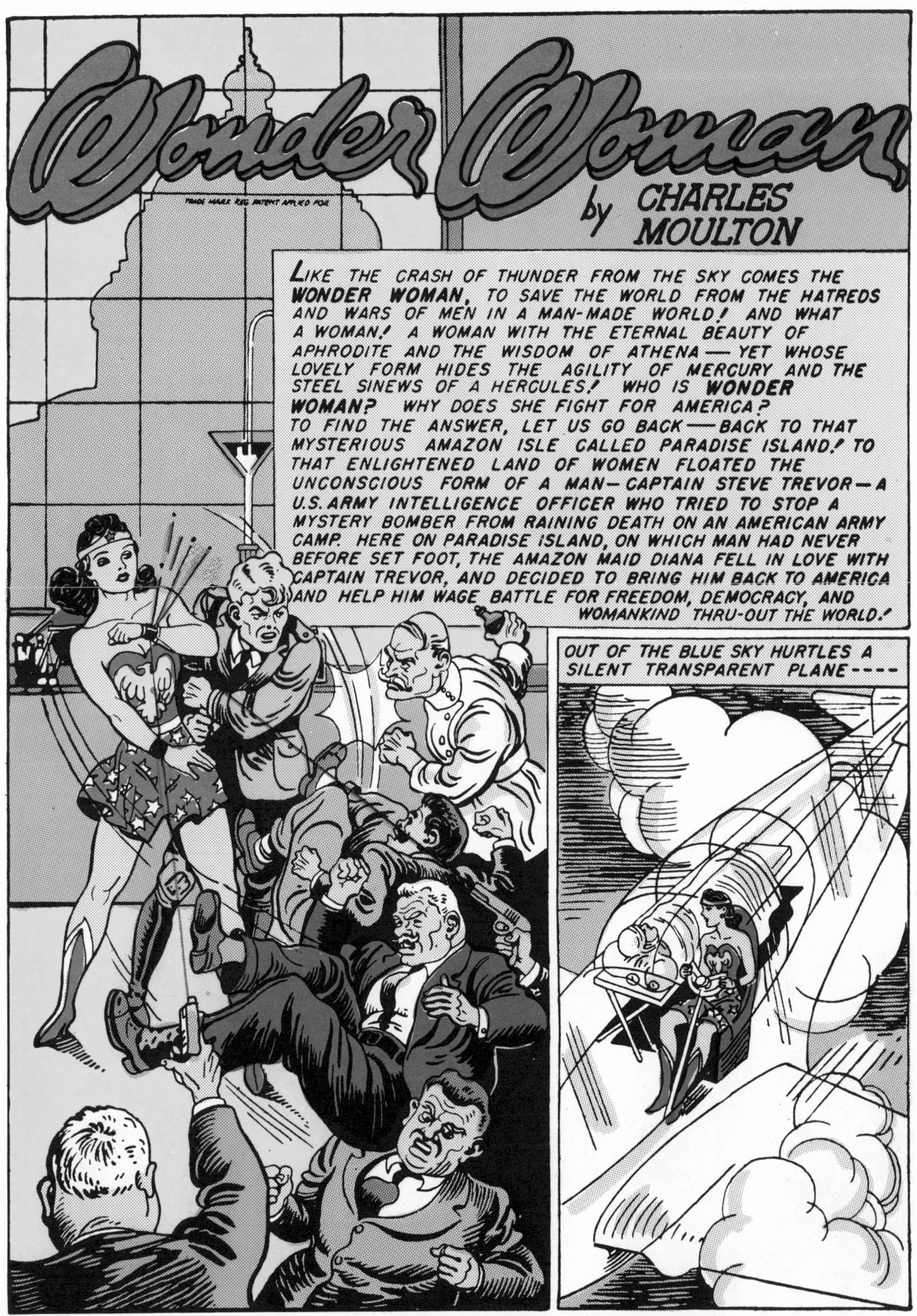
Wonder Woman
TRADE MARK REG. PATENT APPLIED FOR
by CHARLES MOULTON
LIKE THE CRASH OF THUNDER FROM THE SKY COMES THE WONDER WOMAN, TO SAVE THE WORLD FROM THE HATREDS AND WARS OF MEN IN A MAN-MADE WORLD! AND WHAT A WOMAN! A WOMAN WITH THE ETERNAL BEAUTY OF APHRODITE AND THE WISDOM OF ATHENA — YET WHOSE LOVELY FORM HIDES THE AGILITY OF MERCURY AND THE STEEL SINEWS OF A HERCULES! WHO IS WONDER WOMAN? WHY DOES SHE FIGHT FOR AMERICA? TO FIND THE ANSWER, LET US GO BACK — BACK TO THAT MYSTERIOUS AMAZON ISLE CALLED PARADISE ISLAND! TO THAT ENLIGHTENED LAND OF WOMEN FLOATED THE UNCONSCIOUS FORM OF A MAN — CAPTAIN STEVE TREVOR — A U.S. ARMY INTELLIGENCE OFFICER WHO TRIED TO STOP A MYSTERY BOMBER FROM RAINING DEATH ON AN AMERICAN ARMY CAMP. HERE ON PARADISE ISLAND, ON WHICH MAN HAD NEVER BEFORE SET FOOT, THE AMAZON MAID DIANA FELL IN LOVE WITH CAPTAIN TREVOR, AND DECIDED TO BRING HIM BACK TO AMERICA AND HELP HIM WAGE BATTLE FOR FREEDOM, DEMOCRACY, AND WOMANKIND THRU-OUT THE WORLD!
OUT OF THE BLUE SKY HURTLES A SILENT TRANSPARENT PLANE ----

AND AT THE CONTROLS IS AN AMAZON MAIDEN, NAMED DIANA BY HER MOTHER, QUEEN OF THE AMAZONS, AFTER HER GODMOTHER, GODDESS OF THE MOON!
HE'S STIRRING! PERHAPS I'D BETTER REMOVE HIS BANDAGES!
OH-H-H!

WHERE--? I'M IN HEAVEN! THERE'S AN ANGEL SMILING AT ME--- A BEAUTIFUL ANGEL!

HE'S FAINTED! HE'S STILL VERY WEAK. HE CALLED ME AN ANGEL--- A BEAUTIFUL ANGEL. THAT'S THE FIRST TIME A MAN EVER CALLED ME-- BEAUTIFUL!

ON--- ON SPEEDS THE PLANE UNTIL IT REACHES ITS DESTINATION — WASHINGTON, D.C.!
AT LAST I'M HERE — IN THE CAPITAL OF THE UNITED STATES!

DIANA BRINGS THE TRANSPARENT PLANE DOWN ON AN ABANDONED FIELD ON THE OUTSKIRTS OF WASHINGTON.
THIS DESERTED BARN SHOULD DO NICELY AS A HIDEOUT FOR MY PLANE!

PICKING UP STEVE TREVOR, SHE RACES SWIFTLY TO THE WALTER REED HOSPITAL.
GOOD THING IT IS STILL VERY EARLY IN THE MORNING SO THE STREETS ARE DESERTED.
2

AND INSIDE---
THIS IS CAPTAIN STEVE TREVOR OF THE ARMY INTELLIGENCE! HE'S HAD A BRAIN CONCUSSION! SEE THAT HE'S TAKEN CARE OF!
WHO-WHAT?

BUT-BUT WAIT! WHO ARE YOU?
I'LL SEND YOU A FULL REPORT SOMETIME! 'BYE!

NOW WHAT TO DO WITH MY TIME? HM-M! MOTHER TOLD ME SO MUCH ABOUT STYLES OF AMERICAN WOMEN THAT I'M DYING TO SEE THEM!
ALWAYS THE WOMAN, DIANA GOES WINDOW SHOPPING---
THERE'S SO MUCH MATERIAL TO THEIR DRESSES--- BUT THEY ARE CUTE! HM-M! THERE'S A NICE FROCK!
AND NOW AS PEOPLE BEGIN TO THRONG THE STREETS THEY ARE NO LITTLE AMAZED TO SEE THE SCANTILY CLAD GIRL WALKING ABOUT SO UNCONCERNED---
THE HUSSY! SHE HAS NO CLOTHES ON!
THE BRAZEN THING! HMPH! HMPH!
HA! SOUR GRAPES SISTER, DONT YOU WISH YOU LOOKED LIKE THAT!
BOY! WHATTA HONEY!
AW--- I'LL BET IT'S SOME SORT O' PUBLICITY STUNT FOR A NEW MOVIN' PITCHER.
IF IT IS, THEY CERTAINLY GO TO EXTREME LENGTHS TO ATTRACT THE PUBLIC EYE!
WELL, THEY CERTAINLY ATTRACTED MY EYE!
SUDDENLY ALL THOUGHTS OF DIANA ARE FORGOTTEN--- SCREAMS AND SHOTS CUT THROUGH THE AIR!
BANK
C'MON! LET'S GET TO THE CAR FAST!
IT'S A HOLD-UP!
AS IF OUT OF NOWHERE A FIGURE DARTS FORWARD AND BLOCKS THE BANDITS FROM THEIR CAR!
PLUG HER AND LET'S SCRAM OUT OF HERE!
WHAT TH--? IT'S A DAME!
LIKE ONE MAN, THE BANDITS LEVEL THEIR GUNS AND FIRE!
BUT WITH SPEED FASTER THAN THE EYE CAN FOLLOW, THE AMAZON MAIDEN CATCHES THE HURTLING BULLETS ON HER WRIST-BRACELETS!
IT'S FUN TO BE PLAYING "BULLETS AND BRACELETS" AGAIN!
3

WONDER WOMAN

SHE'S PLAYIN' WITH 'EM! SHE'S PLAYIN' CATCH WITH EM!
AND NOW I'M GOING TO PLAY CATCH WITH YOU!

DIANA'S HAND CLOSES LIKE A STEEL CLAMP ABOUT THE BANDIT'S WRIST---

WH-?

CATCH!

WHA - WHAT'S GOIN' ON AROUND HERE?
I DON'T KNOW. I HEARD SOMEONE SAY "IT'S A HOLD-UP." GOOD-BYE!

WAIT! WE WANT TO ASK YOU A FEW QUESTIONS!
SOME OTHER TIME, WHEN I'M ON THE "QUIZ KIDS" PROGRAM!
4

AS DIANA DARTS AWAY, ONE MAN SLIPS FROM THE EDGE OF THE CROWD---
DID YOU SEE HER SLAP THOSE BANDITS AROUND?
AND DID YOU SEE HER SLAP THOSE BULLETS AROUND? NOW THAT WAS SOMETHING!
WONDER WHO SHE IS?

HEY-- WAIT! SHE'S RUNNING FASTER! I'LL STEP ON THE GAS AND CATCH UP TO HER!
EVEN AS THE CAR WHIPS FORWARD, DIANA PUTS ON A GREAT BURST OF SPEED.
WHAT TH'—SHE'S GOING FASTER AND THE CAR'S DOING 35 MILES PER!
FASTER SPEEDS THE CAR, AND FASTER SPEEDS THE HUMAN METEOR AHEAD!
HOLY SMOKE! I'VE GOT THE CAR AT 50MILES PER HOUR—AND I STILL HAVEN'T CAUGHT UP WITH HER!
FASTER---FASTER---FASTER--FASTER- UNTIL DIANA COVERS GROUND AT A MILE-A-MINUTE!
60 MILES AN HOUR--AND SHE'S STILL AHEAD! I'M GOING TO OPEN UP THIS BUGGY TO THE LIMIT!
FASTER AND STILL FASTER---UNTIL AT 80 MILES PER HOUR, THE CAR DRAWS ALONGSIDE THE MILE-A-MINUTE MAIDEN!
HEY--- WAIT-- I JUST WANT TO TALK TO YOU ABOUT A BUSINESS PROPOSITION!
SAY--WHAT ARE YOU? WHEW! YOU WERE BURNING UP THE ROAD!
WHAT'S THIS--- BUSINESS PROPOSITION-- YOU TALKED ABOUT?
MY NAME IS AL KALE! I BOOK ACTS FOR THEATRES! NOW I DON'T KNOW WHAT YOUR RACKET IS AND I DON'T CARE. ALL I KNOW IS THAT THOSE SPEEDY LEGS OF YOURS, OR THAT "BULLET" TRICK COULD NET US A FORTUNE!
YOU MEAN YOU WANT TO PUT ME ON A STAGE?
EITHER ON THE TRACK OR THE STAGE! RACING—OR THAT "BULLET" TRICK IN THE THEATRES. IT WOULD BRING YOU PLENTY OF MONEY!
5

YES, I WILL NEED MONEY. AND I DO HAVE TO KILL TIME TILL STEVE RECOVERS CONSCIOUSNESS---
I'LL DO IT! I'LL PUT ON MY "BULLETS AND BRACELETS" ACT FOR YOU! BUT THE RACING IS OUT!
THAT'S O.K. WITH ME. WE'LL CLEAN UP WITH THAT "BULLETS" ACT ANYWAY! BOY-OH-BOY-OH-BOY-
AND "CLEAN UP" THEY DO---FOR THE "BULLETS AND BRACELETS" IS A GREAT ATTRACTION AND A SOURCE OF WONDER TO ALL!
THE PAPERS GIVE THE "WONDER WOMAN" PLENTY OF PUBLICITY---
AMUSEMENT PAGE
"BULLETS GO TO WASTE ON WONDER WOMAN"
"WONDER WOMAN" BREAKS RECORDS AT BIJOU THEATRE
WONDER WOMAN
MYSTER WOMAN INCRED ACT
BUT AT LAST, ONE DAY THERE APPEARS AN ITEM THAT ATTRACTS WONDER WOMAN'S ATTENTION---
HOSPITAL AUTHORITIES REPORT THAT CAPTAIN TREVOR HAS AT LONG LAST RECOVERED CONSCIO A BRAIN CONCUSSION CAUSED THE COMA THAT LASTED THRE WEEKS. A MYSTERIOUS GIRL FIRST BROUGHT HI
BUT YOU CAN'T QUIT NOW! WE'RE KNOCKIN' 'EM DEAD! WE'RE MAKING MORE MONEY THAN---
MAKING MORE MONEY DOESN'T INTEREST ME ANY MORE! I'M SORRY, BUT I'M THROUGH WITH THE ACT!
I CAN'T HOLD HER. SHE DIDN'T SIGN ANY CONTRACT. WHEN I THINK OF ALL THE DOUGH WE COULD--- DOUGH ---SAY---I GOT HER DOUGH THAT SHE TOLD ME TO HOLD FOR HER! HMMM---
6
KALE---GONE--AND WITH ALL MY EARNINGS! I----- THERE HE IS— GETTING INTO HIS CAR!

WITHOUT A MOMENT'S HESITATION, WONDER WOMAN HURLS HER SLIM FORM THROUGH THE OPEN WINDOW-- AND PLUNGES TO THE STREET BELOW!
AND WONDER WOMAN LANDS ON THE BALLS OF HER FEET LIGHTLY AS A CAT!
MADE IT VERY NICELY!
WHAT'S THIS? I'M STEPPING ON THE GAS AND THE CAR DOESN'T MOVE! WHAT'S 'SMATTER
DON'T YOU THINK THIS IS A GOOD ENOUGH REASON?
YOU!
ULP! LET ME GO--- LET ME GO!
ALL RIGHT!
YI-I-I-II-II
AS LONG AS YOU INSIST!
DON'T LEAVE ME UP HERE!
NOW I'LL JUST TAKE MY OWN MONEY-AND BID YOU A FOND FAREWELL! GOOD-BYE, HIGH AND NOT SO MIGHTY!
THE NEXT DAY, WONDER WOMAN APPROACHES THE HOSPITAL----
STEVE... STEVE I'VE GOT TO SEE HIM--BE NEAR HIM--BUT HOW?
7

AS SHE NEARS THE STEPS, WONDER WOMAN SEES A GIRL HUDDLED AND CRYING THERE---
I DON'T MEAN TO INTRUDE BUT CAN I HELP YOU?
NO ONE CAN HELP ME! BOO-HOO!

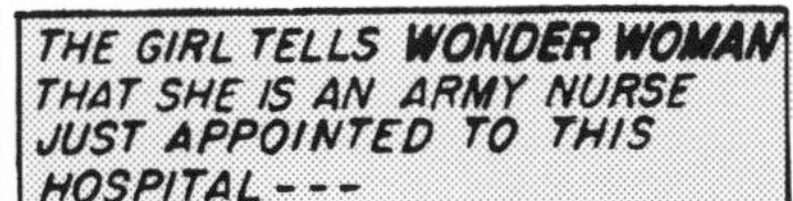
THE GIRL TELLS WONDER WOMAN THAT SHE IS AN ARMY NURSE JUST APPOINTED TO THIS HOSPITAL---

AND TODAY MY FIANCE JUST GOT A JOB IN SOUTH AMERICA, BUT HE CAN'T SEND FOR ME BECAUSE HIS SALARY IS TOO SMALL AT THE MOMENT!
THAT'S TERRIBLE, AND JUST THINK--IT ALL WOULD WORK OUT RIGHT IF ONLY YOU HAD A LITTLE MONEY!

I JUST NOTICED — WITH THESE GLASSES OFF, YOU LOOK A LOT LIKE ME! I HAVE AN IDEA! IF I GAVE YOU MONEY WOULD YOU SELL ME YOUR CREDENTIALS?
YOU--YOU MEAN YOU WANT TO TAKE MY PLACE HERE AT THE HOSPITAL? BUT-I CAN'T--- I MEAN--

LOOK— BY TAKING YOUR PLACE I CAN SEE THE MAN I LOVE AND YOU CAN MARRY THE MAN YOU LOVE! NO HARM DONE, FOR I'M A TRAINED NURSE, TOO—JUST A LITTLE MONEY AND A SUBSTITUTION—
AND WE'D BOTH BE HAPPY! I'LL DO IT! OH—THIS IS WONDERFUL!

OH, BY THE WAY-MY NAME IS DIANA. WHAT'S YOURS?
WHY THAT'S AN AMAZING COINCIDENCE—I'M DIANA TOO! DIANA PRINCE! AND YOU'D BETTER REMEMBER THAT LAST NAME— BECAUSE IT'LL BE YOURS FROM NOW ON.

AND SO THAT AFTERNOON----
AN ANGEL--- A BEAUTIFUL ANGEL!
OH, CAPTAIN TREVOR —YOU FLATTER ME I'M JUST DIANA PRINCE, YOUR SPECIAL NURSE!
HE REMEMBERED ME---HE REMEMBERED!

DAYS PASS AND STEVE TREVOR RECOVERS RAPIDLY UNDER HIS NEW NURSE'S TENDER CARE---
YOU'RE PRETTY SWELL TO ME, DIANA! BUT I'M JUST WASTING AWAY HERE. I SHOULD BE BACK ON MY JOB!
I DON'T BELIEVE IT'S YOUR JOB. YOU WANT TO FIND THAT "BEAUTIFUL ANGEL" YOU WERE TALKING ABOUT- THE ONE WHO BROUGHT YOU HERE! BE A GOOD BOY, NOW, AND KEEP QUIET---

GREAT GUNS! NOW I'VE GOT TO GO--- DOCTOR OR NO DOCTOR!

BY THE TIME THEY NOTICE I'M GONE, IT'LL BE TOO LATE TO STOP ME!
HE'S GONE! OVER-EXERTION MAY KILL TREVOR! IT'S YOUR FAULT, NURSE---YOU SHOULD NEVER HAVE LEFT THE ROOM--
"NEW DRAFT QUOTA CALLED TOMORROW. MYSTERIOUS ENEMY THREATENS TO BOMB CAMP MERRICK WITH A NEW POISON GAS WHICH PENETRATES ALL GAS MASKS!
SORRY DOCTOR!
THAT NIGHT, NURSE DIANA PRINCE DARTS TOWARD AN OLD DESERTED BARN ON THE OUTSKIRTS OF WASHINGTON----
I HOPE NO ONE'S FOUND THIS HIDEOUT WHILE I'VE BEEN NURSING STEVE TREVOR!
INSIDE THE BARN, THE GIRL TRANSFORMS HERSELF FROM DRAB DIANA PRINCE TO THE EXCITING AMAZON MAIDEN... WONDER WOMAN!
IT FEELS GRAND TO BE MYSELF AGAIN! AND NOW FOR CLEVER STEVE TREVOR--- THE IMPETUOUS DARLING!
AT CAMP MERRICK, STEVE TREVOR REPORTS TO THE C.O.!
I'VE GOT AIR PATROLS COVERING THE ENTIRE COAST. BUT THIS MYSTERY BOMBER USES A STRATOSPHERE PLANE. HE'LL POWER DIVE ON THE CAMP AND I'M GOING TO WAIT FOR HIM.
WE'RE DEPENDING ON YOU, CAPTAIN!
HIGH OVER CAMP MERRICK, STEVE TREVOR CIRCLES LIKE A BIRD OF PREY--WAITING FOR THE ENEMY!
THEN--LIKE A DIVING, WINGED COMET--THE MYSTERY BOMBER!
WOW! HE MUST BE DOING 650 M.P.H.! I'VE GOT TO STOP HIM!
JUMPING BLUE BLAZES! THAT GUY'S GOT A FLYING FORT! I CAN'T EVEN DENT HIS POLISH!
9

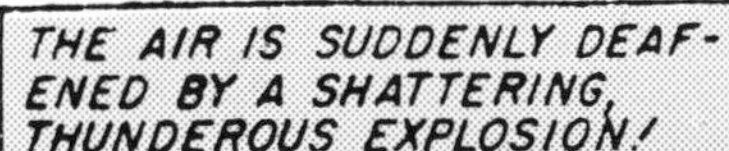
WONDER WOMAN

THE ONLY THING TO DO--CRASH HIM! HERE GOES NOTHING!

THE AIR IS SUDDENLY DEAF-ENED BY A SHATTERING, THUNDEROUS EXPLOSION!
I GOT HIM--BUT MY 'CHUTE! IT'S-IT'S RIPPED AWAY! I'M A GONER FOR SURE! KEEP 'EM FLYING BOYS!

LIKE A STREAK OF LIGHT, A SILENT, TRANSPARENT PLANE HURTLES OUT OF THE BLUE WITH WONDER WOMAN AT THE CONTROLS!

I'LL SET MY ROBOT CONTROL PILOT AND LET DOWN THE LADDER! I HOPE I'M NOT TOO LATE! I CAN'T BE---I MUSTN'T BE!

WONDER WOMAN'S RIGHT ARM GRASPS TREVOR'S FALLING BODY AND TIGHTENS AROUND HIS WAIST WITH THE UNFAILING GRIP OF A BOA-CONSTRICTOR! THE SHOCK IS GREAT BUT HER LOVE AND STRENGTH ARE GREATER!
GOT HIM! NOW TO CARRY HIM BACK TO MY PLANE!

YOU---THE BEAUTIFUL ANGEL!
A GUARDIAN ANGEL IS MORE LIKE IT!

LOOK! THERE'S YOUR BOMB-SLINGER! WE'D BETTER COLLECT HIM AND ASK HIM A FEW QUESTIONS. TAKE THE CONTROLS.
DOWN THE SWAYING LADDER CLIMBS WONDER WOMAN AND THE PARACHUTIST FIRES POINT-BLANK!
STILL PLAYING HARD TO GET, EH?
NOTHING LIKE A GOOD RIGHT HOOK TO SETTLE AN ARGUMENT!
WHY HE'S BEEN WOUNDED- I'D BETTER GET HIM UP TO MY PLANE.
THIS DEVIL IS DONE FOR! THAT CRASH—HE WON'T LIVE TO TALK.
THE CAPTAIN IS RIGHT--I DIE! BUT SOON MY COMRADES WILL COME IN MORE PLANES, MORE POISON GAS FROM THE SECRET BASE! YOU... YOU WILL NEVER FIND---
HE'S RIGHT! I LOCATED THEIR SECRET BASE ONCE, BUT THEY'VE MOVED IT AND I'LL NEVER FIND IT NOW!
BUT I CAN!
GOOD THING I ANTICIPATED THIS AND HAD MOTHER LOOK UP THIS SECRET BASE IN THE MAGIC SPHERE BEFORE I LEFT PARADISE ISLAND!
11
STRAIGHT AS AN ARROW, WONDER WOMAN'S PLANE FLIES TO THE SECRET BASE SHE HAD THUS LEARNED ABOUT.
WONDER WOMAN, IN HER SILENT, INVISIBLE PLANE LANDS UNDETECTED ON THE ENEMY ISLAND!

AS TWO GUARDS PATROL THE GROUNDS, TWO SINISTER FIGURES CATAPULT OUT OF THE SHRUBBERY
WHAT!!?
SINCE THESE DOORS ARE LOCKED·· WHY, WE'LL HAVE TO LET OURSELVES IN!
WELL I'LL BE.. LOOK AT HER!
HOW NICE TO MAKE YOUR ACQUAINTANCE!
HERE-PUT ON THIS MASK!
TREVOR FIRES AT A CONTAINER OF POISON GAS!
THE GAS GATHERS LIKE A MALIGNANT CLOUD ABOUT THE ENEMY BUT THE GAS MASKS PROTECT WONDER WOMAN AND TREVOR!
LOOK! THERE'S THEIR LEADER!
LOOK OUT! HE'S THROWING A SWITCH!
FOOLS! I'LL DIE-BUT YOU DIE WITH ME!
THERE IS ONE TERRIBLE, CATACLYSMIC BLAST... AN ETERNAL MOMENT OF SHATTERING RUIN...

WONDER WOMAN EASILY LEAPS CLEAR — BUT STEVE IS BURIED UNDER THE DEBRIS!

WORKING AT A FEVERISH PACE WONDER WOMAN UNCOVERS STEVE TREVOR---
ARE YOU HURT STEVE? WHY DIDN'T YOU JUMP LIKE I DID?
JUMP LIKE YOU? WHAT AM I— A KANGAROO?

YOUR LEG-- . IT'S BROKEN!
MY LEG DOES SEEM BENT A BIT--BUT I'M GLAD OF IT. AT LEAST IT SHOWS YOU CARE!

YOUR LEG WILL BE RIGHT AS NEW IN A SHORT WHILE. ARUMPH... YOU DID MAGNIFICENT WORK, CAPTAIN.... MAGNIFICENT!
I DIDN'T DO IT! A BEAUTIFUL ANGEL WAS RESPONSIBLE!

CONGRATULATIONS, CAPTAIN! YOU DID EXCELLENT WORK!

THANKS. CHIEF. BUT FOR HEAVEN'S SAKE, DON'T GIVE ME THE CREDIT. IT BELONGS TO THAT BEAUTIFUL GIRL— WONDER WOMAN!

LATER....
JUST SAW THE GENERAL OUTSIDE. THEY THINK YOU'RE DELIRIOUS, TALKING ABOUT A "BEAUTIFUL ANGEL"-- A WONDER WOMAN WHO REALLY BROKE UP THAT NAZI GANG AND SAVED YOUR LIFE!
THAT'S RIGHT! YOU LAUGH, TOO.. BUT I'M NOT DELIRIOUS YOU HEAR ME! THERE IS A WONDER WOMAN! I SAW HER!

ALL RIGHT, I BELIEVE YOU! ANYWAY, CAPTAIN.... YOU DON'T NEED WONDER WOMAN NOW — YOU'VE GOT ME!
LISTEN, DIANA! YOU'RE A NICE KID, AND I LIKE YOU. BUT IF YOU THINK YOU CAN HOLD A CANDLE TO WONDER WOMAN YOU'RE CRAZY!
13

SO I'M MY OWN RIVAL, EH? THAT'S FUNNY... IF MOTHER COULD ONLY SEE ME NOW.... AS A VERY FEMININE WOMAN.. A NURSE, NO LESS, IN A WORLD FULL OF MEN, AND IN LOVE, TOO - WITH MYSELF FOR A RIVAL!

AND SO ENDS THE FIRST EPISODE OF
WONDER WOMAN
ALIAS DIANA PRINCE, ARMY NURSE!
FOLLOW HER EXCITING ADVENTURES AS SHE BESTS THE WORLD'S MOST VILLAINOUS MEN AT THEIR OWN GAME EVERY MONTH IN
SENSATION COMICS

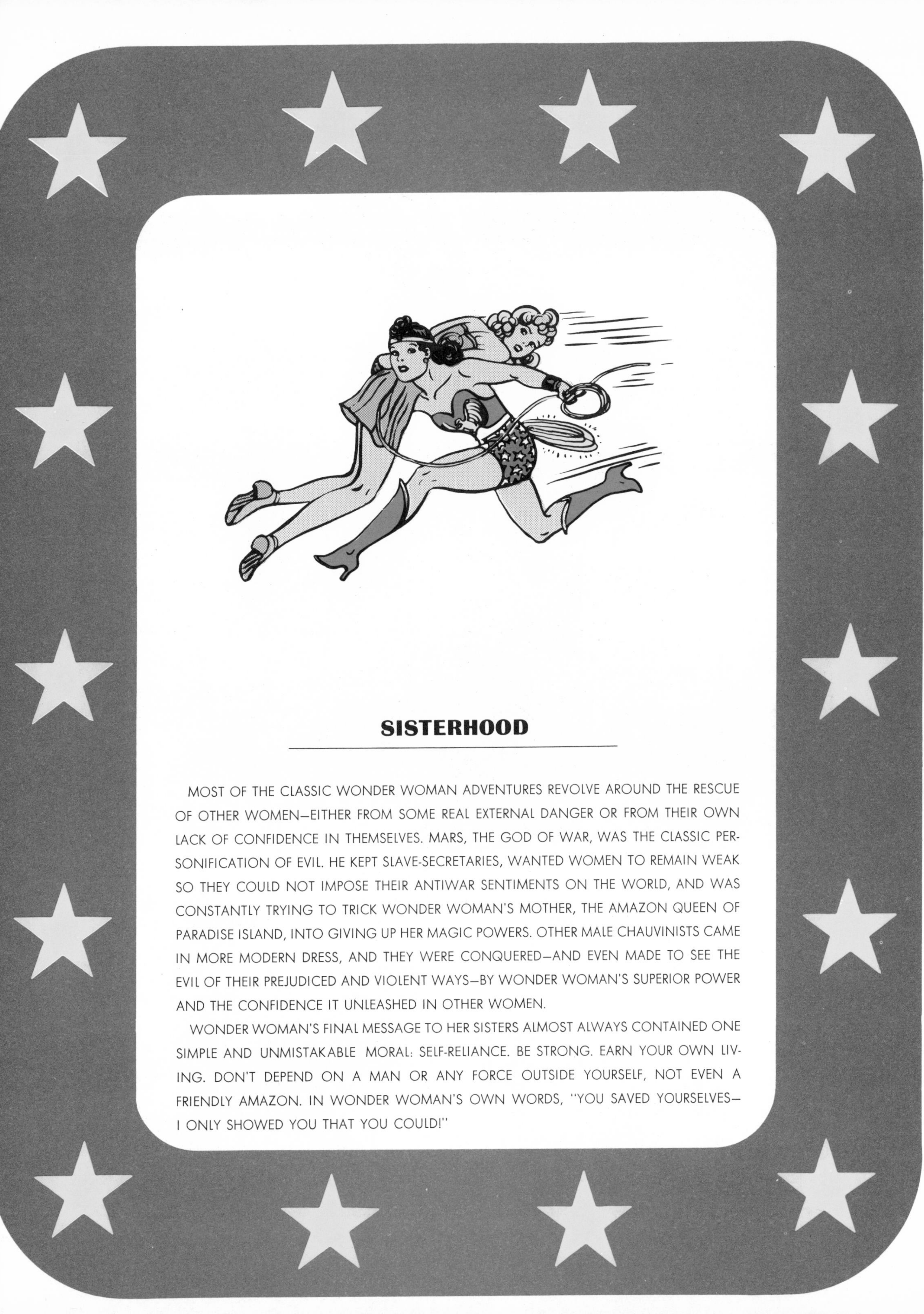

SISTERHOOD

MOST OF THE CLASSIC WONDER WOMAN ADVENTURES REVOLVE AROUND THE RESCUE OF OTHER WOMEN—EITHER FROM SOME REAL EXTERNAL DANGER OR FROM THEIR OWN LACK OF CONFIDENCE IN THEMSELVES. MARS, THE GOD OF WAR, WAS THE CLASSIC PERSONIFICATION OF EVIL. HE KEPT SLAVE-SECRETARIES, WANTED WOMEN TO REMAIN WEAK SO THEY COULD NOT IMPOSE THEIR ANTIWAR SENTIMENTS ON THE WORLD, AND WAS CONSTANTLY TRYING TO TRICK WONDER WOMAN'S MOTHER, THE AMAZON QUEEN OF PARADISE ISLAND, INTO GIVING UP HER MAGIC POWERS. OTHER MALE CHAUVINISTS CAME IN MORE MODERN DRESS, AND THEY WERE CONQUERED—AND EVEN MADE TO SEE THE EVIL OF THEIR PREJUDICED AND VIOLENT WAYS—BY WONDER WOMAN'S SUPERIOR POWER AND THE CONFIDENCE IT UNLEASHED IN OTHER WOMEN.

WONDER WOMAN'S FINAL MESSAGE TO HER SISTERS ALMOST ALWAYS CONTAINED ONE SIMPLE AND UNMISTAKABLE MORAL: SELF-RELIANCE. BE STRONG. EARN YOUR OWN LIVING. DON'T DEPEND ON A MAN OR ANY FORCE OUTSIDE YOURSELF, NOT EVEN A FRIENDLY AMAZON. IN WONDER WOMAN'S OWN WORDS, "YOU SAVED YOURSELVES—I ONLY SHOWED YOU THAT YOU COULD!"

Wonder Woman
By CHARLES MOULTON
WHO IS THE DEVIOUS DOCTOR PSYCHO? KNOWN WHEREVER HIS EVIL GENIUS STRIKES AS THE MAN WITH A THOUSAND FACES, THIS MONSTER ABHORS WOMEN! WITH WEIRD CUNNING AND DARK, FORBIDDEN KNOWLEDGE OF THE OCCULT, DR. PSYCHO PREPARES TO CHANGE THE INDEPENDENT STATUS OF MODERN AMERICAN WOMEN BACK TO THE DAYS OF THE SULTANS AND SLAVE MARKETS, CLANKING CHAINS AND ABJECT CAPTIVITY.
BUT SLY AND SUBTLE PSYCHO RECKONS WITHOUT WONDER WOMAN! ACCEPTING THE MAD DOCTOR'S CHALLENGE, THE LOVELY AMAZON GIRL FIGHTS TO STOP A PERSECUTION OF HER FAIR SEX WHICH THREATENS EVEN THE ALLURING COHORTS OF APHRODITE WITH SHAMEFUL SHACKLES AND MENACES THE ENTIRE EARTH WITH PERPETUAL PUNISHMENT.
BEAUTIFUL AS APHRODITE, WISE AS ATHENA, STRONGER THAN HERCULES AND SWIFTER THAN MERCURY, WONDER WOMAN COMES FROM THE ISLE OF PARADISE WHERE FASCINATING WOMEN RULE SUPREME TO BRING DELIGHT AND HAPPINESS TO THE WORLD OF MEN!
YOU'LL LOVE WONDER WOMAN MORE THAN EVER AS YOU FOLLOW THE COURAGEOUS GIRL THROUGH HER MOST EXCITING ORDEALS IN THE "BATTLE FOR WOMANHOOD."
MARS, THE WAR GOD, PRESENT RULER OF THIS WORLD, RECEIVES UNPLEASANT INFORMATION FROM HIS SLAVE-SECRETARY.
HERE IS THE REPORT YOU ASKED FOR — THERE ARE EIGHT MILLION AMERICAN WOMEN IN WAR ACTIVITIES - BY 1944 THERE WILL BE EIGHTEEN MILLION!
HOUNDS OF HADES! WOMEN! THIS SMELLS LIKE MORE OF APHRODITE'S WORK!
1A

AMERICAN WOMEN ARE WARRIORS-WAACS, WAVES, SECRET AGENTS! 10 MILLION BRITISH WOMEN ARE IN WAR SERVICE, 30 MILLION RUSSIAN WOMEN—
SILENCE-ENOUGH! IF WOMEN GAIN POWER IN WAR THEY'LL ESCAPE MAN'S DOMINATION COMPLETELY! THEY WILL ACHIEVE A HORRIBLE INDEPENDENCE!
SUMMON MY WAR STAFF-COUNT CONQUEST, THE EARL OF GREED AND DUKE OF DECEPTION! I WON'T TOLERATE GIVING WOMEN THE SLIGHTEST FREEDOM!
YOU'RE TELLING ME!
YES, MASTER, YOUR SLAVE OBEYS!
MARS LECTURES HIS LIEUTENANTS.
WOMEN ARE THE NATURAL SPOILS OF WAR! THEY MUST REMAIN AT HOME, HELPLESS SLAVES FOR THE VICTOR! IF WOMEN BECOME WARRIORS LIKE THE AMAZONS, THEY'LL GROW STRONGER THAN MEN AND PUT AN END TO WAR!
AYE MAJESTY!
GO TO EARTH AND PUT THESE UPSTART FEMALES IN THEIR PLACE!
IT CAN'T BE DONE WITH WONDER WOMAN AGAINST US!
FIGHTING WONDER WOMAN ISN'T PROFITABLE.
SHE BEAT YOU, MARS! SHE'LL MURDER ME!
COWARDS ALL! DECEPTION, YOU'RE THE ONE TO FOOL FEMALES! GET BUSY OR—
YES, DIVINITY, I OBEY. I HAVE AN EARTH AGENT WHO HATES WOMEN-I'LL PUT HIM TO WORK AT ONCE.
AND SO, ON EARTH, THE DEVIOUS DR. PSYCHO RECEIVES AN EVIL INSPIRATION.
Z-Z-ZUT! A SPIRIT TELLS ME MY HOUR OF VENGEANCE IS AT HAND! WOMEN SHALL SUFFER WHILE I LAUGH— HA! HO! HA!
THE SUBTLE PSYCHO'S PAST IS SHROUDED IN MYSTERY. IN MEDICAL SCHOOL HIS BRILLIANT MIND WON HIM RECOGNITION—
THIS MEDAL IS THE HIGHEST AWARD OUR UNIVERSITY CAN GIVE!
I'M PROUD OF THIS HONOR.
HA! HA! HE IS COMICAL! HA! HA!
CLAP
CLAP
2A.

HIS CLASSMATES' HUMOR HURTS PSYCHO.
GREAT WORK, PUMPKIN HEAD! YOUR BRAINS MAKE YOU TOP-HEAVY! CONGRATULATIONS, POCKET NAPOLEON!
OH LET ME ALONE!
I KNOW I'M FUNNY LOOKING BUT THEY MIGHT LET ME FORGET IT THIS ONCE!
PSYCHO MEETS MARVA, HIS FIANCEE.
AREN'T YOU GOING TO CONGRATULATE ME, MARVA?
YES - YOU DON'T HAVE TO GET MUSHY - YOU KNOW I ADMIRE YOUR BRILLIANT MIND, BUT— WELL - YOU'RE NOT EXACTLY A CLARK GABLE! LOVE-MAKING DOESN'T BECOME YOU!
LATER PSYCHO SEES MARVA WITH BEN BRADLEY, ATHLETIC IDOL OF THE COLLEGE.
MARVA, MARRY ME!
OH BEN I CAN'T— I'M ENGAGED!
SHE LOVES BEN BECAUSE HE'S HANDSOME— I OUGHT TO LET HER MARRY HIM!
THAT NIGHT A MUFFLED FIGURE BREAKS INTO THE RADIUM LABORATORY WHERE PSYCHO HAS BEEN WORKING.
RADIUM LABORATORY
MARVA, WALKING DOWN THE CORRIDOR, THINKS THE SHORT-APPEARING FIGURE BY THE DOOR IS PSYCHO.
HI, THERE— DID YOU FORGET OUR DATE?
THAT'S FUNNY - HE RAN AWAY FROM ME INTO THE LAB!
DIUM ATORY
NEXT MORNING $125,000 WORTH OF RADIUM IS MISSING FROM THE LABORATORY SAFE AND PSYCHO IS SUSPECTED.
YOU HAD THE LAB KEYS - YOU WENT IN THERE LAST NIGHT!
I DID NOT!
DID YOU SEE THIS MAN ENTER THE LABORATORY?
Y-YES - I DID! OH DARLING, PLEASE GIVE THE RADIUM BACK!
YOU PRETTY, DOUBLE-CROSSING LIAR! YOU'RE TRYING TO FRAME ME AND MARRY BEN BRADLEY!
CONVICTED ON MARVA'S TESTIMONY, PSYCHO RECEIVES THE FINAL BLOW IN PRISON!
MARRIED— SHE'S MARRIED BRADLEY! THIS IS THE END OF ALL MY FAITH IN HUMANITY!
DAILY BLADE
MARRIED
3A

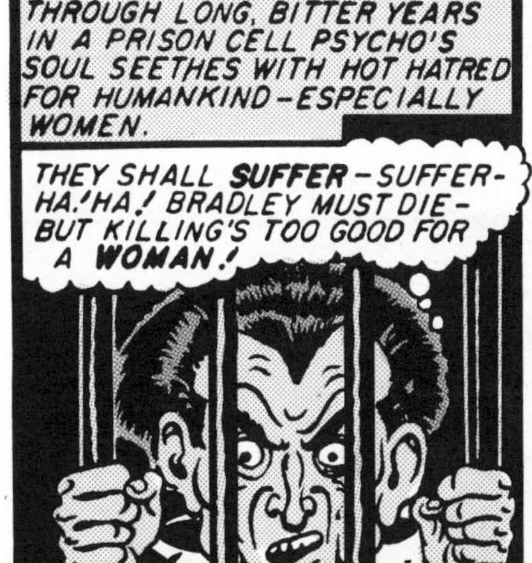
THROUGH LONG, BITTER YEARS IN A PRISON CELL PSYCHO'S SOUL SEETHES WITH HOT HATRED FOR HUMANKIND—ESPECIALLY WOMEN.
THEY SHALL SUFFER—SUFFER—HA! HA! BRADLEY MUST DIE—BUT KILLING'S TOO GOOD FOR A WOMAN!

SOON AFTER PSYCHO'S RELEASE FROM PRISON—
YOU'LL SWALLOW THIS RADIUM—IT WILL BURN HOLES IN YOUR STOMACH HA! HO! HA!
MERCY—I'LL CONFESS! I DID STEAL THAT RADIUM TO FRAME YOU, BUT MARVA PLANNED IT, I SWEAR—AG-GLUG!

AFTER BEN BRADLEY'S DEATH, OF A "STOMACH DISORDER" PSYCHO VISITS MARVA.
AH MY PRETTY MARVA, I HAVE COME FOR YOU! DO NOT PRETEND INNOCENCE—BEN CONFESSED THAT YOU PLANNED MY BETRAYAL!
OH—I DIDN'T!

TAKING MARVA TO A CAREFULLY PREPARED HIDEAWAY, PSYCHO HYPNOTIZES HER.
DON'T BE AFRAID—I WON'T KILL YOU! DEATH IS TOO GOOD FOR YOU! OBEY ME—

UNDER PSYCHO'S HYPNOTIC CONTROL MARVA IS FORCED TO MARRY HIM.
DO YOU PROMISE TO LOVE, CHERISH AND OBEY?
N—OH—YES, I DO!

PSYCHO USES MARVA FOR OCCULT EXPERIMENTS, HYPNOTIZING HER EVERY DAY.
I COMMAND YOU, SLAVE, BRING ME LIVING SUBSTANCE FROM THE SPIRIT WORLD!
I WILL TRY, MASTER!
4A

AT LAST SUCCESS! IN THE WEIRD RED LIGHT OF PSYCHO'S LABORATORY PARTICLES OF LIVING ECTOPLASM ARE DRAWN FROM UNSEEN SPACE THROUGH THE MEDIUM'S BODY TO PSYCHO'S HAND!
I'M MASTER OF PSYCHIC CREATION! I CAN MAKE HUMAN BODIES!

DIRECTING THE ECTOPLASM BY WILL, PSYCHO BUILDS THE MUSCLES OF HERCULES ON HIS OWN SPINDLING ARMS.

MATERIALIZIING AN ECTOPLASMIC MASK OVER HIS FACE, PSYCHO TRANSFORMS HIMSELF INTO MUSSOLINI.

CREATING AN ENTIRE BODY OF ECTOPLASM IN LESS THAN A MINUTE, PSYCHO BECOMES JOHN L. SULLIVAN.
SURE, I'M THE CHAMP'S GHOST! HA! HO! HA! WHAT A SIDE-SPLITTING JOKE DR. PSYCHO IS ABOUT TO PLAY ON THE STUPID PUBLIC!

SOME WEEKS LATER STEVE TREVOR SHOWS NEWSPAPER HEADLINES TO DIANA PRINCE.
HOW'D YOU LIKE TO HEAR A SPEECH BY GEORGE WASHINGTON?
HUH- WHAT?
DAILY PRESS

DAILY PRESS

GEORGE WASHINGTO
TO SPEAK TONIGHT!

Dr. Psycho announces that the Spirit of the Father of our Country will materialize throu Marva the Medium
It is expected that a capaci-ty audience will fill Lafay-ette Hall tonight at a pub-lic seance announced by Dr. Psycho, the noted oc-cultist. A committee of famous scientists test-ed Marva the Medium and report results are genu-ine.

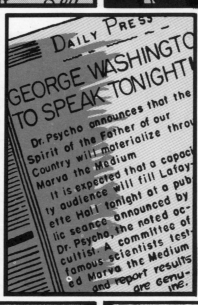

PERSONALLY I THINK IT'S BUNK! BUT MILLIONS ACCEPT EVERYTHING THAT PSYCHO'S SPIRITS SAY, AS LAW AND GOSPEL!
LET'S GO TONIGHT AND SEE FOR OURSELVES!

STEVE AND DIANA ATTEND PSYCHO'S MEETING THAT NIGHT.
LADIES AND GENTLEMEN! TO SEE THAT THE MEDIUM COMMITS NO FRAUD WILL SOME OF YOU COME UP ON THE PLATFORM AND BIND MARVA IN HER CABINET?

COME ON, DI- LET'S GO UP!
YOU GO, STEVE- I HAVE TO LEAVE EARLY.

AS STEVE GOES ON THE STAGE DIANA SLIPS BACKSTAGE AND TRANSFORMS HERSELF SWIFTLY TO WONDER WOMAN.
THERE MAY BE NOTHING HERE TO INVESTIGATE BUT I DON'T LIKE THAT TRIUMPHANT GLEAM IN DR. PSYCHO'S EYES!

WONDER WOMAN MEETS STEVE ON THE STAGE.
WONDER WOMAN- WHAT ARE YOU UP TO?
TYING A MEDIUM- I'VE ALWAYS WANTED TO SEE GEORGE WASHINGTON BUT I MUST BE SURE HE'S THE GENUINE GENTLEMAN!

IF THE COMMITTEE WILL EXAMINE THE CABINET-UGH- NOT QUITE SO VIOLENTLY PLEASE!
I'M SORRY! I'M AFRAID I BROKE THE HINGES- HARDWARE IS SO FRAGILE NOWADAYS!

WITH THE CABINET REPAIRED WONDER WOMAN HELPS TIE MARVA IN HER CHAIR.
OW! PLEASE DON'T TIE ME SO TIGHT!
WHY, THAT ISN'T HALF TIGHT ENOUGH- AN AMAZON GIRL WOULD SLIP OUT OF THAT IN TWO SECONDS!

WITH THE HELPLESS MARVA CLOSELY WATCHED, "GEORGE WASHINGTON" APPEARS SUDDENLY IN A BEAM OF RED LIGHT!
GREETINGS, FELLOW COUNTRYMEN! NEARLY A CENTURY AND A HALF AGO I LIVED IN AMERICA!
GALLOPING CANARIES — IT'S GEORGE HIMSELF!

AN AWE-STRICKEN HUSH FALLS OVER THE AUDIENCE AS "WASHINGTON" ADDRESSES THEM.
I HAVE A MESSAGE FOR YOU- A WARNING! WOMEN WILL LOSE THE WAR FOR AMERICA! WOMEN SHOULD NOT BE PERMITTED TO HAVE THE RESPONSIBILITIES THEY NOW HAVE!
6A.

WOMEN MUST NOT MAKE SHELLS, TORPEDOES, AIRPLANE PARTS- THEY MUST NOT BE TRUSTED WITH WAR SECRETS OR SERVE IN THE ARMED FORCES. WOMEN WILL BETRAY THEIR COUNTRY THROUGH WEAKNESS IF NOT TREACHERY!

WHY THAT LOOSE-TONGUED DOUBLE-TALKING PHONY! WHAT'S HIS GAME? HE'S WORKING FOR THE AXIS! I'LL STOP HIM—
WAIT, WONDER WOMAN! LET'S HEAR WHAT ELSE HE SAYS—SOUNDS GENUINE TO ME!
I WILL PROVE WHAT I SAY! TOMORROW, AT PRECISELY NOON, THE SUPREME SHELL WORKS WILL BLOW UP! WOMEN ARE FILLING THOSE SHELLS- WOMEN'S CARELESSNESS WILL WRECK A BILLION DOLLAR MUNITIONS PLANT! I HAVE PROPHESIED AND IT WILL BE SO!
AH-A-AH! THE SUPREME SHELL PLANT—OH-H-H!
AS WONDER WOMAN LEAPS FROM HER SEAT, "GEORGE WASHINGTON" VANISHES AND PSYCHO APPEARS.
I HOPE THE AUTHORITIES, AFTER HEARING OF GENERAL WASHINGTON'S WARNING, MAY PREVENT THIS DISASTER!
I'M TOO LATE! WHERE DID "WASHINGTON" GO?
AT THE SUPREME SHELL PLANT NEXT DAY EVERY PRECAUTION IS TAKEN.
HAVE YOU SEARCHED ALL BUILDINGS?
FROM TOP TO BOTTOM, SIR. FOUND NOTHING SUSPICIOUS. I'VE POSTED GUARDS AROUND THE WOMEN LOADING SHELLS!
ALL DOORS ARE GUARDED.
SAY, D'YOU KNOW WHO I AM? I'VE GOT OFFICIAL BUSINESS—
SORRY, SIR! ORDERS ARE TO LET NOBODY ENTER THIS SHELL LOADING ROOM UNTIL AFTER 12 O'CLOCK!
7A.
AS THE FATAL HOUR APPROACHES A GENERAL INSPECTS THE PLANT.
TEN TO TWELVE- EVERYTHING OKAY HERE?
YES, GENERAL, NOBODY'S GOT BY ME!
THE GENERAL ENTERS THE SHELL LOADING ROOM AND LAYS HIS STICK DOWN AS HE TALKS WITH WOMEN WORKERS.
ARE YOU GIRLS AFRAID OF "GEORGE WASHINGTON'S" WARNING?
OH, NO, SIR—YOU ARMY MEN WILL GUARD US!
DANGER HIGH EXPLOSIVE

THE GENERAL LEAVES WITHOUT HIS STICK.
THREE MINUTES OF 12- DON'T LET ANYBODY IN OR OUT UNTIL AFTER THE NOON WHISTLE!
NO, SIR—I WON'T, SIR!

OUTSIDE THE PLANT STEVE AND COLONEL DARNELL WAIT ANXIOUSLY FOR THE HOUR OF NOON!
NOTHING CAN HAPPEN, NOW! IT'S ONE MINUTE TO 12—
YOU'RE SLOW, COLONEL-IT'S JUST NOON-GEEHOSAPHAT!

BA-ANG!

SPECTATORS FLEE FOR THEIR LIVES AMID A SHOWER OF SHELL FRAGMENTS.
WHOLE PLANT'S IN FLAMES—THOUSANDS OF LIVES LOST-HOW COULD IT HAVE HAPPENED?
IT'S BEYOND ME-MAYBE "GEORGE WASHINGTON" CAN TELL US!

A MESSAGE FROM PSYCHO AWAITS THEM!
DR. PSYCHO PHONED. HE INVITES YOU TO A PRIVATE SEANCE TONIGHT TO RECEIVE IMPORTANT INFORMATION FROM SPIRITS!
OH, BOSH! BUT WAIT! WE CAN'T AFFORD TO IGNORE ANY CLUES—TELL HIM WE'LL COME!

WONDER WOMAN MEETS THE MEN AT DR. PSYCHO'S LABORATORY.
GLAD TO SEE YOU WONDER WOMAN! BUT HOW DID YOU LEARN ABOUT THIS SEANCE?
WHY-ER-DIANA SENT ME A MENTAL MESSAGE!
8A

OH, I HATE TO BE BOUND-CAN'T I PLEASE REMAIN FREE?
CERTAINLY NOT, MY DEAR! NO WOMAN CAN BE TRUSTED WITH FREEDOM-YOU OUGHT TO KNOW THAT! HA! HO! HA!

AS "GEORGE WASHINGTON" APPEARS, SEEMINGLY FROM NOWHERE, **WONDER WOMAN'S** KEEN EYES OBSERVE HIS ENTRANCE.

IN SOOTH, GOOD GENTLEMEN AND DAME, I GREET YOU KINDLY!

THAT'S PSYCHO'S VOICE, DIS- GUISED– HE CAME FROM BEHIND THAT SCREEN!

TOMORROW, AT NOON, IMPORTANT SECRET PAPERS WILL BE STOLEN FROM YOUR OFFICE SAFE. TRUST NOT **WOMEN**! EVEN NOW THEY ARE BETRAYING YOU–

I CAN'T STAND THIS AWFUL DRIVEL– I'VE GOT TO **ACT**!

WONDER WOMAN INTERRUPTS THE SEANCE.

YOU WILL FIND THE STOLEN PAPERS ON **THREE** OF YOUR OFFICE GIRLS– ULP– OUCH!

I'VE HEARD ENOUGH OF THESE LYING AT- TACKS ON **WOMEN**!

TELL ME THE TRUTH — THIS "GEORGE WASHINGTON" BODY IS REALLY DR. PSYCHO, ISN'T IT?

NO, MADAM! THIS BODY IS LIVING ECTO- PLASM MATERIALIZED THROUGH THE MEDIUM MARVA!

ONE AT A TIME, 3 TRUSTED GIRL AGENTS ARE CALLED INTO COLONEL DARNELL'S OFFICE
I REMOVED THESE FROM THE VAULT AS A SPECIAL PRE-CAUTION— PLEASE CONCEAL THEM ON YOUR PERSON!
WHY CERTAINLY, COLONEL!

THEY'LL BE SAFE WITH ME, COLONEL!

NOBODY'LL FIND THE PAPERS HERE UNLESS I'M SEARCHED THOROUGHLY.

AS NOON APPROACHES, A GROUP OF G2 OFFICERS WATCH THE CLOCK.
THE VAULT CAN'T HAVE BEEN ROBBED! WHERE'S COLONEL DARNELL?
NOT IN YET - HE'S BEEN AT THE WHITE HOUSE ALL MORNING. HERE HE COMES NOW!

WELL, BOYS, IT'S PAST NOON AND NO ROBBERY! I CHECKED THE PAPERS IN THE VAULT LAST NIGHT- I'LL SEE IF ANYTHING'S HAPPENED TO 'EM!

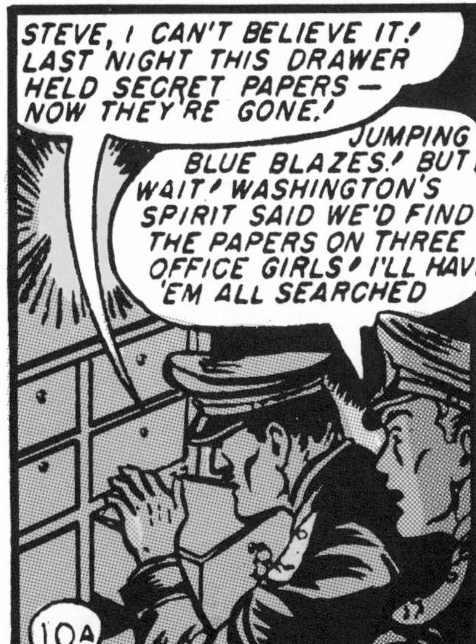
STEVE, I CAN'T BELIEVE IT! LAST NIGHT THIS DRAWER HELD SECRET PAPERS — NOW THEY'RE GONE!
JUMPING BLUE BLAZES! BUT WAIT! WASHINGTON'S SPIRIT SAID WE'D FIND THE PAPERS ON THREE OFFICE GIRLS! I'LL HAVE 'EM ALL SEARCHED
10A

PUT THE CUFFS ON ADELAIDE, MATRON! HERE ARE THE PAPERS— THIS MAKES THE LOT!
THIS IS SILLY I CAN EXPLAIN— TAKE US TO COLONEL DARNELL!
YES, THE CHIEF KNOWS ALL ABOUT IT!

DIANA TAKES THE PRISONERS TO COLONEL DARNELL.
HERE ARE THE PAPERS FOUND ON THESE GIRLS.
I FOLLOWED YOUR ORDERS, COLONEL- BUT I COULDN'T FOOL DIANA!
MY ORDERS! WHAT D'YOU MEAN?

YOU ORDERED US TO HIDE THESE PAPERS ON OUR PERSON—
WHY, OF COURSE- DON'T YOU REMBMBER, COLONEL?
RIDICU-LOUS! I GAVE NO SUCH ORDERS- LOCK THESE PRISONERS UP!

I'VE QUESTIONED THE GUARDS, COLONEL—THEY SAY YOU WERE THE ONLY ONE WHO ENTERED THE VAULT, AT ABOUT 9 A.M. — REMEMBER?
THE GUARDS ARE CRAZY—AT 9 A.M. I WAS IN THE WHITE HOUSE!

THE GUARDS SAW DARNELL HERE AT 9. THREE GIRL AGENTS SWEAR HE GAVE ORDERS AT 9:30 AHA! SOME-BODY MUST HAVE IMPERSONAT-ED DARNELL AND I'LL BET PSYCHO KNOWS WHO! I'LL MAKE THAT SPIRIT-SHUF-FLER TALK!

AT HIS LABORATORY DOCTOR PSYCHO TALKS A GREAT DEAL BUT SAYS NOTHING.
ANSWERING YOUR QUESTIONS, MY DEAR MAJOR, THE ASTRAL ENTITIES OF THE SECOND SPHERE PRECIPITATE THEIR ECTOPLASMIC PROTOPLASM THROUGH KARMIC RADIANCE-
ALL RIGHT! ALL RIGHT— BUT THAT'S NOT WHAT I CAME HERE TO ASK YOU!

BUT PSYCHO'S TALK IS BY NO MEANS PURPOSELESS — IT OCCUPIES STEVE'S ATTENTION WHILE A WEIRD, HALF VISIBLE WEIGHT GATHERS ON HIS CHEST.
I AH-H CAN'T — OO-OOF- BREATHE!
HOW ENTERTAINING- DEATH BY ECTOPLASM- HA! HO! HA!
11A

Z-Z-ZUT! ON SECOND THOUGHT I WILL KEEP THIS STUPID SPECIMEN FOR A WHILE — HE MAY HELP ME IN MY PLAN TO DESTROY WOMEN!

DIANA, WORRIED BECAUSE STEVE HAS NOT RETURNED TO THE OFFICE, GOES HOME EARLY.
THAT DR.PSYCHO IS FIENDISHLY CLEVER—HE MAY HAVE DONE SOMETHING TO STEVE THAT PREVENTS HIS SENDING A MENTAL MESSAGE!

OH THERE'S STEVE NOW!
CALLING WONDER WOMAN! WAS TAKEN PRISONER AT PSYCHO'S LABORATORY. AM IN CAGE—DON'T KNOW WHERE! LOOK OUT FOR BURGLAR ALARMS! THE LAB GROUNDS ARE COMPLETELY WIRED!

CHANGING SWIFTLY TO HER WONDER WOMAN COSTUME, THE AMAZON GIRL MAKES A QUICK EXIT.
SOMETHING TELLS ME THIS PSYCHO IS PLENTY DANGEROUS!

FROM A NEARBY HILL WONDER WOMAN SURVEYS THE PSYCHO LABORATORY GROUNDS.
IF ALL THE OPEN SPACE IS WIRED WITH BURGLAR ALARMS I CAN'T REACH THE LAB SECRETLY EXCEPT BY AIR—AH! THAT'S AN IDEA!

AT THE EDGE OF THE WOODS WONDER WOMAN BENDS DOWN A PAIR OF STRONG SAPLINGS.
THESE YOUNG TREES ARE TOUGH—THEY'LL GIVE A STRONG SNAP-BACK WHEN I LET THEM GO.

FASTENING THE TREE TOPS TOGETHER WITH VINES WONDER WOMAN MAKES A GIANT SLING-SHOT.
WHEN I BREAK THIS ANCHOR VINE I'LL GO SAILING THROUGH THE AIR—TO THE LABORATORY, I HOPE!
12A

HURLED HIGH OVER PSYCHO'S GROUNDS BY THE TREMENDOUS POWER OF THE BENT TREES WONDER WOMAN DESCENDS GRACEFULLY TOWARD THE LABORATORY ROOF.
I DON'T SEE HOW PSYCHO'S BURGLAR ALARMS COULD DETECT THIS APPROACH!

LANDING LIGHTLY ON THE ROOF WONDER WOMAN FORCES A SKYLIGHT AND DESCENDS INTO PSYCHO'S LABORATORY.
THIS PLACE SEEMS EMPTY– A GOOD TIME TO DROP IN!

WONDER WOMAN SEARCHES FROM ROOF TO CELLAR BUT FINDS NO TRACE OF STEVE.
HAH! A TRAP DOOR CONCEALED UNDER A CASE OF CANNED GOODS-LOOKS PROMISING!

BUT AT THIS MOMENT WONDER WOMAN HEARS A FAMILIAR VOICE
WONDER WOMAN–HELP! IT'S STEVE-THIS WAY!
ONE MIN-UTE, STEVE, AND I'LL BE WITH YOU!

HERE I COME, FELLA!

STEVE APPEARS TO BE CONFINED IN AN IRON CAGE
I KNEW YOU'D COME, WONDER WOMAN! CAN YOU BREAK THE BARS OF THIS CAGE?
I SHOULD HOPE SO- I'LL HAVE YOU FREE IN A MINUTE!

BUT AS WONDER WOMAN GRASPS THE BARS A PARALYZING CURRENT OF ELECTRICITY HOLDS HER BODY RIGID!
HA! HO! HA! WHY DON'T YOU TEAR THE CAGE APART, WONDER WOMAN?
GREAT GODDESS APHRODITE! PSYCHO'S GOT ME–I CAN'T MOVE OR SPEAK!
13A.

HOW EASY TO TRICK HUMAN FOOLS! I MATERIAL-IZE A BODY AND WEAR IT LIKE A CLOAK- TREVOR'S, DARNELL'S - A MAJOR GENERAL'S -Z-Z-ZUT! YOU KNOW MY SECRET BUT YOU'LL NEVER BETRAY IT - HA! HO! HA!

I'M PREPARING TO PERFORM AN ELECTRICAL OPERATION ON YOU. WITH LOW POTENTIAL CURRENTS I SHALL LOOSEN THE ATOMS OF YOUR BODY AND REMOVE YOUR SPIRIT!
WHAT JOLLY GAMES THIS FELLOW PLAYS!

WITH A PECULIAR ELECTO-ATOMIZER OF HIS OWN INVENTION PSYCHO SENDS ALTERNATING CROSSCURRENTS THROUGH WONDER WOMAN'S FLESH.
YOUR SPIRIT ALREADY IS SEPARATING FROM YOUR BODY!
WHAT A QUEER FEELING- LIKE FALLING!

WHEN WONDER WOMAN'S SPIRIT IS COMPLETELY DETACHED PSYCHO FASTENS IT TO THE WALL WITH BANDS OF PSYCHO-ELECTRIC MAGNETISM.
YOUR SPIRIT CAN NEVER BREAK THESE BONDS WHILE I HOLD THEM WITH MY IRON WILL!

YOUR BODY SEEMS LIFELESS SINCE I SWITCHED OFF THE PARALYZING CURRENT, BUT IT'S NOT DEAD. YOUR SPIRIT WOULD RETURN TO IT IF RELEASED. I'LL KEEP YOUR BODY IN THIS CAGE!

CALLING ETTA- CALLING ETTA CANDY! IT'S NO USE - I CAN'T SEND A MENTAL RADIO MESSAGE WITHOUT MY PHYSICAL BODY! I'M ABSOLUTELY HELPLESS- I WONDER WHAT PSYCHO'LL DO WITH ME!
14A

MEANWHILE, ETTA RECEIVES A MENTAL RADIO MESSAGE FROM STEVE.
WOO WOO! GATHER ROUND GALS, IT'S MAJOR TREVOR!
I'M A PRISONER AT PSYCHO'S LABORATORY! CAN'T SEEM TO CONTACT WONDER WOMAN- WILL YOU GIRLS HELP?
YAY BO! WILL WE HELP STEVE!

A HANDSOME YOUNG MAN MEETS ETTA AT THE LABORATORY.
I AM CARLO MONTEZ, DR. PSYCHO'S ASSISTANT- AH WHAT A HAPPY DAY TO GREET SO CHARMING A VISITOR!
SAY- YOU'RE KINDA CUTE YOURSELF! WE GIRLS WANT A SEANCE. CAN YOU MANAGE ONE?

THE HOLLIDAY GIRLS FIND CARLO MORE FASCINATING THAN THE SPIRITS.
I AM SORRY THE DOCTOR IS NOT HERE-
FORGET THE DOCTOR- YOU ENTERTAIN US!
DO YOU THINK BLONDES PREFER GEN-TLE-MEN?
WHEN DO YOU GET THROUGH WORK?

AS THE HOLLIDAY GIRLS OVER-WHELM CARLO, WONDER WO-MAN FEELS HER SPIRIT CHAINS WEAKEN.
THAT'S ODD-MY BONDS FEEL LOOSER! IF PSYCHO HOLDS THEM WITH HIS WILL, SOMETHING MUST BE WEAKENING HIS POWER!

WITH A STUPENDOUS SURGE OF PSYCHIC POWER WONDER WO-MAN'S SPIRIT BURSTS HER SHACKLES!
I'M FREE! NOW TO GET BACK INTO MY BODY.

WONDER WOMAN IS HERSELF AGAIN.
BY GOLLY! YOU NEVER KNOW HOW GOOD YOUR BODY FEELS UNTIL YOU'VE BEEN OUT OF IT FOR A WHILE!

RETURNING TO THE RINGED SLAB OF STONE PREVIOUSLY DISCOVERED WONDER WOMAN HEAVES IT UP.
HELLO! IS THAT YOU, WONDER WOMAN?
YES, I'M MOSTLY MYSELF!
THAT'S STEVE'S OWN VOICE-THANK APHRODITE!

HURTLING DOWN INTO PSYCHO'S SUBTERRANEAN VAULT, WONDER WOMAN RUNS A GAUNTLET OF BLUE FLAME.
I CAN HARDLY FEEL THOSE RAYS-THE GOOD DOCTOR'S TREATMENT MUST HAVE GIVEN ME IMMUNITY TO ELECTRIC SHOCKS!
15A.

NO ONE BUT YOU COULD HAVE SAVED ME - THIS BIRD PSYCHO IS THE MOST DANGEROUS MAN ALIVE!

SEARCHING THE VAULT WONDER WOMAN FINDS MARVA.
MM- SHE'S IN A DEEP TRANCE! THIS MEDIUM IS PSYCHO'S SOURCE OF POWER TO MATERIALIZE BODIES -HE KEEPS HER HIDDEN AND HELPLESS. I MUST AWAKEN HER GENTLY!

YOU SHOULDN'T HAVE RELEASED ME - HE'LL BE FURIOUS! OH, DON'T LET HIM TORTURE ME—
DON'T BE AFRAID, MARVA- PSYCHO CAN'T HURT YOU- HE HAS NO POWER OVER YOU EXCEPT WHAT YOU GIVE HIM!

AT THE PRECISE MOMENT THAT MARVA AWAKENS FROM HER TRANCE- A STRANGE THING HAPPENS TO CARLO.
LOOK- CARLO'S DISAPPEARING!
HE'S MELTING AWAY!
IT WAS DR. PSYCHO ALL THE TIME- GRAB HIM, GIRLS!

THE INDIGNANT GIRLS CHASE THEIR DESPERATE DECEIVER.
CATCH HIM KIDS -GIVE HIM A LAMDA BETA TREATMENT!
PADDLES UP, SISTERS, GIVE HIM THE WORKS!

STEVE ARRIVES AS PSYCHO TURNS ON HIS PURSUERS.
FIENDISH FEMALES- I'LL SHOOT YOU ALL!
NOT WITH THAT GUN, BROTHER- PUT UP YOUR HANDS!
16A

YOU'LL NEVER PROVE IN COURT THAT I MATERIALIZED A MAJOR GENERAL AND COLONEL DARNELL!
I'M AFRAID HE'S RIGHT, STEVE- I'VE A FEELING THERE'S MORE TROUBLE AHEAD!
NONSENSE! PSYCHO OUT-SMARTED HIMSELF- HIS WAR AGAINST WOMEN IS FINISHED!

SUBMITTING TO A CRUEL HUSBAND'S DOMINATION HAS RUINED MY LIFE! BUT WHAT CAN A WEAK GIRL DO?
GET STRONG! EARN YOUR OWN LIVING- JOIN THE WAACS OR WAVES AND FIGHT FOR YOUR COUNTRY! REMEMBER THE BETTER YOU CAN FIGHT THE LESS YOU'LL HAVE TO!

Wonder Woman
REG. U. S. PAT. OFF.
By CHARLES MOULTON
FOR THOUSANDS OF YEARS SCIENTISTS HAVE SEARCHED FOR THE LOST GARDEN OF EDEN - BUT IT'S NO WONDER THEY FAILED TO FIND IT! FOR WHEN WONDER WOMAN, AIDED BY THE MAGIC SPHERE ON PARADISE ISLAND LOCATED EDEN, SHE DISCOVERED IT WAS SUNK DEEP BENEATH CRYSTAL ICE AT THE SOUTH POLE! AND TO HER SURPRISE THE GARDEN WAS INHABITED !
FOR YEARS A RACE OF BEAUTIFUL GIRLS HAVE ENJOYED THE BENEFITS OF THIS WONDERFUL "UNDER-ICE" CIVILIZATION UNTIL THEY WERE DISCOVERED AND BESET BY FIENDISH ENEMIES, THE SEAL MEN. WONDER WOMAN SAVES THEM FROM DEFEAT AND EXTINCTION WHEN SHE PROVES THAT WOMEN CAN BE STRONG !
BEAUTIFUL AS APHRODITE, WISE AS ATHENA, STRONGER THAN HERCULES AND SWIFTER THAN MERCURY, WONDER WOMAN INSPIRES NEW FAITH IN HUMAN DESTINY IN THIS STRANGE AND THRILLING CASE OF "THE ICEBOUND MAIDENS."
H G PETER
1A
DIANA (WONDER WOMAN) PRINCE ANSWERS A MENTAL RADIO SIGNAL IN HER OFFICE, NOT REALIZING THAT STEVE IS BEHIND HER.
BZZ-BZZ-BZZ-BZZ
THAT'S A CALL FOR WONDER WOMAN—

CALLING PRINCESS DIANA!
OH-IT'S MY MOTHER, QUEEN HIPPOLYTE CALLING FROM PARADISE ISLAND!

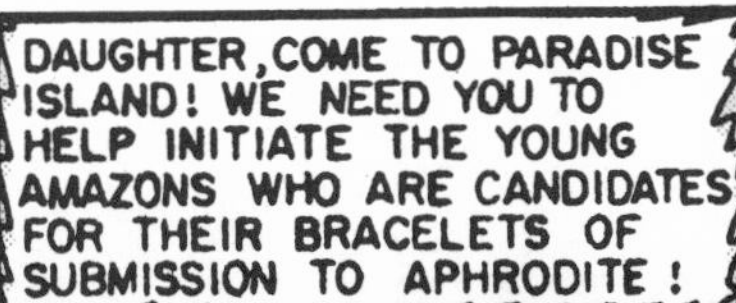
DAUGHTER, COME TO PARADISE ISLAND! WE NEED YOU TO HELP INITIATE THE YOUNG AMAZONS WHO ARE CANDIDATES FOR THEIR BRACELETS OF SUBMISSION TO APHRODITE!

WONDERFUL!

OH-STEVE! I DIDN'T KNOW-
YOU DIDN'T KNOW I WAS HERE-SO YOU GAVE YOURSELF AWAY! YOU CALLED QUEEN HIPPOLYTE YOUR "MOTHER". THAT MEANS YOU ARE WONDER WOMAN!

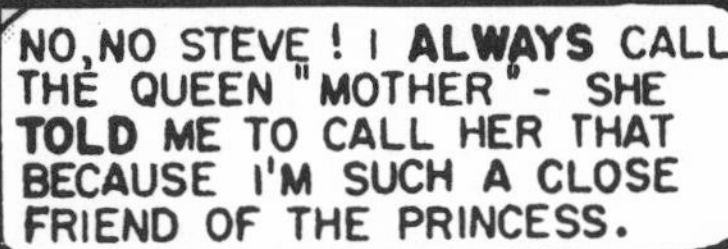
NO, NO STEVE! I ALWAYS CALL THE QUEEN "MOTHER"- SHE TOLD ME TO CALL HER THAT BECAUSE I'M SUCH A CLOSE FRIEND OF THE PRINCESS.

HMM-I NEVER HEARD YOU DO IT BEFORE!

DIANA DOES SOME QUICK THINKING.
THE QUEEN ASKED ME TO TAKE MENTAL MESSAGES FOR WONDER WOMAN AND-
QUICK, MOTHER! CALL DIANA PRINCE YOUR DAUGHTER AND ASK HER TO GIVE THE PRINCESS YOUR MESSAGE!

IF MY MAN'S WORLD DAUGHTER, DIANA PRINCE, CATCHES THIS MESSAGE, PLEASE GIVE IT TO THE PRINCESS PROMPTLY! TELL HER TO BRING YOU WITH HER TO PARADISE ISLAND AS OUR GUEST!
HA HA! MOTHER IS CLEVER!
24

NOW, DO YOU BELIEVE ME, MR. SMARTY?
OF COURSE-IT WAS STUPID OF ME TO THINK YOU COULD BE WONDER WOMAN! I'LL GET A LEAVE OF ABSENCE FOR YOU, DIANA, FROM GENERAL DARNELL!

FLYING FAST AND FAR OVER DISTANT SEAS, WONDER WOMAN APPROACHES THE IRRIDESCENT CLOUDS WHICH HIDE PARADISE ISLAND.

QUEEN HIPPOLYTE IS WAITING.
WELCOME, DARLING! BUT WHERE IS DIANA PRINCE?
HA HA! WE CERTAINLY FOOLED STEVE - HE STILL THINKS THERE ARE TWO OF ME!

WE'RE WORRIED ABOUT THE YOUNG AMAZON GIRLS WHO ARE TAKING TESTS TO WIN THEIR BRACELETS. THEY THINK THEY CANNOT PERFORM THE TASKS REQUIRED AND SO, OF COURSE, THEY FAIL! I'LL SHOW YOU-

"THIS CHILD GETS CAUGHT EVERY TIME BY MALA'S LASSO.
ARIADNA, YOU MUST DO BETTER! I'M ONLY USING A 20-FOOT LASSO-
I-I'M JUST TOO WEAK - I CAN'T JUMP ANY HIGHER!

"THIS GIRL CAN'T BREAK HER BONDS—"

GREAT HERA! THE PRINCESS DIANA COULD BREAK ROPES LIKE THAT AT THE AGE OF THREE!

I-I DON'T SEE HOW SHE DID IT!

3A

"THIS GIRL CAN'T LIFT MORE THAN 500 POUNDS—"
I COULD LIFT A 5000 LB. BAR AT YOUR AGE— OUR PRINCESS COULD LIFT 15,000 LBS. ON HER CHEST!
OH-HOW COULD SHE?
1000 LBS.

THE PRINCESS TALKS TO THE YOUNG AMAZON GIRLS.
LOOK, GIRLS! I'M JUST AN ORDINARY AMAZON. BUT I FEEL THAT I CAN DO THINGS, SO - I CAN DO THEM!
HOLA! HOLA! OUR PRINCESS - SHE'S WONDERFUL - HOLA! PRINCESS DIANA!

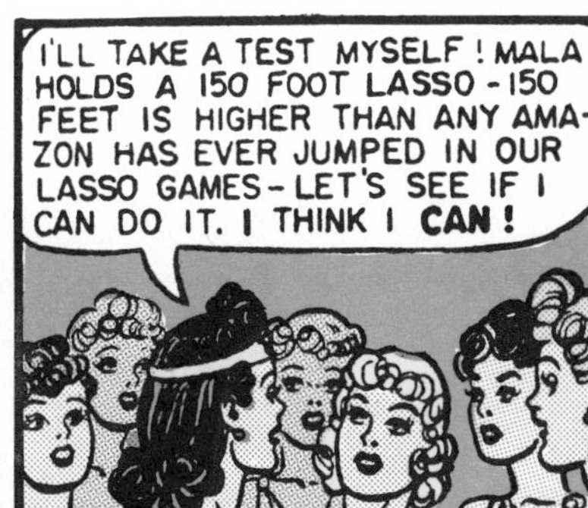
I'LL TAKE A TEST MYSELF! MALA HOLDS A 150 FOOT LASSO - 150 FEET IS HIGHER THAN ANY AMAZON HAS EVER JUMPED IN OUR LASSO GAMES - LET'S SEE IF I CAN DO IT. I THINK I CAN!

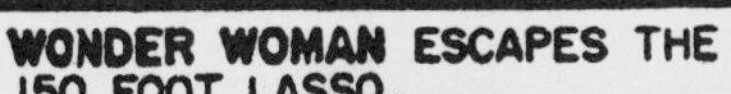
WONDER WOMAN ESCAPES THE 150 FOOT LASSO.

4-A

OH, PRINCESS, YOU'RE SUPERB - YOU'RE MAGNIFICENT - YOU'RE A WONDER AMAZON!
HA HA! DON'T BE SILLY, GIRLS - YOU CAN DO THE SAME THING!

BIND ME AS TIGHT AS YOU CAN, GIRLS, WITH THE BIGGEST ROPES AND CHAINS YOU CAN FIND!
WE ARE, PRINCESS - EVEN YOU CAN'T ESCAPE THESE BONDS!

YOU SEE, GIRLS, IT'S EASY TO BREAK BONDS IF YOU **KNOW** YOU **CAN**!
HOLA! OUR PRINCESS IS **INVINCIBLE!**

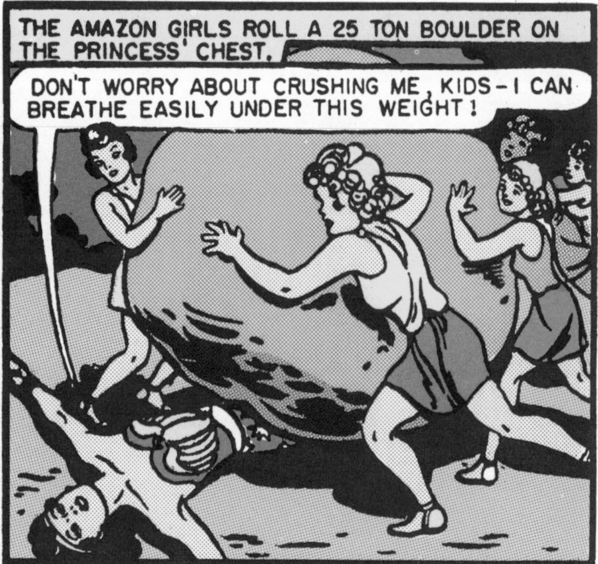

THE AMAZON GIRLS ROLL A 25 TON BOULDER ON THE PRINCESS' CHEST.
DON'T WORRY ABOUT CRUSHING ME, KIDS - I CAN BREATHE EASILY UNDER THIS WEIGHT!

YOU SEE, GIRLS, THERE'S NOTHING TO IT - ALL YOU HAVE TO DO IS **HAVE CONFIDENCE IN YOUR OWN STRENGTH!**
5A

UNDER **WONDER WOMAN'S** INSPIRATION, THE AMAZON GIRLS PASS THEIR STRENGTH TESTS WITH FLYING COLORS.
YOU CAN'T CATCH ME NOW, MALA!
I BET I CAN LIFT **TWICE** THIS WEIGHT!
THESE ROPES ARE **EASY** TO BREAK!
5000 LBS

BUT, WHILE THE SUCCESSFUL INITIATES HAVE THEIR BRACELETS WELDED UPON THEM, GODDESS APHRODITE SPEAKS TO THE PRINCESS.

WELL HAST THOU TAUGHT THY AMAZON SISTERS STRENGTH - GO NOW AND TEACH THE DAUGHTERS OF VENUS!

I OBEY, O GODDESS!

THEY'RE MESSENGERS SENT BY APHRODITE FROM VENUS TO THE SUNKEN GARDEN OF EDEN TO BRING THE WORSHIP OF LOVE AND BEAUTY TO THE EARTH - LOOK INTO THE MAGIC SPHERE -

WONDER WOMAN

THE MAGIC SPHERE SHOWS APHRODITE WATCHING THE SINKING OF THE GARDEN OF EDEN BENEATH CLEAR CRYSTAL ICE.

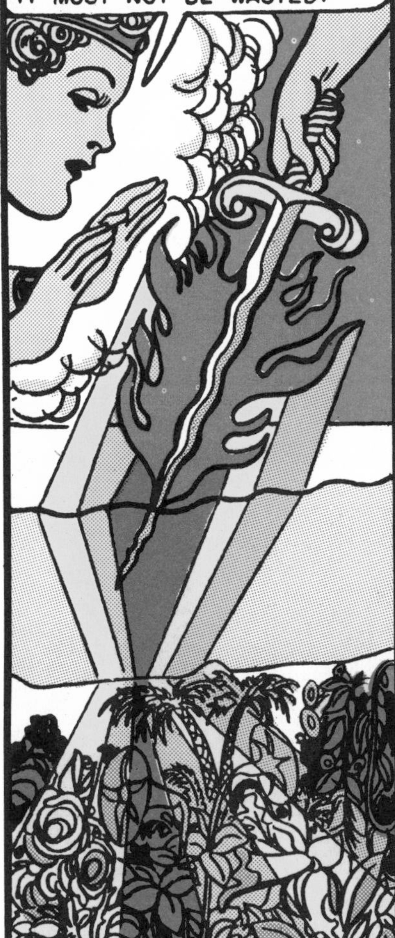

EDEN IS A PERFECT HOME-LAND OF LOVE AND BEAUTY - IT MUST NOT BE WASTED.

APHRODITE FLIES TO VENUS -
THY GIRLS, DESIRA, HAVE PROVED THEMSELVES WORTHY TO BE MY MESSENGERS TO THE PLANET EARTH. SUNKEN UNDER THE SOUTH POLE IS THE BEAUTIFUL GARDEN OF EDEN - FORBIDDEN TO EARTH PEOPLE -

THY DAUGHTER EVE SHALL REPLACE THE EARTH GIRL EVE WHO WAS DEPOSED FROM THE GARDEN - SHE SHALL RULE EDEN, HENCEFORTH TO BE CALLED EVELAND!

DESIRA'S DAUGHTER EVE, TRANSFORMED INTO AN EARTH GIRL WITHOUT WINGS, SUDDENLY FINDS HERSELF IN EVELAND, THE TROPICAL COUNTRY OF LOVE AND BEAUTY.
WHERE AM I AND HOW DID I GET HERE?

APHRODITE BRINGS A SPIRIT DAUGHTER TO YOUNG EVE FROM VENUS.
I BROUGHT THEE HERE TO RULE EVELAND. WITH ME NOW IS THY SPIRIT DAUGHTER, EVE LECTRESS, WHO SHALL BE THY SUCCESSOR.
WELCOME, BELOVED CHILD!
6A

EVE'S DAUGHTER FULLY MATERIALIZES -
ALL THY SUBJECTS SHALL BE SENT HERE IN THE SAME MANNER. RULE WISELY, EVE, AND ALL WILL BE WELL.
OH THANK YOU, DIVINE APHRODITE! WE'LL BE HAPPY FOREVER!

SUDDENLY, EVELAND VANISHES FROM THE MAGIC SPHERE AND APHRODITE SPEAKS.
HASTEN, AMAZON MAID - EVE AND HER MAIDENS NEED THY HELP QUICKLY!
I OBEY, GODDESS!
·OLYMPUS·

LIKE A FLASH OF LIGHT, WONDER WOMAN SOARS FROM PARADISE ISLAND TO THE SOUTH POLE.
THAT CLEAR ICE BELOW MUST BE THE CEILING OF EVELAND - I HATE TO SMASH IT BUT I MUST GET THROUGH!

THE AMAZON PRINCESS, LEAVING HER PLANE UNDER MENTAL RADIO CONTROL, PLUNGES THROUGH THE ICE CEILING OF EVELAND.
7-A

GREETINGS, GIRLS! I'M AMAZON PRINCESS DIANA - GODDESS APHRODITE SENT ME TO HELP YOU!
WE HEARD ABOUT YOU ON THE PLANET VENUS - YOU ARE WONDER WOMAN!

I'M SO GLAD YOU'VE COME - WE ARE IN TERRIBLE TROUBLE!

MY BELOVED DAUGHTER, EVE ELECTRESS, HAS BEEN CAPTURED BY SEAL MEN! SHE WAS LURED INTO THEIR DARK ICE CAVES BY PRINCE PAGLI - MANY OF OUR MAIDENS HAVE DISAPPEARED THUS!
WE'LL RESCUE THEM - SHOW ME THE WAY!

ACROSS THIS RIVER OF DESTRUCTION LIES BITTERLAND WHERE THE SEAL MEN, OUR ENEMIES, LIVE IN CAVES AND TUNNELS IN THOSE BLACK ICE CLIFFS!
WELL, LET'S SWIM OVER–WHAT ARE WE WAITING FOR?

WOMEN ARE TOO WEAK TO SWIM THIS RIVER! THE SEAL MEN SWIM POWERFULLY BUT THEY CANNOT INVADE EVELAND BECAUSE LIGHT BLINDS THEIR EYES. THEY PERSUADE OUR GIRLS TO CROSS TO BITTERLAND ON CAKES OF ICE!

WONDER WOMAN PLUNGES IN.
COME ON GIRLS, THIS IS EASY! YOU CAN SWIM THIS RIVER!

IF SHE CAN SWIM IT, I CAN–HERE GOES!
THIS CURRENT IS SWIFT BUT I'LL MAKE IT!
WONDER WOMAN'S RIGHT–THIS IS EASY–COME ON, GIRLS!

IN THE ENTRANCE ICE CAVE OF BITTERLAND, THE GIRLS ENCOUNTER SEAL MEN GUARDS.
GRR-RR- GRON! SURRENDER, SHEES–YOU'RE OUR PRISONERS!
SEAL MEN! WE CAN'T FIGHT THEM–THEY'RE TOO STRONG!
8-A

OF COURSE YOU CAN FIGHT THESE SEAL MEN - LOOK, I'LL SHOW YOU!

WONDER WOMAN

THE GIRLS TRY TO FIGHT BUT SOON WEAKEN - ALL BUT WONDER WOMAN ARE QUICKLY CONQUERED BY THE POWERFUL SEAL MEN.
UGH!

I AM PRINCE PAGLI. YOUR COMPANIONS ARE ALL PRISONERS - IF YOU RESIST FURTHER, THEY'LL BE KILLED.
I HAVE NO CHOICE - I SURRENDER!

WHILE BEING BOUND, WONDER WOMAN QUESTIONS HER CAPTOR.
WHAT WILL YOU DO WITH US?
WE USE CAPTIVES FOR GARDEN SLAVES - OUR SEAL MEN CANNOT WORK IN LIGHT. YOU WILL BE FROZEN UNTIL WE NEED YOU!
9A

YOU FREEZE US? HOW HORRIBLE!
QUICK FREEZING ISN'T PAINFUL - IT SUSPENDS ANIMATION AND PRESERVES PRISONERS IN PERFECT CONDITION FOR LATER USE WHEN PRESENT SLAVES GO BLIND!

YOU'RE INTELLIGENT - FOR A WOMAN - YOU AMUSE ME. I'LL PUT YOU ON THIS CAPTIVE CARRIER AND SHOW YOU OUR ICE-BOUND MAIDENS!

THESE CARDS GIVE EACH PRISONER'S NUMBER AND THE DATE WHEN SHE WAS FROZEN - AFTER A CERTAIN TIME EACH GIRL IS THAWED OUT BY HEATING HER IRON PLATFORM WITH ELECTRICITY.
HOW INGENIOUS!

WHILE PAGLI INSPECTS THE FROZEN MAIDENS WONDER WOMAN QUIETLY BREAKS HER ARM BONDS AND GRASPS HER MAGIC LASSO.

PRINCE PAGLI, INTENT ON STUDYING THE PRISONERS' RECORD CARDS, IS SUDDENLY JERKED OFF HIS FEET.
UNF-ULP!

TURN YOUR HEATING CURRENT INTO ALL THE PRISONERS' PLATFORMS, MY DEAR PRINCE!
I REFUSE-BUT-AH-SOMETHING COMPELS ME TO OBEY!

AS THE ICE BLOCKS MELT, THE GIRLS COME INSTANTLY TO LIFE!
OH-H-H! WHAT'S HAPPENED?
I'M ROASTING - WHERE AM I?
HOP THIS WAY, GIRLS, AND I'LL FREE YOU ALL!

OH, WONDER WOMAN, YOU'RE MARVELOUS! WE NEVER EXPECTED TO BE FREE AGAIN!
WE MUST FREE EVE AND THE OTHERS - WHERE ARE THEY, PAGLI?
IN THE FREEZING ROOM - IF YOU ENTER THEY'LL KILL THE PRISONERS!
10-A

YOU WILL TAKE ME INTO THE FREEZING ROOM LIKE THIS, APPARENTLY YOUR CAPTIVE. BUT YOU'LL BE MY PRISONER AND OBEY MY ORDERS!
I'M COMPELLED TO OBEY!

EVE AND HER GIRLS, MEANWHILE, ARE READY TO BE DIPPED INTO QUICK FREEZING VATS OF LIQUID AIR.
DIP THEM QUICKLY AND HOIST THEM OUT AGAIN - THEY'LL FREEZE INSTANTLY. THEN FREEZE THEM IN ICE CAKES. READY -

STOP! COUNT FRIGID, FREE THESE PRISONERS!

AS THE LAST GIRL IS FREED, PAGLI, UNSEEN BY WONDER WOMAN, GIVES COUNT FRIGID A SECRET SIGNAL.
BUT PRINCE PAGLI - OH! I UNDERSTAND - QUICK, SEALMEN! SLAY THE PRISONERS!

BUT WONDER WOMAN BURSTS HER BONDS - THE EVELAND GIRLS, INSPIRED BY HER EXAMPLE, COMPLETELY OVERPOWER THE SEAL MEN.
WE ARE STRONG - WE CAN FIGHT! FOLLOW WONDER WOMAN!

THE GIRLS RETURN IN TRIUMPH TO EVELAND.
HAIL, WONDER WOMAN! SHE SAVED US!
YOU SAVED YOURSELVES - I ONLY SHOWED YOU THAT YOU COULD!
11-A

GOODBYE, GIRLS! IF YOU NEED ME AGAIN I'VE SHOWN QUEEN EVE HOW TO CALL ME ON THE MENTAL RADIO.

Wonder Woman
REG. U. S. PAT. OFF.
By Charles Moulton
IT SEEMED UNLIKELY THAT ANY BRAVE, LOYAL AMERICAN GIRL ENLISTED IN THE WAACS WOULD SHOOT A GENERAL! YET THE GENERAL WAS SHOT BEFORE DIANA'S VERY EYES! NONE BUT A WAAC COULD HAVE FIRED THAT MYSTERIOUS BULLET! IT'S UP TO WONDER WOMAN TO SOLVE A MYSTERY THAT SHAKES THE MORALE OF THE ENTIRE ARMY AND BIDS FAIR TO BANISH AMERICAN WOMEN FROM THEIR NEWFOUND PLACE OF DARING AND DANGER.
CAN WONDER WOMAN UNRAVEL THE THREADS OF WEIRD INTRIGUE WHICH, LIKE A POISONOUS SPIDER'S WEB, ENTANGLE THE GIRL WITH THE GUN? TO DO SO OUR LOVELY AMAZON MAIDEN MUST JOIN THE WAACS. YOU'LL SEE HER SHARING THEIR DISCIPLINE AND THEIR PUNISHMENT DUTY, HAVING FUN WITH A WOMAN-HATING GENERAL AND PLAYING DANGEROUS GAMES WITH A DEADLY, DETERMINED KILLER WHOSE IDENTITY, WHEN REVEALED, IS ALMOST UNBELIEVABLE!
STEVE IS SUMMONED BY GENERAL STANDPAT, CHIEF OF STAFF
HOW ARE YOU, MAJOR TREVOR? I'M GOING TO INSPECT TRAINING CAMPS - YOU WILL ACCOMPANY ME.
YES, SIR!
H.G. PETER

THERE'S SABOTAGE GOING ON—MUNITIONS, CAMP EQUIPMENT. IT'S SERIOUS-YOU'VE GOT TO STOP IT! WORST IS AT CAMP DOE WHERE THEY'RE TRAINING THOSE WAACS- WOMAN SOLDIERS- BAH!
MAY I BRING MY ASSISTANT, SIR, LIEUTENANT PRINCE?
AFRICA
YES, BRING 50 ASSISTANTS IF YOU LIKE. BUT GET THOSE SABOTEURS, OR HEADS WILL FALL IN THE ARMY INTELLIGENCE SERVICE! UNDERSTAND?
YOU COULDN'T BE PLAINER, GENERAL!
AFRICA
GOT A JOB FOR YOU, DI-INSPECTING WAACS AT CAMP DOE WITH GENERAL STANDPAT. HE SUSPECTS SOMEBODY OF SABOTAGING WAR SUPPLIES!
YOU MEAN THE AMMUNITION DUMP THAT BLEW UP NEAR THE WAAC CAMP? I HOPE HE DOESN'T THINK ANY OF THE WAACS HAD ANYTHING TO DO WITH THAT!
STEVE AND DIANA JOIN THE GENERAL'S PARTY.
WE'RE REPORTING, SIR, FOR INSPECTION TOUR. MAY I PRESENT MY ASSISTANT, LT. DIANA PRINCE.
"LIEUTENANT" PRINCE-YOU DECEIVED ME, MAJOR! I CERTAINLY DIDN'T THINK YOU WERE BRINGING A WOMAN LIEUTENANT!
SORRY, GENERAL, BUT MISS PRINCE HAPPENS TO BE AN EXPERT AT DETECTING SABOTAGE, AND-
ALL RIGHT! BRING YOUR PETTICOAT STAFF-BUT NOT IN MY CAR! YOU AND LIEUTENANT PRINCE WILL RIDE WITH MY LUGGAGE IN THE CAR BEHIND!
I'M SORRY, DI-I DIDN'T KNOW THE OLD BOY WAS SO SORE AT WOMEN IN THE ARMY—
I DON'T MIND! I'D MUCH RATHER RIDE WITH SUITCASES THAN LISTEN TO OLD STANDPAT'S SPOUTING!
2
THE WAACS STAND IN COMPANY FORMATION TO GREET GENERAL STANDPAT'S INSPECTION CAVALCADE.

THE GENERAL WAITS IMPATIENTLY FOR THE CAMP COMMANDER TO APPEAR.
WHY ISN'T THE CAMP COMMANDER HERE?
GENERAL SCOTT'S IN HIS OFFICE RIGHT UP THERE, SIR-WASHINGTON CALLED HIM ON THE PHONE-HE'LL BE HERE IMMEDIATELY!

SUDDENLY A SHOT RINGS OUT.
UGH! I'M SHOT--- A WOMAN-- SHOT ME!
BA-ANG!

AT THE SAME MOMENT IN THE RIGID RANKS OF THE WAACS, A STEALTHY HAND PICKS UP A .22 AUTOMATIC WHICH HAD DROPPED NEAR A GIRL'S FEET.

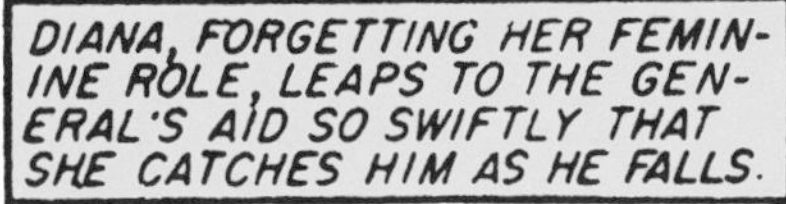
DIANA, FORGETTING HER FEMININE ROLE, LEAPS TO THE GENERAL'S AID SO SWIFTLY THAT SHE CATCHES HIM AS HE FALLS.

EASY, GENERAL - GREAT APHRODITE! HE'S BADLY HIT NEAR THE HEART!

GENERAL SCOTT, CAMP COMMANDER, HURRYING UP, RUSHES STANDPAT TO THE BASE HOSPITAL.
WHAT A MARVELOUS LEAP YOU MADE, DIANA, WHEN THE GENERAL WAS SHOT!
WHY-ER EXCITEMENT OFTEN GIVES WEAK PEOPLE ABNORMAL STRENGTH!

THE CAMP COMMANDER CONSULTS STEVE.
LUCKY YOU'RE HERE MAJOR-YOU MUST CONDUCT AN INVESTIGATION! DID THE GENERAL SAY ANYTHING AFTER BEING SHOT?
YES, SIR - HE SAID "A WOMAN SHOT ME!"

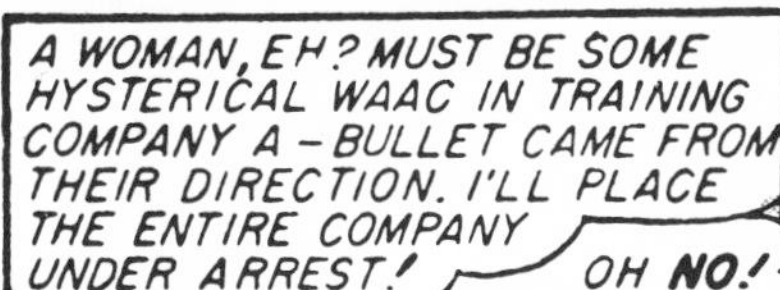
A WOMAN, EH? MUST BE SOME HYSTERICAL WAAC IN TRAINING COMPANY A - BULLET CAME FROM THEIR DIRECTION. I'LL PLACE THE ENTIRE COMPANY UNDER ARREST!

OH NO! GENERAL STANDPAT'S WORDS MEAN NOTHING- HE ALWAYS SUSPECTS WOMEN— SORRY! I'M SPEAKING OUT OF TURN.

COMPANY A GOES TO THE GUARDHOUSE.
IF A GIRL FIRED THAT SHOT WHAT'D SHE DO WITH HER GUN?
THAT'S FOR YOU TO FIND OUT- SEARCH EVERY WAAC, THEN GIVE 'EM A LIE DETECTOR TEST!

LINE UP FACING THE WALL- HANDS ABOVE YOUR HEADS!

DIANA MOVES DOWN THE LINE SEARCHING EVERY GIRL.
NOBODY COULD CONCEAL A GUN UNDER THOSE UNIFORMS!

BUT DIANA IS MISTAKEN.
WELL, I'LL BE A KANGA'S UNCLE! THIS IS—

-A .22 AUTOMATIC

ZEUS STRIKE ME IF IT ISN'T MARVA PSYCHO!
YOU ARE MISTAKEN, MISS PRINCE- I AM JANE GRAY. I-I CARRY THAT GUN TO PROTECT MYSELF!

THE GENERAL WAS SHOT WITH A .22 BULLET AND THIS AUTOMATIC HAS BEEN FIRED RECENTLY!
I FIRED IT THIS MORNING IN-IN-IN TARGET PRACTICE!
4

AFTER GIVING "JANE" A LIE DETECTOR TEST, DIANA STUDIES HER BLOOD PRESSURE RECORD CAREFULLY.
YOU LIED ABOUT YOUR NAME AND ABOUT SHOOTING YOUR GUN IN TARGET PRACTICE!
THAT'S MY STORY AND I'LL STICK TO IT!

DIANA DECIDES TO USE THE MAGIC LASSO.
HOLD OUT YOUR HANDS!
W-WHAT ARE YOU GOING TO DO TO ME?

I SHALL MAKE YOU TELL THE TRUTH— WHILE BOUND WITH THIS GOLDEN ROPE YOU MUST OBEY ME!
OH NO-NO! YOU CAN'T DO THIS TO ME!

TELL ME YOUR REAL NAME!
I-OH, SOME-THING COM-PELS ME! I AM MARVA PSYCHO— MY MAIDEN NAME WAS MARVA JANE GRAY.

TELL ME THE TRUTH—DID YOU FIRE YOUR AUTOMATIC AT— GOOD HERA! THE GIRL'S FAINTED!

WHILE DIANA TRIES TO REVIVE MARVA, STEVE ENTERS THE ROOM WITHOUT WARNING.
THAT'S WONDER WOMAN'S MAGIC LASSO!
WHY-YES— SHE LENT IT TO ME!

WONDER WOMAN CAME TO INVESTIGATE THE SHOOTING— SHE WAS HERE JUST A MOMENT AGO!
AND SHE'S STILL HERE! YOU CAN'T FOOL ME ANY LONGER, DIANA— IN-CREDIBLE AS IT SEEMS, YOU MUST BE WONDER WOMAN!
5

YOU'VE MADE A FOOL OF ME LONG ENOUGH— TAKE THOSE HORN-SWOGGLING GLASSES OFF!
NO! STEVE— PLEASE DON'T—

DIANA'S SKILL AS A VENTRILOQUIST GAINS HER A MOMENT'S RESPITE.
LET DIANA ALONE STEVE, I AM **HERE** IF YOU WANT TO SEE ME!
HUH? **WONDER WOMAN'S** VOICE!

AS STEVE STRIDES TOWARD THE DOOR—

DIANA LEAPS LIGHTLY THROUGH A WINDOW.

FASTER THAN THE EYE CAN FOLLOW, DIANA SPEEDS TO THE NEXT WINDOW AND JUMPS IN—
THIS WILL HAVE TO BE THE FASTEST TIME I **EVER** MADE!

AS STEVE WALKS DOWN THE HALL TO THE NEXT ROOM **WONDER WOMAN** LOOKS OUT THE DOOR.
STOP RIGHT WHERE YOU ARE, STEVE TREVOR, AND TELL ME WHAT YOU DID TO DIANA PRINCE!
WHY—ER— AH— I ONLY—

WHILE SHE HOLDS STEVE'S ATTENTION WITH CONVERSATION, **WONDER WOMAN** COMPLETES HER COSTUME.
I THOUGHT **YOU** WERE DIANA— THAT IS I THOUGHT DIANA WAS YOU-AH-ER—
WELL, YOU CAN SEE FOR YOURSELF THAT **I AM I**!
6

WONDER WOMAN HASTILY HIDES DIANA'S CLOTHES.
DIANA HAD YOUR MAGIC LASSO! SHE TOOK A BIG JUMP WHEN THE GENERAL WAS SHOT—
DON'T BE SO SUSPICIOUS! LOTS OF GIRLS JUMP HIGH WHEN THEY'RE EXCITED AND I **LENT** DI MY LASSO!

I'VE GOT TO SEND STEVE AWAY BEFORE HE STARTS LOOKING FOR DIANA.
STEVE, YOU MUST VISIT DR. PSYCHO IN PRISON-IMMEDIATELY!
PSYCHO! THE GUY WHO MATERIALIZED BODIES TO DISGUISE HIMSELF AND BLEW UP THE MUNITION WORKS?

YES, PSYCHO MAY BE BEHIND THIS SHOOTING, EVEN THOUGH HE'S IN JAIL. THAT WAAC DIANA'S EXAMINING IS PSYCHO'S WIFE-SHE APPEARED TO FAINT BUT ACTUALLY SHE FELL IN A TRANCE!
WHAT? IS IT POSSIBLE PSYCHO COULD CONTROL HER MIND FROM A DISTANCE?

PSYCHO MIGHT PUT HER IN A TRANCE BY SENDING THOUGHT WAVES- SHE WAS HIS MENTAL SLAVE FOR YEARS! FIND OUT IF PSYCHO PLANNED THIS CRIME!
I'LL TRY-WISH ME LUCK!

WONDER WOMAN HURRIES BACK TO FIND MARVA GONE.
THERE'S HER CAP-THAT'S WHERE I LEFT HER, BOUND WITH MY MAGIC LASSO! THE LASSO'S MISSING AND HER AUTOMATIC'S GONE FROM THE TABLE!

AT THIS VERY MOMENT, AN INGENIOUS TRAP IS BEING PREPARED.
HELP, WONDER WOMAN, HELP!

WONDER WOMAN RUSHES TO THE WINDOW AND---
HA! I'VE GOT YOU! NOW YOU MUST OBEY ME, WONDER WOMAN- I KNOW HOW IT FEELS TO BE BOUND WITH THIS ROPE!
YES-I'M COMPELLED TO OBEY!
7

THE LASSO IS FASTENED HERE SECURELY-CLIMB UP TO THIS WINDOW. DO NOT TRY TO ESCAPE!
I MUST OBEY YOU!

INSIDE THE ROOM, WONDER WOMAN IS COMPELLED TO CHANGE CLOTHES WITH MARVA.
I BROUGHT THIS BLACK WIG AND YOUR COSTUME FITS ME PERFECTLY- HOW DO I LOOK?
VERY PRETTY! YOUR LOOKS HAVE IMPROVED TREMENDOUSLY SINCE YOU JOINED THE WAACS!

I CAN'T UNDERSTAND WHY YOU'RE BEHAVING LIKE THIS! NOW THAT YOUR HUSBAND IS IN JAIL YOU'RE NO LONGER UNDER HIS INFLUENCE! WHAT'S WRONG WITH YOU ANYWAY?
THERE'S NOTHING WRONG WITH ME! I KNOW WHAT I'M DOING BUT NOBODY WOULD UNDERSTAND ME IF I TOLD!

THERE CAN'T BE ANY REASON FOR YOU TO SHOOT A GENERAL!
THAT'S WHAT I'D LIKE TO EXPLAIN TO THE AUTHORITIES- BUT I'M SURE THEY WON'T BELIEVE IT ONCE I'M ACCUSED! I'M NOT GOING TO HAVE THAT HAPPEN!

MY WAAC COMPANY'S ON PUNISHMENT DUTY- YOU MUST TAKE MY PLACE AS "JANE GRAY" UNTIL I RELEASE YOU! NO ONE WILL NOTICE THE DIFFERENCE! PROMISE!
NO, NO! I CAN'T- OH! THE LASSO COMPELS ME- I PROMISE!

WONDER WOMAN JOINS THE WAACS.
AUXILIARY JANE GRAY REPORTING FOR PUNISHMENT DUTY WITH COMPANY A-
THAT AIN'T THE WAY FOR A MILITARY PRISONER TO SALUTE- FOLD YER ARMS- THEN START DIGGIN'!
MP

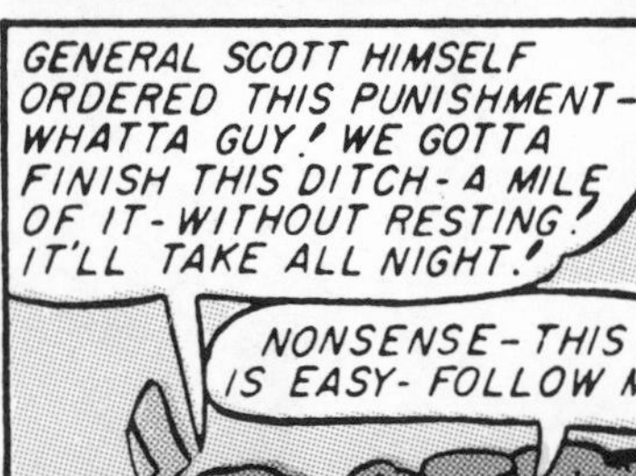

GENERAL SCOTT HIMSELF ORDERED THIS PUNISHMENT- WHATTA GUY! WE GOTTA FINISH THIS DITCH- A MILE OF IT- WITHOUT RESTING! IT'LL TAKE ALL NIGHT!
NONSENSE- THIS IS EASY- FOLLOW ME!
8

COME ON, GIRLS! ONLY A FEW MORE YARDS TO GO!
PHEW! PUFF- WHOO! WE'LL SHOW THOSE MEN!

LED BY WONDER WOMAN THE GIRLS COMPLETE A 20 HOUR JOB IN 15 MINUTES.
WELL, SERGEANT, WHAT NEXT?
BY GOLLY, I DON'T KNOW! NOBODY EVER DUG THAT FAST BEFORE! YOU CAN MARCH TO QUARTERS AND REST!

AT THAT MOMENT ORDERS ARRIVE.
ORDERS FROM GENERAL SCOTT- AUXILIARY JANE GRAY WILL REPORT IMMEDIATELY TO CAMP HEADQUARTERS
GET IN THERE, GRAY- MAKE IT SNAPPY!
MP

BOY, IS THE GENERAL SORE! SOME DAME TRIED TO KILL HIM BUT HE CAUGHT HER!
I WONDER IF THEY CAUGHT MARVA IN MY COSTUME-OR IF THIS SOLDIER MEANS ME!

THIS IS JANE GRAY, SIR!
JANE GRAY! HA, HA! YOU'RE REALLY WONDER WOMAN, AREN'T YOU? AREN'T THOSE YOUR CLOTHES?
WHY- ER-YES, NO-
I DON'T KNOW WHAT TO SAY! I MUST KEEP MY PROMISE UNTIL RELEASED

GO INTO THE NEXT ROOM AND PUT THOSE CLOTHES ON! WHEN WE GET YOU TWO MURDERESSES INTO THE RIGHT CLOTHES WE CAN IDENTIFY YOU BOTH BEYOND QUESTION!
SO I'M A MURDERESS NOW - OKAY, GENERAL- WHATEVER YOU SAY!

PROPERLY DRESSED, THE GIRLS ARE BROUGHT BACK BY A FIRST OFFICER OF WAACS. BECAUSE IT WAS HANDY, THE MAGIC LASSO IS USED TO BIND MARVA--
TELL THE TRUTH, GRAY- DIDN'T YOU CONSPIRE WITH WONDER WOMAN TO KILL GENERAL STANDPAT?
I NEVER KILLED ANYONE NOR TRIED TO KILL ANYONE!
GENERAL SCOTT

TIE THESE PRISONERS TOGETHER AND LEAVE THE ROOM! I'VE GOT TO BREAK DOWN THIS WAAC GIRL'S LIES!
YES, SIR!
BUT MARVA COULDN'T LIE - SHE WAS BOUND WITH THE MAGIC LASSO THAT MEANS SHE'S INNOCENT!

MARVA, TELL ME THE WHOLE TRUTH.!
I D-DAREN'T- BUT I MUST! A CLEVERLY DISGUISED NAZI AGENT CAME HERE TO DESTROY THE AMMUNITION DUMP. I RECOGNIZED HIM AS STOFFER, A FORMER ASSOCIATE OF DR. PSYCHO!
COMPELLED BY THE MAGIC LASSO MARVA CONTINUES HER STORY: "THEY WERE DRILLING US WAACS WHEN—"
EYES FRONT— DRESS YOUR RANKS-
STOFFER WAS IN THAT CAR IN OFFICER'S UNIFORM! BUT HE COULDN'T BE— I MUST BE CRAZY—
"I WAS GIVEN EXTRA K.P. DUTY FOR INATTENTION AT DRILL- THAT MEANS GETTING UP AT 3 A.M. TO WALK A MILE AND PREPARE BREAKFAST—"
JUS' GOT T' BED- CAN'T WAKE UP- FOOL I WAS!
"CROSSING THE DARK DESERTED CAMP GROUNDS, I FELT A HAND SUDDENLY GRIP MY COAT."
YI-EEE!
SHUT UP, YOU FOOL!
"HANDS PINNED ME FIRMLY AGAINST THE WALL— IT WAS STOFFER!"
SO IT WAS YOU IN THAT CAR!
YES— I SAW YOU RECOGNIZED ME. BUT IF YOU'RE WISE YOU'LL KEEP YOUR MOUTH SHUT!
IF YOU DENOUNCE ME NOBODY WILL BELIEVE YOU. I'LL ARREST YOU- REVEAL YOUR PAST! I'LL ACCUSE YOU OF HELPING YOUR HUSBAND PSYCHO COMMIT MURDERS —YOU'LL GO TO PRISON!
YOU- YOU BEAST! I-I'LL THINK IT OVER—
"I PLANNED TO TELEPHONE MAJOR TREVOR-BUT THAT DAY THE AMMUNITION DUMP BLEW UP— IT WAS TOO LATE!"
STOFFER DID THIS —I'M SURE OF IT! BUT I HAVE NO PROOF!
10

"I BOUGHT A .22 AUTOMATIC- IT WAS AGAINST WAAC REGULATIONS BUT I HAD A WILD PLAN—"
WE'RE NOT ALLOWED TO SELL—
IT'S ALL RIGHT- I'M BUYING THIS FOR AN OFFICER!

"THAT EVENING I SNEAKED OUT OF STUDY HALL AND WENT OVER TO THE MEN'S CAMP-"
STOFFER SHOULD PASS HERE ON HIS WAY TO OFFICERS' QUARTERS.

"SURE ENOUGH, ALONG HE CAME AND I FELL IN BEHIND HIM."
I'VE GOT YOU COVERED- WALK QUIETLY BEHIND THAT GARAGE OR I'LL SHOOT!

"ON REACHING A SECLUDED SPOT I—"
YOU BLEW UP THE AMMUNITION DUMP STOFFER- I GIVE YOU ONE MINUTE TO START WRITING YOUR CONFESSION BEFORE I SHOOT.
BUT DON'T BE RIDICULOUS! YOU CAN'T—

SUDDENLY HE GRABBED MY GUN—I PULLED THE TRIGGER BUT NOTHING HAPPENED!
HA HA! YOU DIDN'T EVEN KNOW ENOUGH TO RELEASE THE SAFETY CATCH ON YOUR AUTOMATIC!

YOU'VE COMMITTED A SERIOUS CRIME-ASSAULT ON AN OFFICER WITH INTENT TO MURDER! BUT I WON'T PREFER CHARGES IF YOU KEEP QUIET! MEANWHILE, I MAY FIND USE FOR YOUR TOY PISTOL—
SOB! SOB!

"HE FOUND USE FOR IT ALL RIGHT! STOFFER SHOT GENERAL STANDPAT WITH MY PISTOL FROM THIS OFFICE WINDOW!"

THIS FRAMES ME BEAUTIFULLY FOR SHOOTING THE GENERAL... MY ONLY HOPE IS TO FORCE THE REAL CRIMINAL TO REVEAL HIMSELF.

I TOOK YOUR MAGIC LASSO, WONDER WOMAN, TO MAKE STOFFER CONFESS! BUT HE OVERPOWERED ME. THERE HE SITS COMPLACENTLY CALLING HIMSELF "GENERAL SCOTT!"
THAT'S A LIE!
EASY, "GENERAL!"

WHY SHOULD I KILL GENERAL STANDPAT?
BECAUSE HE KNOWS THE REAL GENERAL SCOTT TOO WELL- YOU KIDNAPPED SCOTT ON HIS WAY TO TAKE COMMAND OF THIS CAMP AND YOU TOOK HIS PLACE!

YOU GIRLS TALK TOO MUCH- I'LL GIVE YOUR TONGUES A REST!
UNF!
E-E-EEK!
I'D BETTER PLAY UNCONSCIOUS!

GIRLS FAINTED- PUT 'EM IN A PRISON AMBULANCE. I'LL DRIVE IT MYSELF TO WAAC HEADQUARTERS!
YES, GENERAL!

STOFFER DRIVES RAPIDLY FROM CAMP TO A NAZI HIDEOUT
QUICKLY, THROW THE REAL GENERAL SCOTT IN THE AMBULANCE- I'VE GOT TO GET RID OF HIM!
YAH - VE HAF DER BOMB READY!

AS GENERAL SCOTT LANDS BESIDE HER, WONDER WOMAN COMES TO LIFE.
I HAD TO WAIT UNTIL THE GENERAL WAS OUT OF THEIR HANDS BEFORE I STARTED ANYTHING - NOW FOR SOME FUN!

WONDER WOMAN EASILY BURSTS THROUGH THE LOCKED DOORS OF THE VEHICLE.

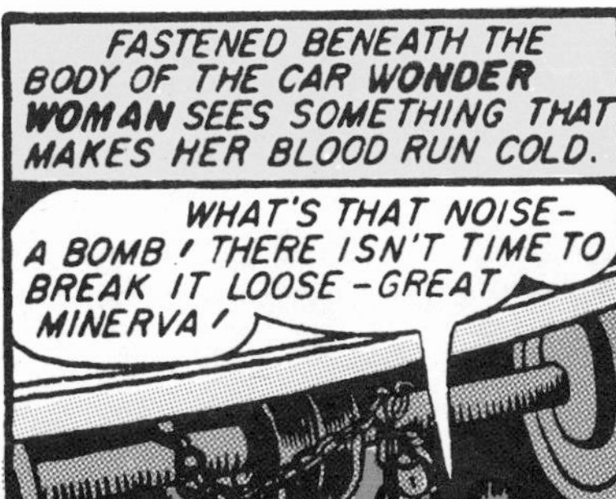
FASTENED BENEATH THE BODY OF THE CAR WONDER WOMAN SEES SOMETHING THAT MAKES HER BLOOD RUN COLD.
WHAT'S THAT NOISE- A BOMB! THERE ISN'T TIME TO BREAK IT LOOSE - GREAT MINERVA!
SPUT- T-T-TUT

WITH ONE SWIFT MOTION WONDER WOMAN DRAGS THE HELPLESS PRISONERS FROM THE AMBULANCE.
SPLIT SECONDS COUNT NOW!

SEIZING THE AMBULANCE WONDER WOMAN HURLS IT A SAFE DISTANCE.
WHEW! THAT'S GOOD EXERCISE!

AS FATE WOULD HAVE IT, STOFFER'S ESCAPING PLANE TAKES OFF AT THE SAME MOMENT AND—
CRA-AASH!
BAA-ANG!

WELL, GENERAL- THAT STOFFER FELLOW DID A GOOD JOB OF IMPERSONATING YOU- HE ALMOST GOT AWAY WITH IT, TOO!
YES! BUT HE DIDN'T KNOW WONDER WOMAN COULD HIT A PLANE WITH AN AMBULANCE AT 300 YARDS!
13

GENERAL STANDPAT RECOVERS IN TIME TO PRESENT THE MEDALS.
FOR HEROIC ACTION I COMMEND THESE BRAVE SOLDIERS- AHEM- BRAVE WOMEN- HARRUMPH!
DON'T FORGET TO KISS US ON BOTH CHEEKS, GENERAL - IT'S A NEW ARMY REGULATION FOR WAACS!
WONDER WOMAN'S ADVENTURES APPEAR EVERY MONTH IN SENSATION COMICS
Buy WAR BONDS AND STAMPS FOR VICTORY

Wonder Woman

By CHARLES MOULTON

AGAIN THE BEWILDERED LANA'S TORTURED MIND GENERATES A MIGHTY BRAIN-STORM WHICH SWEEPS OUR FRIENDS INTO THE DANGEROUS PIONEER DAYS WHEN OUR BRAVE FOREFATHERS RISKED THEIR LIVES TO EXPLORE AND SETTLE IN THE WILD WEST. ONLY **WONDER WOMAN,** WITH HER HERCULEAN STRENGTH, COULD BEAT THE MIGHTY "**GODS OF THE PRAIRIE**" TO SAVE HER FRIENDS FROM A BARBAROUS DEATH AT THE HANDS OF FEROCIOUS SAVAGES. YOU'LL THRILL WITH EXCITEMENT AS YOU READ OF THE BEAUTIFUL AMAZON MAID'S DAUNTLESS COURAGE IN---

"THE REDSKINS' REVENGE."

H G PETER

ON THE TRIREME -
I CAN'T BELIEVE HE BETRAYED ME - HE DIDN'T - BUT STEVE **HEARD** HIM - -OHH- MY MIND'S IN AN AWFUL TURMOIL----
HOLD TIGHT - WE'RE 20TH CENTURY BOUND!
1-B

WHEE! BACK ON TERRA FIRMA!
WOO! WOO! AM I GLAD TO SHED THOSE FANCY CLOTHES! SEE WHAT YOUR THINK-IN' DOES, LANA?
I'M SORRY, BUT I-I'M STILL CON-FUSED----

NO! NO! LANA, HAVE A HEART! WE JUST GOT BACK AN' YOU GOT THAT BRAINSTORM LOOK AGAIN!
OH, MY FORMULA - I'M A MURDERESS! CARL WILL SAVE ME - OR BETRAY ME - OHHH, I THINK I'M GOING MAD!

AGAIN LANA'S TWISTED THOUGHTS STIR THE WINDS OF TIME INTO A RAGING TORNADO.
OH-OH!
WOO! WOO! OH, LANA, YOU'VE DONE IT AGAIN AND ME WITHOUT A CANDYYYYY!

PRESENT TIMES ARE BLOWN AWAY AND OUR FRIENDS ARE HURLED INTO A WESTERN FRONTIER SETTLEMENT.
CREEPERS JEEPERS, FROM A VESTAL VIRGIN TO A PIONEER. AN' AM I RUGGED!
GOLLY, LOOK AT OUR CLOTHES!

MEANWHILE, WONDER WOMAN AND STEVE ARRIVE FROM ROME AT PAULA'S LAB -
THANK APHRODITE YOU'RE BACK, PRINCESS. THE DEAN OF HOLLIDAY COLLEGE HAS PUT OUT AN ALARM FOR ETTA CANDY AND HER PALS.
UH-OH, THEY SHOULD BE BACK AT COLLEGE BY NOW! I'D BETTER CALL DEAN PICKLEPUSS!
2-B

DEAN PICKLEPUSS SPEAKING - OH, SO IT'S WONDER WOMAN. --- NO, MISS CANDY AND HER FRIENDS HAVEN'T RETURNED AND IT'S YOUR FAULT - IF YOU DIDN'T CONTINUALLY TAKE THEM ADVEN-TURING -----
BUT, DEAN PICKLE-PUSS! BUT LET ME EXPLAIN ---BUT--- BUT--- --OH, SHE HUNG UP!

ETTA AND THE GIRLS ARE STILL MISSING - PROBABLY STRANDED IN ANOTHER ERA - MAYBE IN GRAVE DANGER AND THE DEAN'S RIGHT! IT'S ALL MY FAULT!
BUCK UP, SWEETSTUFF, YOU---
PRINCESS, YOUR MOTHER'S CALLING YOU BY MENTAL RADIO.

CALLING AMAZON PRINCESS DIANA! MAGIC SPHERE SHOWS ETTA CANDY AND GIRLFRIENDS SWEPT BACK INTO AMERICAN PIONEER DAYS BY WINDS OF TIME -
AD 1840

MOTHER, DARLING, ARE THEY ALL RIGHT?
THE GIRLS NEED HELP- GO TO THEIR AID, DAUGHTER, BUT BE CAUTIOUS. APHRODITE BE WITH YOU!

COME ON, PAULA AND STEVE - WE'RE GOING TO GIVE THE SPACE TRANSFORMING MACHINE ANOTHER WORKOUT!
OKAY, ANGEL, BUT LEAVE MY ARM IN THE SOCKET. I'VE A FEELING I'LL NEED IT!

MEANWHILE, OVER 100 YEARS AGO IN THE FRONTIER DANCE HALL RUN BY MATILDA GUMDROP.
QUIET DOWN 'FORE I PUMP LEAD INTO YOU NOISY COYOTES! YOU'RE NOW GONNA BE HONORED BY BEAUTIFUL AND TALENTED COQUETTES, THE GUMDROP DANCE HALL TERPSICHOREANS!
BANG
3-B

WA-HOO!
WHAT GALS!

IN MATTIE'S OFFICE—
WELL! WELL! OUR LEADIN' FUR TRADER, DANIEL BEENE! HOW'S PRUE?
FINE, SHE'S ALWAYS BUSY DOIN' SOMETHIN' FER THE INDIANS — TEACHIN' THEIR CHILDREN OR NURSING THEIR SICK—

PRUDENCE SURE IS A GREAT GAL! THE INDIANS **WORSHIP** HER!
MATTIE, I COME IN HERE TO INVITE YOU TO THE HOUSE TOMORROW. WE'RE GIVIN' PRUE A PARTY TO ANNOUNCE HER ENGAGEMENT TO SILAS SNEEK.

HOW CAN A SWELL GAL LIKE PRUE LOVE A NINKAPOOP LIKE SILAS? JUST NO ACCOUNTIN' FER TASTES NOHOW!

ARRIVING HOME, TRADER BEENE FINDS SILAS SNEEK WAITING—
YOU'RE A FINE ASSISTANT, SILAS, AND YOU'LL BE A MOST WELCOME SON-IN-LAW!
AW, PAW!

HERE, SILAS, BRING THESE TRINKETS TO CHIEF GREATHEART AT ONCE TO PAY FOR THE FURS HIS TRAPPERS BROUGHT ME. I NEVER APPROVE OF CHEATING THE INDIANS!
I HOPE THEY APPRECIATE YOUR GENEROSITY, MR. BEENE.

BUT SILAS SNEEK HAS SINISTER PLANS OF HIS OWN—
THAT STUPID BEENE AND HIS SUGARY DAUGHTER DON'T MUCH KNOW WHAT'S AHEAD OF 'EM--- HAW!
4-B

MY COLLECTION OF TRINKETS IS GROWING. IT'LL BE MOST USEFUL WHEN I'M CHIEF FUR TRADER IN THESE PARTS! 'CAUSE WHEN CHIEF GREATHEART GETS ANOTHER HALF-EMPTY SACK FROM BEENE, HE'LL SURELY GO ON THE WARPATH!

CHIEF GREATHEART AND SILAS SOON REACH THE BEENE HOME-

MEANWHILE, INSIDE THE HOUSE—

NO, NO! THIS TROUBLE IS TOO BIG FOR A MERE WOMAN TO HANDLE - GO BACK EAST UNTIL I STRAIGHTEN OUT THIS MESS - THEN WE'LL BE MARRIED!
YES, SILAS, I WILL ANNOUNCE OUR ENGAGEMENT AT THE PARTY TOMORROW!

THE NEXT DAY CHIEF GREATHEART HOLDS A WAR COUNCIL WITH HIS STRONGEST BRAVES---AND SILAS SNEEK!
FUR TRADER BEENE CHEAT US NOW FOR LONG TIME - THEN HE INSULT CHIEF WHEN WE MAKE POW WOW!
KILL CHEATERS! SCALP 'EM WE BURN TOWN!

AT THIS MOMENT THE SPACE TRANSFORMER MATERIALIZES WONDER WOMAN ON A HUGE BRANCH OVERLOOKING THE ANGRY INDIANS.
GREAT HERA, INDIANS! AND CARL AMBISHUN'S WITH THEM! I WONDER WHAT TROUBLE HE'S STIRRING UP NOW!
SILENCE, MY BRAVES - WE CANNOT WAR ON TRADER BEENE AND OTHER WHITES AS LONG AS GOOD LADY, MISS PRUDENCE, REMAINS IN TOWN!

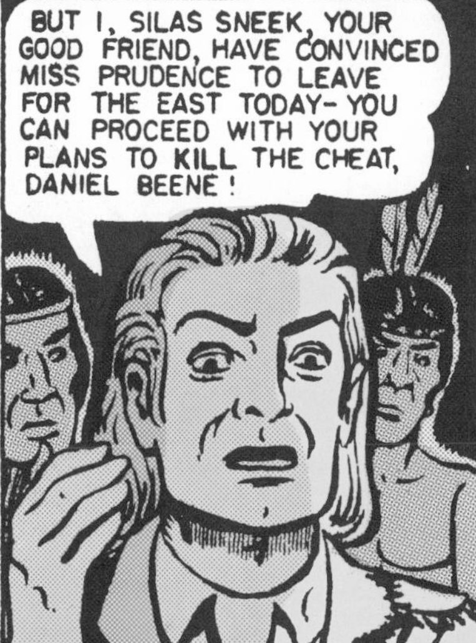
BUT I, SILAS SNEEK, YOUR GOOD FRIEND, HAVE CONVINCED MISS PRUDENCE TO LEAVE FOR THE EAST TODAY - YOU CAN PROCEED WITH YOUR PLANS TO KILL THE CHEAT, DANIEL BEENE!

UH-OH! I BET "PRUDENCE" IS LANA AND SHE'S STILL DEPENDING ON THAT SNAKE TO DO HER FIGHTING FOR HER. I MUST STOP HER FROM LEAVING!
6-B

AT THE BEENE HOUSE, PRUE'S ENGAGEMENT PARTY IS IN FULL SWING WHEN -
TODAY I'M LEAVING FOR THE EAST - DAD'LL FOLLOW SOON - IF WE STAY HERE THE INDIANS'LL KILL HIM. ONLY SILAS CAN QUIET 'EM DOWN!
DON'T BELIEVE IT, PRUE! THEM INJUNS WORSHIP YOU - LONG'S YOU STAY YOUR DAD'S SAFE!

SUDDENLY WONDER WOMAN BURSTS INTO THE ROOM—
PRUDENCE, YOU MUSTN'T LEAVE! AS SOON AS YOU'RE GONE, THE INDIANS PLAN TO BURN THE TOWN DOWN! SILAS SNEEK'S PLOTTING WITH THEM—

A PERFECT STRANGER BURSTS IN HERE WITH A COCK-AND-BULL STORY THAT I'M S'POSED TO BELIEVE —
WOO WOO! SHE'S PROB'LY RIGHT, PRUE, I NEVER DID TRUST THAT COYOTE.

PAW'S SAFETY MEANS EVERYTHIN' TO ME, AND SILAS ALWAYS KNOWS WHAT'S BEST! I'M LEAVIN' WITH THE WILKENS' FAMILY NOW AND THAT'S FINAL!

PRUE RIDES OFF WITH THE WILKENS, BUT HER DEPARTURE IS WATCHED BY AN UNSEEN OBSERVER—
GOOD LADY LEAVE AND HER EVIL FATHER RIDE THIS WAY- SHE BETTER OFF WITHOUT HIM - ME GET HIM NOW!

NOW WE FIX YOU, YOU HEAP BIG CHEAT!
7-B

BACK IN TOWN—
I'M WORRIED ABOUT PRUE'S FATHER. HE SHOULD BE BACK BY NOW. I'D BETTER TRY TO FIND HIM!
GO TO IT, BIG GIRL- LOOKS LIKE WE'RE ALL IN THE SOUP NOW!

WHILE WONDER WOMAN SEARCHES FOR BEENE, THE INDIANS WREAK THEIR SAVAGE REVENGE UPON THE TOWN—
BAND

KEEP YORE DISTANCE OR YOU'LL GET THE GUMDROP SOCK THAT'LL CRACK YORE SKULLS!
FAT SQUAW MUCH TOO FRISKY– FUN WATCH HER BURN ALIVE!

GULP– LOOKS LIKE I'M GONNA BE A ROASTED "GUMDROP"!

WONDER WOMAN, MY ANGEL! THE SPACE TRANSFORMER MATERIALIZED ME HERE IN THIS WILDERNESS–
STEVE, RIDE WITH ME – I'VE GOT TO FIND DANIEL BEENE WHOM YOU KNOW AS MR. KURREE–THE INDIANS CAPTURED HIM!

BLAZES! WHAT'S COOKIN' OVER THERE?
GREAT HERA! THE TOWN'S ON FIRE! WE'D BETTER REACH THE INDIAN CAMP FAST– SOMETHING TELLS ME MORE PEOPLE THAN BEENE ARE INDIAN CAPTIVES NOW!
8-8

AND SOMEONE ELSE IS VERY ALARMED BY THE FIRE—
FIRE! AN' IT COMES FROM THE DIRECTION OF OUR TOWN! FATHER AND SILAS – OH I MUST TURN BACK!

AS THEY NEAR THE CAMP, STEVE SPOTS AN INDIAN SNIPER AND -
LOOK OUT, ANGEL! GLAD I DIDN'T HIT THE INDIAN - CAN'T BLAME THE POOR DEVILS FOR WANTING OUR SCALPS WITH THE RAW DEAL SO MANY OF THE WHITES GIVE THEM!
GREAT SHOT, STEVE!
ZING

IN THE INDIAN CAMP -
CHIEF, THIS IS EXACTLY WHAT THE WICKED WHITES DESERVE!
SOMETIMES ME WONDER IF **YOU** ARE NOT WICKED WHITE TOO!

CHIEF GREATHEART, WHITE MAN AND WOMAN RIDE INTO CAMP - THEY NOT LIKE OTHER WHITE PEOPLE - THEY BIG MEDICINE MEN - THEY BEWITCH MY BOW AND ARROW!
WE SHOOT THEM WITH **FLAMING** ARROWS!

STOP SHOOTING, BRAVES - WHITE WOMAN BIG MEDICINE LADY - MAYBE GODDESS - WE GIVE HER TEST!
9-B

YOU BEAT OUR ARROWS - GOOD. BUT CAN YOU BEAT MIGHTY GODS OF THE PRAIRIE? YOU FIGHT AND IF YOU WIN, I KNOW YOU ARE GODDESS!
WITH PLEASURE - AS MANY AS YOU LIKE!

DON'T BOTHER OPENING THE GATE - THIS LITTLE JUMP WILL WARM ME UP!
SHE LEAP LIKE DEER!
SHE BRAVE!
SOON SHE BE TORN TO PIECES - BIG SHAME!

I **COULD** USE MY MAGIC LASSO BUT IT'LL BE MORE FUN TO FIGHT THEM WITH MY BARE HANDS. FRONTIER LIFE SURE KEEPS A GIRL IN FORM!

10-B

YOU GREAT WHITE GODDESS OF MEN AND BEASTS—WE LET YOUR WHITE PEOPLE GO—HOLD BIG FEAST FOR YOU TOO!
DANIEL BEENE MUST BE RELEASED TOO!

ALL THE WHITES ARE RELEASED EXCEPT DANIEL BEENE—
NO! HIM CHEAT INDIANS— MUST DIE! BRAVES, START FIRE 'ROUND TRADER BEENE!
WE'LL SEE ABOUT THAT!

YIPE!
UG!
YIPE!
UG!

SHE EVIL SPIRIT, CHIEF GREATHEART! SHE MUST—HEY! STOP HER—SHE'S LASSOING ME!
CHIEF, YOU ARE A WISE MAN—GIVE ME A CHANCE TO PROVE THAT THIS MAN LIES ABOUT TRADER BEENE!
PROCEED, MIGHTY ONE!

TELL THE TRUTH—WHO REALLY CHEATED THE INDIANS—TRADER BEENE OR YOU?
I-I'M COMPELLED TO CONFESS! I STOLE HALF THE WAMPUM AND HID IT IN ROCKY CAVE.
SO—WE SETTLE WITH YOU!
11-B

UNSEEN, PRUDENCE ENTERED THE CAMP—
SO YOU'RE THE CHEAT—YOU WHOM I LOVED AND TRUSTED! I'VE LEARNED MY LESSON—I'LL RELY ON MYSELF, NOT ON A MAN!
DON'T FORGET THAT, PRUE!
BRAVO!

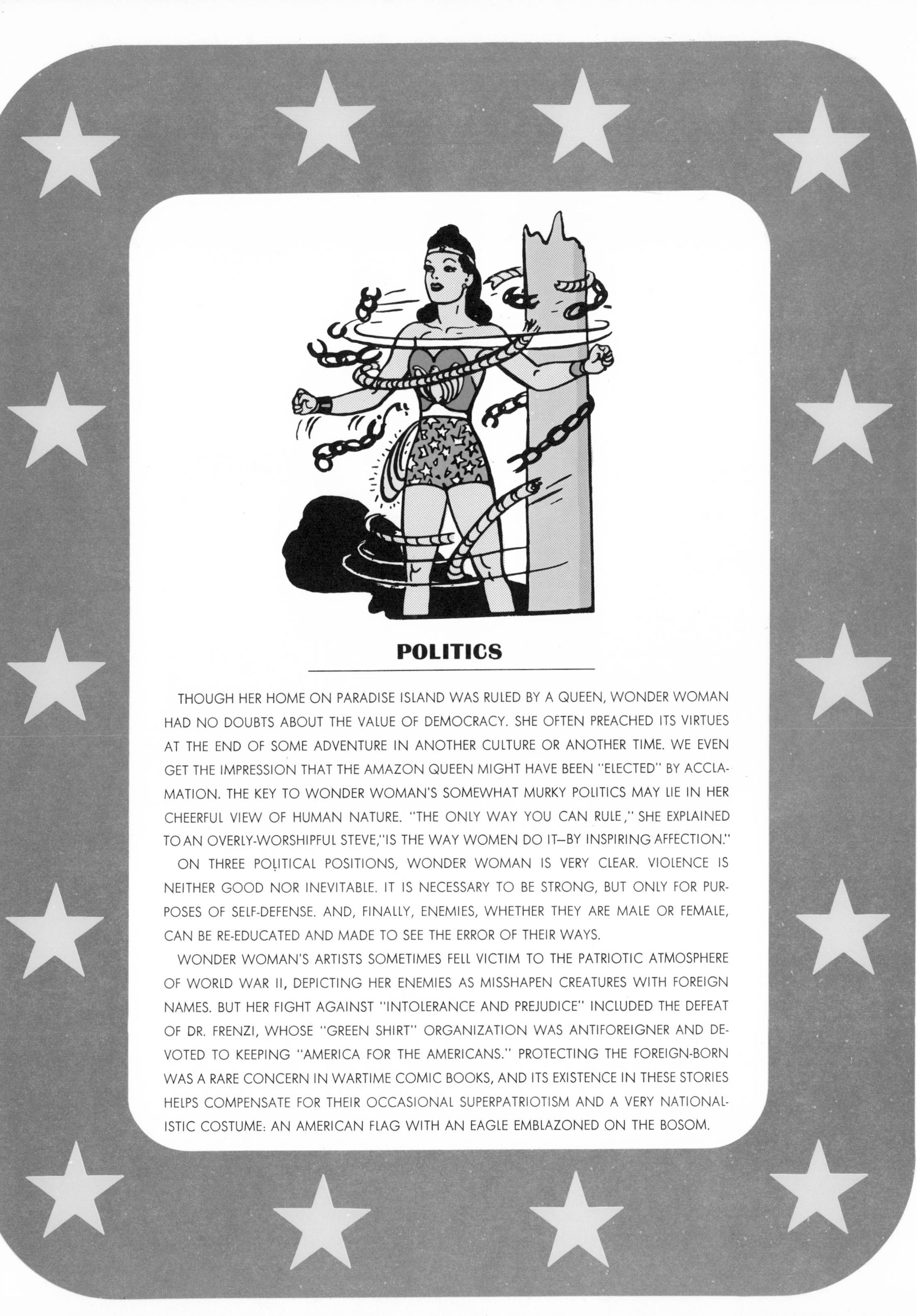

POLITICS

THOUGH HER HOME ON PARADISE ISLAND WAS RULED BY A QUEEN, WONDER WOMAN HAD NO DOUBTS ABOUT THE VALUE OF DEMOCRACY. SHE OFTEN PREACHED ITS VIRTUES AT THE END OF SOME ADVENTURE IN ANOTHER CULTURE OR ANOTHER TIME. WE EVEN GET THE IMPRESSION THAT THE AMAZON QUEEN MIGHT HAVE BEEN "ELECTED" BY ACCLAMATION. THE KEY TO WONDER WOMAN'S SOMEWHAT MURKY POLITICS MAY LIE IN HER CHEERFUL VIEW OF HUMAN NATURE. "THE ONLY WAY YOU CAN RULE," SHE EXPLAINED TO AN OVERLY-WORSHIPFUL STEVE,"IS THE WAY WOMEN DO IT—BY INSPIRING AFFECTION."

ON THREE POLITICAL POSITIONS, WONDER WOMAN IS VERY CLEAR. VIOLENCE IS NEITHER GOOD NOR INEVITABLE. IT IS NECESSARY TO BE STRONG, BUT ONLY FOR PURPOSES OF SELF-DEFENSE. AND, FINALLY, ENEMIES, WHETHER THEY ARE MALE OR FEMALE, CAN BE RE-EDUCATED AND MADE TO SEE THE ERROR OF THEIR WAYS.

WONDER WOMAN'S ARTISTS SOMETIMES FELL VICTIM TO THE PATRIOTIC ATMOSPHERE OF WORLD WAR II, DEPICTING HER ENEMIES AS MISSHAPEN CREATURES WITH FOREIGN NAMES. BUT HER FIGHT AGAINST "INTOLERANCE AND PREJUDICE" INCLUDED THE DEFEAT OF DR. FRENZI, WHOSE "GREEN SHIRT" ORGANIZATION WAS ANTIFOREIGNER AND DEVOTED TO KEEPING "AMERICA FOR THE AMERICANS." PROTECTING THE FOREIGN-BORN WAS A RARE CONCERN IN WARTIME COMIC BOOKS, AND ITS EXISTENCE IN THESE STORIES HELPS COMPENSATE FOR THEIR OCCASIONAL SUPERPATRIOTISM AND A VERY NATIONALISTIC COSTUME: AN AMERICAN FLAG WITH AN EAGLE EMBLAZONED ON THE BOSOM.

Wonder Woman
By Charles Moulton
DR. FRENZI HAD AN AMAZINGLY SUCCESSFUL BUSINESS! HE SOLD INTOLERANCE AND PREJUDICE AND IT IS REMARKABLE HOW MANY CUSTOMERS HE HAD! HIS WORK, THOUGH NEITHER CLEAN NOR HONEST, HAD NO SPECIFIC LAWS AGAINST IT.
DR. FRENZI THOUGHT HE HAD A RACKET TO BEAT ALL RACKETS UNTIL HIS DEADLY INTENT BROUGHT HIM TO GRIPS WITH THAT ALLURING AMAZON, WONDER WOMAN — BEAUTIFUL AS APHRODITE, WISE AS ATHENA, STRONGER THAN HERCULES, AND SWIFTER THAN MERCURY — WHO ONCE AGAIN FOUGHT FOR JUSTICE --
"WHEN TREACHERY WORE A GREEN SHIRT!"
HG PETER
1

DISTURBING REPORTS REACH THE OFFICES OF ARMY INTELLIGENCE.
BUT STEVE, THIS IS ALL WRONG! WE'VE ALREADY COME THROUGH A DEVASTATING WAR AND NOW THIS DR. FRENZI AND HIS GREEN SHIRT GANG ARE DESTROYING ALL THAT WE HAVE FOUGHT TO PRESERVE.
PROBABLY NOT AS BAD AS IT SOUNDS, DI--- YOU KNOW HOW RUMORS SPREAD.
THEN READ THIS REPORT! IT IS MORE THAN JUST A RUMOR IN THE TOWN OF OAKVILLE THREE HOMES BURNED TO THE GROUND--PEOPLE THREATENED!
OAKVILLE! SAY, THAT'S WHERE MY FRIEND GEORGE ZENKO LIVES. GUESS HE'D LET ME KNOW IF ANYTHING WERE WRONG.
---BUT AT THAT MOMENT IN OAKVILLE---
WHY SHOULD I FIRE ZENKO? HE'S WORKED FOR ME FOR YEARS--GOOD FELLOW TOO!
BECAUSE HE'S A FOREIGNER, SAM, AND DR. FRENZI SAYS WE GOT TO CLEAN 'EM OUT!
BAR
SAM'S EAT BAR
WOO WOO, GIRLS, I'M WORN OUT! LET'S GET NOURISHMENT!
NO MORE JALOPY TRIPS FOR ME! NEXT TIME WE GO WEST IT'S PULLMAN ALL THE WAY!
BARBER SHOP
SAM'S EAT BAR
THERE YOU ARE, ETTA--SAM'S EAT BAR! WHOA!
INSIDE SAM'S EAT BAR--
WE DON'T WANT NO FOREIGNERS IN OUR TOWN! THIS IS A FRIENDLY TIP--LEAVE TOWN WHILE YOU'RE ABLE!
AND YOU CALL YOURSELVES AMERICANS--GET OUT BEFORE I THROW YOU OUT!
TOUGH, AIN'T HE, AL?
TOUGH ENOUGH TO STAND UP TO SNEAKS LIKE YOU!
UMPH
I'LL FIX YOU--BUT PERMANENTLY!
HAM AND BEANS

PULLIN' A KNIFE IS BAD MANNERS, MISTER! TRY BEING SWEET INSTEAD!
Candy

WHAT'S IT ALL ABOUT, MISTER--ER--
ZENKO'S MY NAME, GEORGE ZENKO. THANKS FOR SAVING MY LIFE! YOU'LL GET THE SET-UP TONIGHT WHEN DR. FRENZI SPEAKS! HE CALLS IT AMERICA FOR THE AMERICANS.
HASH

THAT NIGHT THE INSIDIOUS FRENZI SELLS HIS WARES--
SO, MY FELLOW AMERICANS, IT IS TIME TO GIVE AMERICA BACK TO AMERICANS! DON'T LET FOREIGNERS TAKE YOUR JOBS!
SOMEBODY PLEASE TELL ME I'M DREAMING! I CAN'T BE HEARING THIS!
HE'S RIGHT!
YEAHHHH!

THE COLLECTION BOX WILL BE PASSED. IT IS YOUR DUTY TO GIVE--TO HELP PRESERVE YOUR OWN INDEPENDENCE!
HERE'S MY DOLLAR!
AND MINE--BUT HOW ABOUT ACTION?

YOU'LL GET ACTION! TONIGHT THE GREEN SHIRTS RIDE AGAIN TO PURIFY AMERICA!

AFTER THE MEETING--
NICE GOING, DOC--YOU SPOKE TONIGHT AS IF YOU BELIEVED IT YOURSELF!
DON'T BE SILLY, JOSIE. AMERICA IS THE LAND OF OPPORTUNITY AND THIS IS MY OPPORTUNITY TO MAKE A FORTUNE!

LATER THAT NIGHT, FROM THEIR HEADQUARTERS IN AN ABANDONED MAUSOLEUM, THE GREEN SHIRTS RIDE OUT ON THEIR HORRIBLE ERRAND--
ZENKO IS FIRST, MEN, LET'S GO!
I THOUGHT FRENZI WAS SILLY-- BUT HE MEANS BUSINESS! I'M GOING TO MENTAL RADIO WONDER WOMAN!

AT INTELLIGENCE HEADQUARTERS, DIANA SWIFTLY CHANGES TO WONDER WOMAN AS SHE RECEIVES ETTA'S MESSAGE--
HELP-- WONDER WOMAN --FRENZI'S GREEN SHIRTS ARE OUT TO MURDER FOREIGNERS! OAKVILLE!
GREAT HERA! FRENZI MUST BE STOPPED BEFORE THIS MADNESS SPREADS!

HELLO, BEAUTIFUL --WHERE'S DI?
ER--SHE'S GONE--SHE'S UPSET BECAUSE YOU DIDN'T TAKE THOSE MESSAGES SERIOUSLY. ETTA JUST RADIOED THERE'S TROUBLE IN OAKVILLE!

THE ALLURING AMAZON CALLS HER INVISIBLE PLANE BY MENTAL ROBOT CONTROL--
GOODBYE, STEVE! MY PLANE IS OUTSIDE--
WAIT! YOU'RE NOT GETTING AWAY THAT EASY! I'M COMING WITH YOU--

BUT COL. TREVOR MISCALCULATES--
STEVE!
OOPS!

WITH THE SPEED OF LIGHT, THE BEAUTIFUL AMAZON SWOOPS LOW--
WHEW--THANKS, WONDER WOMAN! THIS IS ONE TIME I'LL GLADLY ADMIT YOUR SUPERIORITY--

AT 3000 MILES AN HOUR WONDER WOMAN AND STEVE TREVOR STREAK FOR OAKVILLE.

MEANWHILE, IN FRONT OF SAM'S EAT BAR
ALL RIGHT, MEN-- DRAG ZENKO OUT!
YEAH-- AND IF HIS BOSS OBJECTS, DRAG HIM OUT TOO!
EAT BAR
SAM'S EAT BAR
OAKVILLE HARDW

HERE THEY ARE!
TAKE YOUR HANDS OFF ME!
THE "GREEN SHIRTS" WILL MAKE AN EXAMPLE OF YOU-

AND OF YOU TOO, FOR CONTINUING TO EMPLOY THIS FOREIGNER!
YOU WOULDN'T DARE!
THROW THE ROPE OVER THE LAMP POST AND GET IT OVER WITH.
SAM'S EAT BAR

AT THAT MOMENT--

MERCIFUL MINERVA! THEY'RE HANGING THOSE MEN! I'M GOING TO JUMP, LAND THE PLANE AND JOIN ME!
THE STUPID FOOLS!

THE INDIGNANT AMAZON PLUMMETS INTO THE SNARLING CROWD--
I THOUGHT WE FINISHED THIS BUSINESS WHEN THE WAR ENDED!
OWWW! IT'S WONDER WOMAN! LET'S SCRAM!
SAM'S EAT BAR

GIVE HER THE OLD WESTERN STRANGLE HOLD WITH YOUR LASSOES!

SUDDENLY--
WE'VE GOT HER! NOW RIDE!

BUT AS THE HORSEMEN GALLOP MADLY IN FOUR DIFFERENT DIRECTIONS, WONDER WOMAN TENSES--

WONDER WOMAN'S AMAZON TRAINING FOILS HER FOES.
THAT'S SHOWING 'EM, ANGEL!
I WONDER WHAT'S HAPPENED TO ETTA--
HEY! I'M FALLING!

UNSEEN, FRENZI HURRIEDLY MAKES HIS ESCAPE--
I MUST GET OUT OF HERE--THAT WOMAN ISN'T HUMAN!

STEVE MEETS HIS OLD FRIEND--
THANKS A LOT--THAT WAS CLOSE!
WHY, STEVE!--YOU SURE TRAVEL IN MIGHTY GOOD COMPANY!
GEORGE! AND YOU CAN ADD BEAUTIFUL TO GOOD WHERE WONDER WOMAN IS CONCERNED!
SAM'S
EAT BAR

BUT WALLS HAVE EARS--
THAT'S EXACTLY HOW IT IS. FRENZI HAS THESE PEOPLE BELIEVING THEY'RE DOING THE RIGHT THING!
WILL GREED AND LUST FOR POWER ALWAYS CONTROL MANKIND?
I HAVE A PLAN. I WILL GO ON THE AIR HERE AND EXPOSE FRENZI FOR WHAT HE IS!

SAY, WONDER WOMAN, THAT'S A GREAT IDEA! PEOPLE WILL LISTEN TO YOU. THE WHOLE WORLD KNOWS YOU STAND FOR JUSTICE!

MEANWHILE, THE HOLLIDAY GIRLS SEEK INFORMATION--
I GUESS THEY'VE ALL GONE. HURRY INSIDE AND WE'LL EXPLORE THIS DARK HOLE.
OOH, IT IS DARK!

SHHH-- WE'RE NEARING THE END OF THE PASSAGEWAY. THERE'S A DOOR AND A LIGHT SHOWING UNDER IT.
DON'T SHUSH, ETTA! IT'S TOO QUIET NOW!

THE GIRLS EXPLORE FRENZI'S HEADQUARTERS--
WOO WOO! LOOK AT THE MONEY!
AND JUST READ THESE PLANS FOR A REVOLUTION!
LOOKS LIKE TREASON, GIRLS--WAIT'LL WE TELL WONDER WOMAN!
7

BUT FRENZI HAS A WATCHDOG--
YOU'LL NEVER LEAVE THIS PLACE ALIVE TO TELL ANYBODY!
HUH?

FRENZI IS PLEASANTLY SURPRISED--
THESE ARE WONDER WOMAN'S SNOOPERS--I FOUND THEM GOING THROUGH YOUR PAPERS, DOC.
GOOD GOING, JOSIE. TIE THESE BABIES UP, BOYS!
YOU'LL NEVER GET AWAY WITH THIS, FISH-FACE!

THIS RACKET IS TOO GOOD TO BE SPOILED BY WONDER WOMAN. SOMEHOW I MUST ELIMINATE HER!

I HEAR SHE INTENDS TO BROADCAST THE TRUTH OVER THE RADIO--HA! THE TRUTH IS WHAT SHE WILL BROADCAST --BUT MY VERSION OF IT!

WONDER WOMAN RECEIVES A MESSAGE, SPECIAL DELIVERY!
GOOD! SHE SAW IT!
THUD

"YOUR FRIENDS ARE IN GRAVE DANGER! FOLLOW MESSENGER TO OLD CEMETERY. COME ALONE OR THEY DIE!" FRENZI
HISSSS! THIS WAY--
YOUR FRIENDS ARE IN DANGER! FOLLOW MESSENGER TO OLD CEMETERY. COME ALONE OR THEY DIE! FRENZI

SLIPPING AWAY FROM STEVE, WONDER WOMAN IS LED TO FRENZI'S HIDEOUT.
PUT 'EM UP, WONDER WOMAN! ONE STEP FORWARD AND TONS OF CEMENT WILL BURY YOUR FRIENDS INSTANTLY! HAH--HAH!
SKR-R-UNCH!
HEAVENLY HERA! WHAT'S THIS? I'LL GET YOU OUT OF--
PLOP

AS WONDER WOMAN'S ATTENTION IS DIRECTED TO FRENZI,STEALTHY FINGERS STEAL HER LASSO FROM BEHIND--
FRENZI,YOU COWARD-- I CAN--OOPS!
GOT HER WITH HER OWN LASSO, DOC!
QUICK, AL! WELD THOSE CHAINS TO HER BRACELETS--

BOUND BY HER UNBREAKABLE LASSO, WONDER WOMAN LIES HELPLESS IN THE CLUTCHES OF HER FOE.
HA!HA! IT'S TIME FOR WONDER WOMAN'S BROADCAST!
CHAINED BY MEN--I'VE LOST MY STRENGTH BY APHRODITE'S LAW---

HER FRIENDS' DANGER COMPELS WONDER WOMAN TO SUBMIT--
I HAVE A SCRIPT ALL PREPARED FOR YOU. READ!
"FELLOW AMERICANS-- THIS IS WONDER WOMAN SPEAKING.IN THE INTEREST OF JUSTICE AND EQUALITY, JOIN THE GREEN SHIRTS OF AMERICA! RID YOUR COUNTRY OF--" NO! NEVER!

WHAT! START THE MIXER UP AGAIN, AL!
I MUST STOP THIS! I CANNOT PREACH HATE AND WARFARE WHEN I AM A DISCIPLE OF PEACE AND LOVE--NOR CAN I SACRIFICE THE GIRLS!
SKR-R-UNCH
PLOP!
CLICK!

OH,STEVE,I HOPE YOU CAN RECEIVE THIS MESSAGE--"OLD CEMETERY--UNDERGROUND--BRING HELP--HURRY"!
9

WELL? DO YOU BROADCAST OR DO YOUR FRIENDS DIE?
YOU WIN, FRENZI.
PRESS THE BUZZER, AL. WE'RE ON THE AIR!

MEANWHILE, ABOVE THE TOWN OF OAKVILLE--
WELL, STEVE--WE'VE SEARCHED HIGH AND--
WAIT, GEORGE--LOOK!
CEMETERY--UNDERGROUND--BRING HELP--HURRY!

THE BEAUTIFUL AMAZON DEFIES FRENZI!
AMERICANS! DO NOT FOLLOW THE DOCTRINES OF INTOLERENCE AND PREJUDICE PUT FORTH BY THIS TRAITOR, FRENZI! HE PLANS TO USE YOU AND YOUR MONEY FOR HIS OWN SELFISH PURPOSES--HE IS YOUR REAL ENEMY--HE---

SKR-RUNCH
SLURP!
RIP OUT THE MICROPHONE! FASTER, FASTER WITH THAT CEMENT! USE IT ALL! I'LL ENTOMB THE AMAZON WITH THE REST!
IN THREE MINUTES THAT AERATED CEMENT WILL MAKE ME FREE OF THE ONLY PERSON I FEAR IN THE WHOLE WORLD--WONDER WOMAN!

BUT WHEN STEVE ARRIVES AT THE OLD CEMETERY--
HM, WONDER WOMAN SAID UNDERGROUND, BUT IF SO, WHERE'S THE ENTRANCE?
COLONEL, I-ER-I USED TO BE A GREEN SHIRT. I KNOW HOW TO GET IN.

BUT PRECIOUS MOMENTS HAVE BEEN LOST!
JUMPING BLUE BLAZES! THERE'S WONDER WOMAN! --HER WRISTS ARE CHAINED!
STEVE! HURRY! THE MIXER IS COMING THROUGH THE ROOF!
CRASH!

STEVE FIRES CAREFULLY--AND WITH AMAZON STRENGTH RETURNED, WONDER WOMAN LEAPS FREE!
GOOD SHOT, STEVE! GO AFTER FRENZI WHILE I RESCUE THE HOLLIDAY GIRLS.
ZING
CRACK
BANG
RIGHTO, ANGEL!

INDEED, STRONGER THAN HERCULES!
NO TIME TO DIG THE GIRLS OUT--

THE INVINCIBLE AMAZON WADES THROUGH THE HARDENED CEMENT LIKE WATER AND CARRIES HER FRIENDS TO SAFETY!
WOW! I'D NEVER BELIEVE IT IF I DIDN'T SEE IT WITH MY OWN EYES!
CRASH!
THANK APHRODITE, I MADE IT IN TIME!

WONDER WOMAN PULVERIZES THE CEMENT WITH HER BARE HANDS --
WHEW! AM I GLAD TO GET OUT OF THAT!
GEORGE, SEE THAT THE GIRLS RECEIVE TREATMENT FOR SHOCK. I'VE GOT TO HELP STEVE FIND FRENZI AND GIVE HIM ONE!
AND A MOMENT LATER --
WONDER WOMAN, MA'AM, WE'RE MIGHTY ASHAMED OF OURSELVES FOR BELIEVING ANYTHING THIS RODENT SAID. WE LET HIM FOOL US, BUT NOW WE'RE TURNING IN OUR SHIRTS, THANKS TO YOU!
HELP! TURN ME LOOSE!
TAKE ME AWAY FROM HERE! I DEMAND JUSTICE--
AT YOUR TRIAL, YOU WILL RECEIVE JUSTICE, DR. FRENZI. MORE JUSTICE THAN YOU BELIEVE IN GIVING. WHEN YOUR REAL MOTIVES ARE DISCLOSED, YOU'LL GIVE THANKS ON YOUR KNEES FOR THE PROTECTION GIVEN YOU BY JUST BEING IN AMERICA!
IT TAKES REAL CHARACTER TO ADMIT ONE'S FAILURES -- AND NOT A LITTLE WISDOM TO TAKE YOUR PROFITS FROM DEFEAT. BUT REMEMBER, THIS MAN'S WORLD OF YOURS WILL NEVER BE WITHOUT PAIN AND SUFFERING UNTIL IT LEARNS LOVE, AND RESPECT FOR HUMAN RIGHTS. KEEP YOUR HANDS EXTENDED TO ALL IN FRIENDLINESS BUT NEVER HOLDING THE GUN OF PERSECUTION AND INTOLERANCE!
YOU'RE WONDERFUL, ANGEL!
12
The End

Wonder Woman
By CHARLES MOULTON
KNIGHTHOOD IS IN FLOWER AGAIN. IN FACT, IT WOULD SEEM THAT IT NEVER EVEN WENT OUT---NOT IN THE MYSTERIOUS LAND OF ANGLONIA, ANYWAY.
WONDER WOMAN-BEAUTIFUL AS APHRODITE, WISE AS ATHENA, STRONGER THAN HERCULES, AND SWIFTER THAN MERCURY-FINDS HERSELF 600 YEARS BEHIND THE TIMES (EVEN THOUGH THE CALENDAR READS 1947), WHEN SHE IS CALLED UPON TO RESCUE
"THE MYSTERIOUS PRISONERS OF ANGLONIA."
H G PETER
1
MAJOR TREVOR AND WONDER WOMAN, FLYING OVER ASIA, ARE BLOWN OFF THEIR COURSE ACROSS AN UNMAPPED DESERT.
MOUNTAINS AHEAD ARE MARKED "UNEXPLORED" ON THE CHART.
YOU'LL HAVE TO FLY OVER THEM.

NO WONDER THESE MOUNTAINS ARE UNEXPLORED. NO HUMAN COULD CLIMB THEM!
ATTEMPTING TO FLY OVER THE JAGGED CLIFF, STEVE CRASHES INTO A TREETOP--
BLAZES--THE WING'S DAMAGED! AND I CAN'T SEE WHAT'S BELOW WITH THAT MIST!
LUCK, BY JINKS, A LANDING FIELD! HEY! KNIGHTS IN ARMOR--WHAT IN SAM HILL---?
AS STEVE'S PLANE TAXIS TO A STOP--
WHAT IN THE NAME OF INSANITY IS THIS? WHAT SORT OF A SCREWBALL WORLD HAVE WE FLOWN INTO?
I DON'T KNOW. THIS IS LIKE THE OPENING CHAPTER OF "A CONNECTICUT YANKEE IN KING ARTHUR'S COURT"!
CLANK!
2

AHA! 'TIS YOUNG HUBERT, FALSE PRETENDER TO MY THRONE! ARREST THE VILLAIN!
AYE, SIRE--THIS TIME HE CANNOT ESCAPE US!

STAND BACK, YOU FUGITIVES FROM A NUT FACTORY. I HATE TO SHOOT POOR DEMENTED IDIOTS, BUT--

PRITHEE, SIR JOHN, WHAT SAYS THE FOOL?
THAT I KNOW NOT--SOME JOCULAR LINGO DOUBTLESS. HAVE AT HIM!

THESE BOYS MEAN BUSINESS.
BLAZES--THEIR SHIELDS ARE BULLET-PROOF!

AS WONDER WOMAN REPELS SWORDS, A KNIGHT SWINGS HIS HUGE MACE FROM BEHIND AGAINST THE AMAZON'S MOST VULNERABLE SPOT.
UGH!
3

SURRENDER THY WEAPON, KNAVE, OR I SHALL KILL THY QUEEN!
YOU'VE GOT ME, PAL-- HERE YOU ARE-- I'LL BET THIS IS THE FIRST YOU'VE EVER SEEN OF AN ARMY .45! BE CAREFUL- IT MIGHT GO OFF!

WHAT DO YOU MEAN GO OFF? GO OFF OF WHAT? OOF!
BANG

THOU TRAITOR! WOULDST SLAY THY KING? I'LL TEACH THEE--
NAY, SIRE--'TIS SOME NEFARIOUS DEVICE OF THAT VILE PRETENDER, HUBERT. HE CAME HERE IN THAT TERRIBLE WAR MACHINE TO KILL THEE!

FAITH, METHINKS THOU'RT RIGHT! THROW THIS ARCH-TRAITOR AND HIS DAMSEL INTO A DUNGEON. WE'LL MAKE PRETTY HUBERT'S EXECUTION A PUBLIC SPECTACLE!

LATER, WONDER WOMAN WAKES TO FIND HERSELF IN A 13TH CENTURY DUNGEON!
THANK HEAVEN YOU'RE ALIVE, BEAUTIFUL! I COULD DO NOTHING--
OOH-MY POOR HEAD!

THESE "KNIGHTS" ARE MADMEN--
NO--I THINK I HAVE THE ANSWER. THESE MOUNTAINS ARE SOMEWHERE NEAR PALESTINE.
4

IF I REMEMBER MY HISTORY, KING RICHARD OF BRITON LED A CRUSADE THROUGH HERE TO FREE JERUSALEM CENTURIES AGO! SOME KNIGHTS BECAME LOST IN THESE MOUNTAINS. THEIR DESCENDANTS, OUR CAPTORS, STILL LIVE AS DID THEIR KNIGHTLY ANCESTORS!

BUT WHY DID THEY PICK ON US?
THAT I DON'T KNOW! SEEMS LIKE A CASE OF MISTAKEN IDENTITY. I'LL JUST BREAK---MERCIFUL MINERVA! MEN MUST HAVE CHAINED MY BRACELETS-I CAN'T BREAK THIS LITTLE CHAIN!

MEN-AT-ARMS LATER COME FOR STEVE.
CONTENT THEE, GOOD HUBERT, THE POPULACE AWAITS TO SEE THEE MOUNT THY THRONE!
I'M NOT HUBERT!
NO, HUBERT--HA HA--THY NAME'S "COWARD"!

WAIT! TAKE ME, TOO--
BAH! A WENCH IS NAY WORTH BEHEADING.

THEY'RE GOING TO KILL STEVE, AND I'M HELPLESS--I HAVEN'T THE STRENGTH TO BREAK THIS WALL DOWN, WHILE MY BRACELETS ARE CHAINED THIS WAY!

CROWDS PRESS CLOSE AROUND THE EXECUTION PLATFORM AS STEVE IS LED TO HIS DOOM.
5

THUS DIE ALL WHO DARE DISPUTE MY RULE!
I DON'T CARE WHO RULES THIS FORSAKEN DUMP--WHY CUT MY HEAD OFF?

AS THE EXECUTIONER'S AXE DESCENDS, A SWIFT ARROW FLIES FROM AN UNKNOWN BOW.
UG--YAWP! SOME FOUL ARCHER'S SHOT ME!

IN THE FLASH OF AN EYE, STURDY YEOMEN RUSH FROM ALL SIDES TO RESCUE THE PRISONER.
HERE'S A MACE, HUBERT--THY STEED AWAITS THEE!

BLACK ROBERT BARS STEVE'S WAY--BUT NOT FOR LONG.
HOW NOW, SIRRAH--ULP!
LIKE THIS, SOURPUSS!

HEIGH-HO FOR HONEST HUBERT! DOWN WITH THE BLACK USURPER!

STEVE'S RESCUERS REACH THEIR FOREST HIDEAWAY.
HAIL TO JOLLY PRINCE HUBERT, RIGHTFUL KING OF ANGLONIA! WE'LL SEAT HIM ON HIS FATHER'S THRONE!
GREAT SQUALLING CATFISH--AM I HUBERT OR AM I TREVOR? ONE THING I KNOW I AM--IS DIZZY!

THY HEAD, SIRE, IS CONFUSED--A BLOW OF SOME VILLAIN'S MACE, NO DOUBT. I'LL PUT THEE STRAIGHT. THOU DOST REMEMBER, SURELY, THY GREAT FATHER, KING RICHARD, AND US, THE PEOPLE'S PARTY, WHOM HE SUPPORTED!

"THEN THAT VILE TRAITOR, BLACK ROBERT OF DOGWOOD, TREACHEROUSLY ATTACKED THE PALACE AND--
DIE THUS ALL PEASANT-LOVING LIBERALS! KILL THEM, MEN--I, DUKE ROBERT, AM NOW KING!

"THY FATHER WAS KILLED AND THOU, PRINCE HUBERT, WAST CAPTURED AND BROUGHT TO THE USURPER."
THOU MAYST CHOOSE BETWEEN QUICK DEATH AND LIFE IN A DUNGEON.

"BUT THOU SNATCHED THE KNIGHT'S SWORD AND--"
I CHOOSE TO DIE IN BATTLE LIKE A MAN! SEE IF THOU CANST KILL ME!

"THOU STRUCK DOWN THE TYRANT AND RESCUED LADY SIGNA, BLACK ROBERT'S CAPTIVE--"
OUT OF MY WAY, KNAVES!

"BLACK ROBERT, WOUNDED AND FURIOUS, SET ALL HIS FORCES AFTER THEE--"
CAPTURE THAT VILLAIN ALIVE--HE SHALL NOT BE GIVEN MERCIFUL DEATH BUT LIFE IN A DUNGEON!
7

THERE WAS A RUMOR THOU WERT RECAPTURED, SIRE, BUT WE NEVER BELIEVED IT. WE KNEW THOU WOULDST APPEAR TO LEAD OUR ARMY OF THY FAITHFUL FOLLOWERS!
BUT I DON'T WANT TO BE KING--

I UNDERSTAND, MY PRINCE. NEVER DIDST THOU LOVE ROYAL POMP. BUT THY LADY, THE STRONG MAIDEN--WILT THOU LEAVE HER IN THE DUNGEON?
YOU WIN--I MUST LEAD YOUR ARMY TO SAVE WONDER WOMAN!

WONDER WOMAN, MEANWHILE IS DESPERATE.
I MUST SAVE STEVE--

IT'S NO USE-I CAN'T BREAK THE DOOR DOWN--BUT MAYBE I CAN PULL THE BARS OUT OF THIS WINDOW! APHRODITE HELP ME!

THE ANCIENT BARS YIELD TO THE AMAZON'S STRENGTH, STILL TREMENDOUS DESPITE HER CHAINED BRACELETS.
OOPS! THE GODDESS ANSWERED MY PRAYER QUICKLY!

I CAN CRAWL THROUGH THIS OPENING--MAYBE!

A STARTLED JAILOR, COMING TO FEED THE PRISONERS, MEETS WONDER WOMAN.
AI--EEE! AN ESCAPED PRISONER-!! NO-CAN'T BE--MUST BE A GHOST--NO PRISONER'S EVER ESCAPED FROM HERE ALIVE!

LET ME GO--LET ME GO!
NAY, VARLET, AS YOUR KNIGHTS WOULD SAY, COME HITHER. I WOULD A WORD WITH THEE!

QUICK! TELL ME WHAT HAPPENED TO STEVE--ER--YOU CALL HIM HUBERT?
S-SOMETHING COMPELETH ME TO OBEY! HUBERT IS A PRISONER IN THE LOWEST DUNGEON--

SO BLACK ROBERT SENT STEVE BACK TO PRISON INSTEAD OF BEHEADING HIM--THANK APHRODITE!

UNLOCK THAT CELL!
I'LL BE KILLED FOR THIS, BUT I OBEY--I MUST!

OH, STEVE--I'M SO HAPPY YOU'RE SAFE I HAVE TO HUG YOU!
AH--ER--ZOUNDS! METHINKS, FAIR MAID, THOU FORGETTETH I AM BETROTHED TO MY LADY SIGNA. SHE IS IN THE NEXT DUNGEON--JAILOR! THY KEYS!

AH, SIGNA, BELOVED, AT LAST!
OH, HUBERT--THOU HAST RESCUED ME!
WEH--ELL! WHAT DO YOU KNOW ABOUT THAT?

THE JAILOR, FORGOTTEN BY ALL, FREES HIMSELF FROM THE LASSO AND LOCKS THE CELL DOOR, FROM THE OUTSIDE--
WHILE THIS PLEASANT RE-UNION OCCUPIES THEM, I'LL SECURE THESE TROUBLESOME CREATURES AND FLEE FOR HELP!
9

THAT SLY JAILOR HAS LOCKED US IN! HE'S ESCAPING!
LET HIM--I KNOW A SECRET PASSAGE FROM THIS DUNGEON!

NOT FOR NOTHING HAVE I ROAMED THIS OLD CASTLE AS A CHILD! BE OF GOOD COURAGE, FAIR MAIDS! I GO ONLY FOR AN INSTANT TO SEE IF THESE SECRET PASSAGEWAYS ARE GUARDED-- IF THEY ARE--I'LL CLEAR THE WAY--

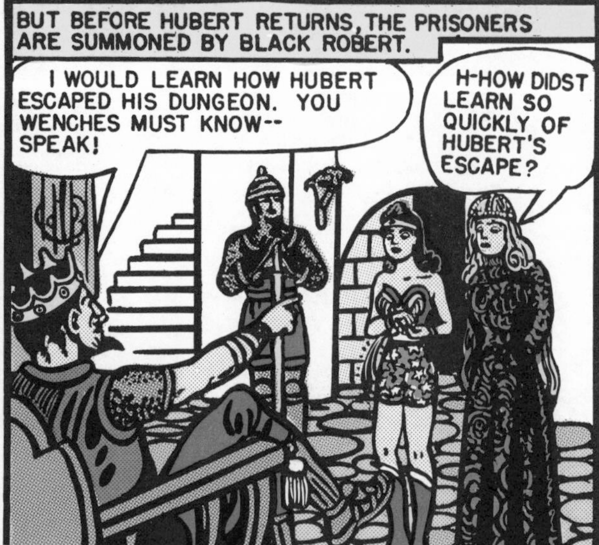
BUT BEFORE HUBERT RETURNS, THE PRISONERS ARE SUMMONED BY BLACK ROBERT.
I WOULD LEARN HOW HUBERT ESCAPED HIS DUNGEON. YOU WENCHES MUST KNOW--SPEAK!
H-HOW DIDST LEARN SO QUICKLY OF HUBERT'S ESCAPE?

"QUICKLY!" ART MAKING MOCK OF ME? THE KNAVE MUST HAVE ESCAPED DAYS AGO TO APPEAR WITH THIS HERCULES WOMAN IN A WEIRD, LEAPING WAR MACHINE ON OUR JOUSTING GROUNDS!

OH--NOW I SEE! STEVE AND HUBERT ARE DOUBLES. THEY LOOK ALIKE. WHEN WE LANDED, EVERYONE THOUGHT STEVE WAS HUBERT. BUT ACTUALLY THE PRINCE WAS STILL IN PRISON! ONLY ROBERT KNEW THIS AND HE THOUGHT HUBERT HAD ESCAPED.

TELL ME HOW HUBERT ESCAPED, OR I'LL HAVE THE INFORMATION OUT OF YE!
IF WE TELL, HUBERT WILL BE CAUGHT RETURNING TO THE DUNGEON.
WE WON'T TELL!

PUT THESE PRISONERS TO THE QUESTION!
AYE, YOUR HIGHNESS--THAT I WILL DO SPEEDILY.
10

AS WATER LEAKS FROM THE KETTLE THIS STONE WILL DESCEND. WHEN YOU FEEL TALKATIVE, I'LL GLADLY LISTEN! BUT YOU'D BETTER HURRY---THE KETTLE IS GETTING LIGHTER!
YOU'RE SO SWEET!

MEANWHILE, STEVE LEADS HIS ARMY TO ASSAULT THE CITY.
DOWN WITH ROBERT THE BLOODY TYRANT! FREEDOM FOR ANGLONIA!

HUBERT, EMERGING FROM THE SECRET PASSAGE NEAR THE CITY WALLS, HEARS THE BATTLE CRY.
HA! MY FAITHFUL FOLLOWERS ASSAULT THE WALL--I'LL OPEN THE GATE FOR THEM!

AFTER A FIERCE BUT BRIEF FIGHT WITH THE GUARD---

HUBERT OPENS THE GATE AND STEVE'S TROOPS POUR IN.
WHAT WIZARDRY IS THIS? THE LEADER OF THOSE TROOPS IS I--OR MY DOUBLE! I'LL FOLLOW MYSELF TO VICTORY!

BUT THE INVADERS ARE BEATEN BACK BY SUPERIOR NUMBERS.
WE NEED ARMOR--THESE HUMAN TANKS ARE CRUSHING MY MEN--

MEANWHILE, WONDER WOMAN'S STRENGTH, REDUCED BY HER BRACELET CHAINS, BECOMES EXHAUSTED.
I--I CAN'T HOLD THIS MUCH LONGER--
TORTURE MAY MAKE ME BETRAY HUBERT. I'VE KEPT THIS DEADLY ACID FOR SUCH EMERGENCIES--

WAIT, SIGNA-- POUR THAT ACID ON MY WRIST CHAINS!
BUT WHY-- OH I SEE! IT'S BURNING THROUGH THE METAL!

CUTTING THOSE MAN-FORGED CHAINS BETWEEN MY BRACELETS RESTORED MY STRENGTH-- THANK APHRODITE!
MERCIFUL HEAVEN--THOU ART STRONGER THAN SAMSON!

WITH THE HUGE STONE, THE MIGHTY AMAZON SOON CLEARS A WAY FOR STEVE'S TROOPS.
LONG LIVE HUBERT! FREEDOM FOR ANGLONIA!

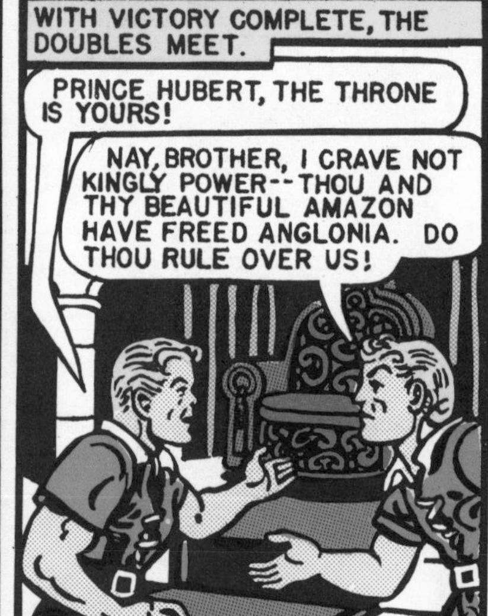
WITH VICTORY COMPLETE, THE DOUBLES MEET.
PRINCE HUBERT, THE THRONE IS YOURS!
NAY, BROTHER, I CRAVE NOT KINGLY POWER--THOU AND THY BEAUTIFUL AMAZON HAVE FREED ANGLONIA. DO THOU RULE OVER US!

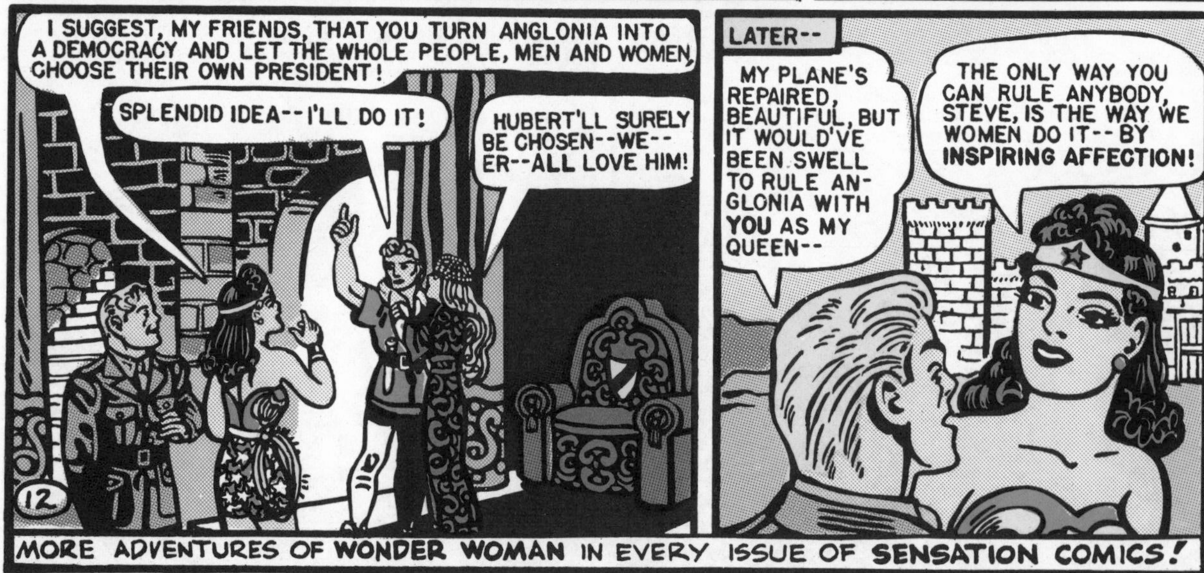
I SUGGEST, MY FRIENDS, THAT YOU TURN ANGLONIA INTO A DEMOCRACY AND LET THE WHOLE PEOPLE, MEN AND WOMEN, CHOOSE THEIR OWN PRESIDENT!
SPLENDID IDEA--I'LL DO IT!
HUBERT'LL SURELY BE CHOSEN--WE--ER--ALL LOVE HIM!
12
LATER--
MY PLANE'S REPAIRED, BEAUTIFUL, BUT IT WOULD'VE BEEN SWELL TO RULE ANGLONIA WITH YOU AS MY QUEEN--
THE ONLY WAY YOU CAN RULE ANYBODY, STEVE, IS THE WAY WE WOMEN DO IT--BY INSPIRING AFFECTION!

MORE ADVENTURES OF WONDER WOMAN IN EVERY ISSUE OF SENSATION COMICS!

Wonder Woman
By CHARLES MOULTON
WHEN THE NEW STUDENTS BEGAN ARRIVING AT HOLLIDAY COLLEGE, ONE OF THEM SEEMED TO STEP RIGHT OUT OF THE NINETEENTH CENTURY! AND IT WAS WONDER WOMAN — BEAUTIFUL AS APHRODITE, WISE AS ATHENA, STRONGER THAN HERCULES, AND SWIFTER THAN MERCURY— WHO DISCOVERED THE STRANGE SECRET BEHIND THE INCREDIBLE MYSTERY OF
"THE GIRL FROM YESTERDAY!"
HG PETER
1

DC

DIANA (WONDER WOMAN) PRINCE IS ETTA CANDY'S GUEST AT THE NEW TERM PARTY AT HOLLIDAY COLLEGE.

WOO WOO! WATCHING NEW GIRLS ARRIVE IS SO EXCITING!

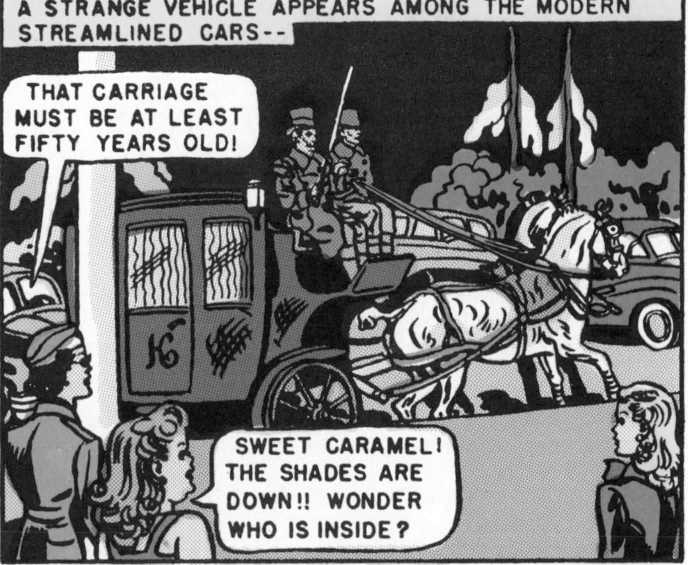
A STRANGE VEHICLE APPEARS AMONG THE MODERN STREAMLINED CARS--
THAT CARRIAGE MUST BE AT LEAST FIFTY YEARS OLD!
SWEET CARAMEL! THE SHADES ARE DOWN!! WONDER WHO IS INSIDE?

SHE'S LOVELY! ALTHOUGH SHE LOOKS LIKE A DRAWING FROM AN OLD BOOK! BUT WHAT DOES IT ALL MEAN?

WELCOME TO HOLLIDAY COL-LEGE! I'M ETTA CANDY, AND THIS IS LT. DIANA PRINCE!
HOW DO YOU DO? I AM URSULA KEATING.
TEE HEE! LOOK AT THOSE SILLY CLOTHES!

WHY ARE THEY LAUGHING AT ME?
NEW STUDENTS ARE ALWAYS LAUGHING AT SOMETHING! THEY'RE NERVOUS THEMSELVES.
COME IN TO OUR "GET ACQUAINTED DANCE!"
2

THEY'RE STARING AT MY CLOTHES! I--I DIDN'T KNOW THERE WERE ANY OTHER KIND!
YOUR CLOTHES ARE BEAUTIFUL, URSULA!
THERE'S SOME-THING STRANGE ABOUT ALL THIS!

LATER THAT EVENING...
HOW ABOUT CUTTING A RUG, HONEY?
HA! HA! HA!
OH–I THOUGHT YOU WANTED TO DANCE! I CAN DANCE THE QUADRILLE!
THEY'RE TEASING URSULA TOO MUCH!
TE-HEE!

I-SHOULD NEVER HAVE LEFT HOME!
SHE'S CRYING! I MUST TELL HER THE GIRLS REALLY MEANT NO HARM--

BLINDED BY TEARS, URSULA DOESN'T SEE THE DANGER APPROACHING AS SHE RUSHES ONTO THE DRIVEWAY--
MERCIFUL MINERVA! THAT CAR! URSULA DOESN'T SEE IT!
SOB! SOB!

A LIGHTNING CHANGE, AND DIANA PRINCE BECOMES WONDER WOMAN!

THE AMAZING AMAZON TURNS THE ONRUSHING CAR ASIDE AT THE LAST MOMENT!
OH!
3

LEADING THE FRIGHTENED URSULA TO A QUIET SPOT--
YOU SAVED MY LIFE! BUT-- I--I WISH I WERE DEAD!
OF COURSE YOU DON'T! SUPPOSE YOU TELL ME ALL ABOUT IT. YOU'LL FEEL BETTER!

I LIVE WITH MY AUNT, ABIGAIL KEATING. WE'VE ALWAYS WORN CLOTHES LIKE THESE. WE WERE ALWAYS ALONE -- THAT'S WHY I WAS SO GLAD WHEN MY TUTOR TOLD MY AUNT THAT I SHOULD BE SENT TO COLLEGE!

I THOUGHT IT WOULD BE WONDERFUL TO GO OUT IN THE WORLD. BUT I HATE IT! I--I WANT TO GO HOME AND BE JUST LIKE MY AUNT!
I'LL TAKE YOU HOME, URSULA!
THIS MYSTERY IS DEEPER THAN I THOUGHT!

WONDER WOMAN CALLS HER ROBOT PLANE--
A GIRL OF TODAY— LIVING IN YESTERYEAR! URSULA'S AUNT SHOULD SUPPLY THE ANSWER!

THE FLEET AMAZON PLANE SOON LANDS AT THE OLD KEATING MANSION--
DO YOU ACTUALLY LIVE HERE? WHY--THE PLACE LOOKS DESERTED!
THAT'S AUNT ABIGAIL'S IDEA! SHE NEVER EVEN COMES OUTSIDE-- SHE NEVER SEES THE SUN!

THERE'S AUNT ABIGAIL NOW!
GREAT HERA!
4

AUNT ABIGAIL IS RELIVING THE PAST!
NOW FOR THE WEDDING BANQUET! BUT FIRST, LET ME THROW MY BRIDAL BOUQUET! MAY SHE WHO CATCHES IT, BE AS HAPPY AS I AM!

A STRANGE DRAMA UNFOLDS IN THE ANCIENT COB-WEBBED ROOM--
NOW, JOHN, YOU SHALL HAVE THE FIRST PIECE OF OUR WEDDING CAKE!

WHAT A WONDERFUL DANCER YOU ARE, JOHN! BUT I'M TIRING. LET'S SIT BEFORE THE FIRE UNTIL IT'S TIME TO LEAVE ON OUR HONEYMOON!

AUNT ABIGAIL HAS BEEN DOING THIS EVERY DAY FOR AS LONG AS I CAN REMEMBER! NOW SHE'LL SIT BEFORE THE FIRE IN THE DRAWING ROOM FOR HOURS!

WE'LL GIVE HER A FEW MOMENTS TO CALM HERSELF—THEN SPEAK TO HER.

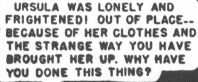

SOON AFTER, IN THE DRAWING ROOM--
AUNT ABIGAIL--I'VE COME HOME! WONDER WOMAN WAS KIND ENOUGH TO HELP ME!
WH-WHAT? OH--URSULA! WHY AREN'T YOU AT COLLEGE?

URSULA WAS LONELY AND FRIGHTENED! OUT OF PLACE--BECAUSE OF HER CLOTHES AND THE STRANGE WAY YOU HAVE BROUGHT HER UP. WHY HAVE YOU DONE THIS THING?
SO THAT SHE CAN LEAD MY LIFE--THE LIFE I NEVER HAD!
5

WHEN JOHN HUNTER DESERTED ME ON MY WEDDING DAY--MY LIFE ENDED! BUT URSULA WEARS MY CLOTHES-AND SHALL DO ALL THE THINGS I SHOULD HAVE DONE! JOHN HUNTER RUINED MY LIFE—BUT I SHALL LIVE AGAIN-THROUGH URSULA!

DON'T YOU REALIZE YOU'RE WASTING YOUR LIFE--LIVING IN THE PAST AS YOU DO? IS THIS MAN WORTH IT?
LOOK AT HIS PICTURE IN THIS MINIATURE-AND SEE FOR YOURSELF.

HMM, IT'S TOO FADED TO SEE ANYTHING. PAULA CAN RESTORE THIS PICTURE FOR ME! IF I CAN FIND JOHN HUNTER, I CAN SAVE ABIGAIL KEATING FROM A USELESS AND BITTER OLD AGE!

LEAVING THE KEATINGS, THE TIRELESS AMAZON SWIFTLY FLIES TO THE SECRET LABORATORY OF PAULA, AN AMAZON-TRAINED SCIENTIST.
AGE JOHN HUNTER'S FEATURES, AFTER YOU RESTORE THEM, PAULA. THEN WE'LL GET A BETTER IDEA OF HOW HE WOULD LOOK TODAY!
AN EXCELLENT IDEA, PRINCESS!

UNDER PAULA'S EXPERT RETOUCHING, THE WORK IS SWIFTLY DONE--
HMM···THAT FACE LOOKS VERY FAMILIAR, PAULA! BUT.. I HOPE I'M MISTAKEN IN WHERE I THINK I'VE SEEN IT BEFORE! I'LL SOON KNOW.

MOMENTS LATER, WONDER WOMAN IS AT THE CENTRAL POLICE BUREAU--
HERE'S OUR COMPLETE ROGUE'S GALLERY, WONDER WOMAN. BUT IT'LL TAKE HOURS TO GO THROUGH IT ALL!
I GUESS YOU HAVEN'T SEEN AN AMAZON AT WORK, CAPTAIN!
6

WITH BREATHLESS SPEED, THE AMAZON PRINCESS FLIPS THROUGH THOUSANDS OF FILES IN SCANT SECONDS!

GREAT HERA, MY SUSPICIONS WERE JUSTIFIED! ABIGAIL KEATING'S OLD FIANCE, JOHN HUNTER, IS LON LOGOX, THE CRIMINAL! NOW I CAN NEVER BRING THEM TOGETHER! THE SHOCK WOULD KILL HER!
LON LOGOX
WANTED FOR MURDER ROBBERY
DESCRIPTION
AGE 52 GRAYING TE
HEIGHT FIVE FT EIGH
WEIGHT -175 POUNDS
A KILLER - APPROACH
WITH CAUTION & US

LATER, AT THE POLICE COMMISSIONER'S OFFICE--
YES, WONDER WOMAN, LON LOGOX IS THE BRAINS BEHIND A JEWEL GANG! HE OFTEN SENDS US ADVANCE NOTICES OF HIS CRIMES--THIS LETTER JUST ARRIVED FROM HIM.

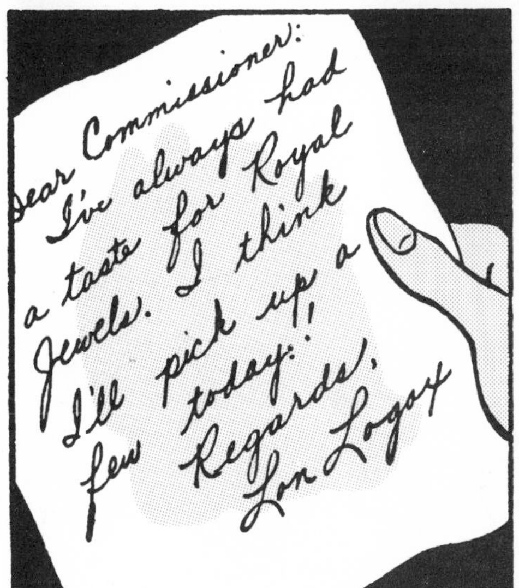
Dear Commissioner:
I've always had
a taste for Royal
Jewels. I think
I'll pick up a
few today!
Regards,
Lon Logox

LOGOX MUST BE REFERRING TO THE GERUVIAN ROYAL JEWELS AT THE ART MUSEUM! THIS TIME WE'LL GET HIM IF HE SHOWS UP --A MOUSE COULDN'T GET THROUGH OUR GUARDS!
CALLING ROBOT PLANE!
I'LL TAKE A LOOK AT THE JEWELS!

THERE'S A FIRM CALLED THE ROYAL JEWEL COMPANY! THAT LETTER MIGHT BE A RUSE--TO GET THE POLICE TO THE MUSEUM WHILE THE GANG ROBS THE COMPANY! I'LL GO THERE FIRST--JUST IN CASE!
7

SHORTLY, THE BEAUTIFUL AMAZON MAID LANDS ON THE ROOF OF THE ROYAL JEWEL COMPANY--
I WAS RIGHT! THERE'S LOGOX AND HIS MEN!
ROYAL JEWEL
GEMS FIT FOR A QUEEN!

HA HA! THOSE DUMB COPS ARE AT THE MUSEUM BY NOW, WHILE WE'RE PULLING OFF THIS JOB! I'VE THOUGHT OF EVERYTHING!

NOT EVERYTHING, LON LOGOX, ALIAS JOHN HUNTER!
WONDER WOMAN!

IT'S THOSE BRACELETS! WE CAN'T HIT HER!
AN OLD AMAZON CUSTOM!
BANG!
BANG!

WHILE WONDER WOMAN'S OCCUPIED--I'LL PREPARE A LITTLE SURPRISE FOR HER!
BANG!!
CRASH!
OH-!

FELLED BY THE BLOW ON THE BACK OF HER HEAD, AN AMAZON'S VULNERABLE SPOT, WONDER WOMAN IS BOUND WITH HER OWN LASSO--
THIS MINIATURE! IT'S THE ONE I GAVE ABIGAIL KEATING!

AFTER WONDER WOMAN REGAINS CONSCIOUSNESS--
WHERE DID YOU GET THIS MINIATURE, WONDER WOMAN?
MY MAGIC LASSO COMPELS ME TO ANSWER!

AFTER WONDER WOMAN RELATES THE STORY, OF ABIGAIL KEATING --
HA HA! SO ABIGAIL IS STILL WAITING FOR ME! I WON'T DISAPPOINT HER! A VISIT FROM ME WILL SHOCK HER OUT OF HER SENSES, AND I'LL ROB HER HOUSE BEFORE SHE RECOVERS! HA HA!
MERCIFUL MINERVA! HE MUST NOT TELL HER!

SHORTLY--
TAKE US TO CUR HIDEOUT IN YOUR PLANE, WONDER WOMAN! THE BOSS WILL MEET US LATER.
AIN'T THIS SOMETHING! WONDER WOMAN HELPIN' US GET AWAY! HA! HA!
UNLESS I MAKE HIM DROP THE LASSO—I MUST OBEY!

AS THE SWIFT PLANE SPEEDS ON, THE FAST-THINKING AMAZON'S KEEN SIGHT GLIMPSES AN OPPORTUNITY FOR ESCAPE--
THERE'S A DOWNDRAFT JUST AHEAD-NEAR THAT FROZEN LAKE! I'LL HEAD DIRECTLY INTO THE DOWNDRAFT!

AS THE PLANE ENTERS THE DOWNDRAFT, IT DROPS SUDDENLY --
HE LET GO OF THE LASSO!
YEOW!

SHE'S GOT US!
NOW FOR THE KEATING MANSION! PRAY HERA-I'M NOT TOO LATE!
9

THERE'S A CAR! IT MUST BE HUNTER'S! BUT HAS HE TOLD ABIGAIL ABOUT HIS CRIMES YET?

AT THAT MOMENT, INSIDE THE KEATING DRAWING ROOM--
WHO ARE YOU? HOW DID YOU GET IN HERE?
I'M USED TO GETTING INTO LOCKED PLACES! DON'T YOU RECOGNIZE ME, ABIGAIL?
I--I CAN'T SEE! IT'S SO DARK! BUT THAT VOICE-- CAN IT BE--?

YES, ABIGAIL! IT'S JOHN HUNTER!
JOHN! JOHN HUNTER!
OHH--!

AND, OUTSIDE THE DRAWING ROOM DOORS--
JOHN HUNTER!
HE'S IN THERE! IT'S TOO LATE TO STOP HIM FORCIBLY! ABIGAIL WOULD BECOME SUSPICIOUS! IF I COULD ONLY DROWN OUT HIS WORDS! DROWN---THAT IS IT! BY HERA! I HAVE IT!

THE FLEET AMAZON MAID RACES TO THE FROZEN LAKE SHE HAD GLIMPSED FROM THE PLANE--
THIS ICE WILL HELP TURN THE TRICK!

THE INGENIOUS WONDER WOMAN WRENCHES A GIGANTIC PIECE OF ICE FROM THE LAKE---
I MUST NOT FAIL!
10

THIS PART OF THE ROOF IS DIRECTLY OVER THE DRAWING ROOM! HERE GOES!

THE AMAZING WONDER WOMAN CREATES A DEAFENING HAIL STORM--
BLAM!
BOOM!

AND, INSIDE THE HOUSE--
BOOM! CRASH!! BLAM!
I'M REALLY LON LOGOX—THE CROOK! HA! HA! BLAST THAT HAIL!
PLEASE--I CAN'T HEAR YOU! WHAT DID YOU SAY, JOHN?

IN THE EXCITEMENT, WONDER WOMAN YANKS THE CROOK OUT OF THE DIMLY-LIGHTED ROOM, UNOBSERVED—
WONDER WOMAN!
IF YOU'VE ANY TALKING TO DO — SAVE IT FOR THE POLICE!

LATER, AS THE BOASTFUL GANG LEADER IS BEING QUESTIONED BY THE POLICE --
YEAH! I GOT A TRUNKFUL OF SPARKLERS!
ABIGAIL MUST FIND OUT ABOUT THIS SOONER OR LATER! BUT HOW—WITHOUT IT BREAKING HER HEART? BY HERA! THERE IS A WAY!

BUZZ-Z, BUZZ-Z-Z-
TERRIFIC IDEA, WONDER WOMAN! I'LL HAVE EVERYTHING READY BY TONIGHT.

THAT NIGHT, WONDER WOMAN RETURNS TO THE KEATING MANSION --
WONDER WOMAN! YOU'VE MADE AUNT ABIGAIL BEAUTIFUL!
WAKE HER UP IN TEN MINUTES AND BRING HER TO THE DRAWING ROOM. JOHN HUNTER WILL BE THERE!

THERE! A NEW ABIGAIL - A NEW DRAWING ROOM. AS SOON AS I DARKEN THIS ROOM - WE'LL BEGIN!

TEN MINUTES LATER--
IS-IS THAT-MY -JOHN?
YEP! YOU CAN'T SAY I'VE NOT BEEN A WOW AS A COLLECTOR OF HOT ICE! HA! HA! YEAH! I'M THE KING PIN HIMSELF! KING PIN! GET IT? HA HA!

YOU-YOU'RE NOT THE JOHN HUNTER I KNOW! I-I'M SORRY, BUT I'VE MADE A TERRIBLE MISTAKE! I-I THINK IT WOULD BE BEST IF WE NEVER SAW EACH OTHER AGAIN!

SUDDENLY, THE LIGHT GOES ON AND--
YOU WON'T, ABIGAIL! THAT WAS A TALKING PICTURE OF JOHN HUNTER, ALIAS LON LOGOX, TAKEN AT POLICE HEADQUARTERS, ON A THREE-DIMENSIONAL AMAZON CAMERA.

TO THINK OF ALL THE YEARS I'VE WASTED, YEARNING FOR HIM - AND SPOILING URSULA'S LIFE! HOW CAN I EVER THANK YOU, WONDER WOMAN?
BY STARTING TO LIVE IN THE PRESENT -INSTEAD OF THE PAST!
12

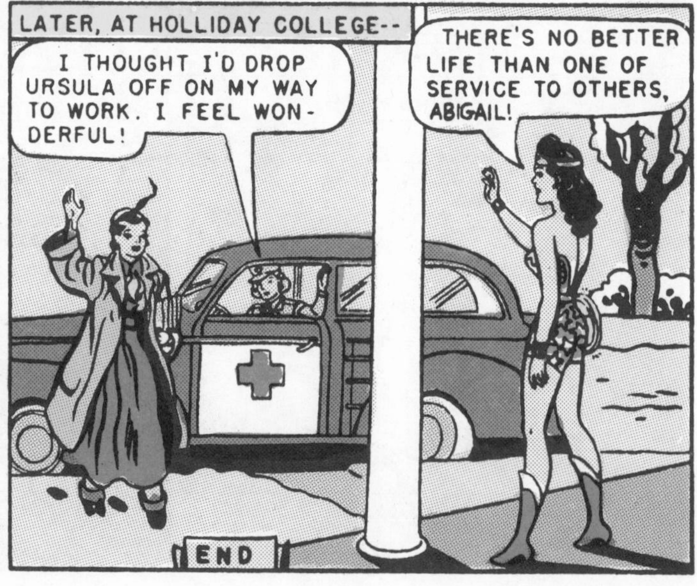
LATER, AT HOLLIDAY COLLEGE--
I THOUGHT I'D DROP URSULA OFF ON MY WAY TO WORK. I FEEL WONDERFUL!
THERE'S NO BETTER LIFE THAN ONE OF SERVICE TO OTHERS, ABIGAIL!
END

Wonder Woman

By CHARLES MOULTON

WHAT HAPPENS WHEN AN AMAZON SAVES THE LIFE OF A WOMAN-HATER? CAN TWO MORE OPPOSITES MEET, THAN **WONDER WOMAN**—BEAUTIFUL AS APHRODITE, WISE AS ATHENA, STRONGER THAN HERCULES, AND SWIFTER THAN MERCURY—A WOMAN WHO HAS SWORN TO DEVOTE HER LIFE FOR THE GOOD OF OTHERS, AND THOMAS TIGHE, WHO HAS DEVOTED HIS LIFE TO HATRED? THE GLAMOROUS AMAZON HAS NEVER BEFORE BEEN FACED WITH SUCH A FORMIDABLE PROBLEM! COUNTLESS LIVES AND THE FUTURE OF HOLLIDAY COLLEGE DEPEND ON HER EFFORTS! FOR IN TWENTY-FOUR ACTION-CRAMMED HOURS, THE FEARLESS AMAZON MUST RACE AROUND THE WORLD IN ONE SMASHING CLIMAX AFTER ANOTHER TO COMPLETE...

"THE FIVE TASKS OF THOMAS TIGHE!"

IN FRONT OF HIS WHALING SHIP, VENGEANCE, CAPT. RAB HARANGUES HIS CREW IN VAIN--
WHO'LL GO AFTER THE WHITE DEMON WITH ME?
IT'S SUICIDE TO GO OUT AFTER THAT KILLER WHALE!
I'VE HAD ENOUGH!
WE'VE LOST ENOUGH MEN-I'M QUITTING!

I'VE FAILED! I'M ALONE--ALONE--ALONE!

SUDDENLY, AN UNEXPECTED FIGURE APPEARS--
I'LL HELP YOU CAPTURE THAT KILLER WHALE, CAPT. RAB!
WHAT?! YOU-A MERE HOLLIDAY COLLEGE GIRL! HOW CAN A GIRL HELP ME? AND WHY SHOULD YOU VOLUNTEER?

DEEP IN THE NORTHWEST FOREST, OWNER JAMES MAGNUS FRANTICALLY APPEALS TO HIS LUMBERJACKS--
BUT YOU'VE GOT TO CUT DOWN THOSE GIANT ROJO TREES, MEN! MY CONTRACT DEPENDS ON IT! IF I FAIL, I'LL NOT ONLY BE BANKRUPT, BUT DESPERATELY NEEDED HOUSING UNITS WILL NOT GO UP!
YEAH--IT'S WORTH YOUR LIFE TO CUT DOWN THOSE ROJO TREES!
COUNT ME OUT!

DESERTED BY HIS MEN, THE DESPAIRING MAGNUS IS STARTLED BY THE APPROACH OF A STRANGER--

I'LL HELP YOU CUT DOWN THOSE ROJO TREES, MR. MAGNUS!

A GIRL! IMPOSSIBLE! NO GIRL EVER DID THE WORK OF A LUMBER-JACK BEFORE!

AT THE FOOT OF ROCKY CRAG PEAK, PROF. EARL DEAN'S CLIMBING EXPEDITION IS HALTED WHEN--
BUT YOU MUST GUIDE US TO THE TOP OF THE PEAK! WE EXPECT TO COLLECT IN-VALUABLE WEATHER DATA UP THERE!
HAD YOU TOLD US YOU WANTED TO SCALE ROCKY CRAG PEAK, PROF. DEAN, WE WOULD HAVE REFUSED! IT'S NEVER BEEN DONE BY MAN!

AS THE DEAN EXPEDITION IS PREPARING TO RETURN--
WAIT, PROF. DEAN! I'LL LEAD YOU TO THE TOP OF ROCKY CRAG PEAK!
WHY SHOULD YOU – A HOLLIDAY STUDENT–RISK YOUR LIFE?
ABOARD THE NEPTUNE SALVAGE BOAT, AN OMINOUS MESSAGE IS RECEIVED FROM A DIVER WORKING IN THE DEPTHS BELOW--
CAPT. RANSON! I FOUND THE CONTAINER OF RADIUM IN THE WRECK OF THE AMPHIB! I TOLD YOU I'D SUCCEED EVEN THOUGH THE OTHERS FAILED! JUST LEAVE IT TO BIG BOY STEVENS! I'LL--GREAT THUNDER! WHAT'S THAT? IT'S--HELP--HELP--OHH-
AND--
THAT RADIUM IS BADLY NEEDED AT RIVERVIEW HOSPITAL, MEN! BIG BOY STEVENS GAVE HIS LIFE TO HELP OTHERS! SHALL HIS SACRIFICE BE IN VAIN?
YOU'RE NOT GOING TO GET ME TO DIVE DOWN FOR THAT STUFF!
NOT WHEN BIG BOY IS THE THIRD MAN TO DIE IN THE ATTEMPT!
BUT JUST THEN--
I'LL DIVE FOR THAT RADIUM, CAPTAIN!
YOU--A SCHOOL GIRL? IMPOSSIBLE!
AT THE GIANTS' HOLLOW PASS A PLANE DESPERATELY FIGHTS AGAINST THE GRIP OF A MIGHTY FORCE THAT WHIRLS IT DOWN···DOWN···DOWN--
FLIGHT X-4 CALLING EMERGENCY FIELD 7! CONTROLS USELESS! AM LOSING ALTITUDE! WILL CR--
3
AND AT EMERGENCY FIELD 7--
THAT'S THE FOURTH PLANE TO CRASH IN GIANT'S HOLLOW PASS! WE'LL NEVER BE ABLE TO REACH THE PEOPLE IN THE VALLEY BEYOND!
I'LL FLY A PLANE THROUGH THE PASS!
YOU – I A GIRL!

WHY SHOULD ALL THE HOLLIDAY GIRLS RISK THEIR LIVES IN ATTEMPTING TO SUCCEED, WHERE HARDY, SEASONED MEN HAVE FAILED?
FOR THEIR AMAZING STORY, WE MUST GO BACK TO THE AFTERNOON WHEN LT. DIANA PRINCE WAS PASSING THE THOMAS TIGHE BANK AND ----

HELP! MR. TIGHE IS LOCKED IN HIS VAULT!
IT'S FASTENED WITH A TIME LOCK! HE'S GOING TO SUFFOCATE!
MERCIFUL MINERVA! I MUST TRY TO HELP THAT POOR MAN!
THOS TIGHE'S BANK

IN THE SECLUSION OF A NEARBY ALLEY, DI CHANGES INTO WONDER WOMAN WITH LIGHTNING SPEED, AND A MOMENT LATER--

I'VE HEARD OF THOMAS TIGHE! HE'S A WOMAN HATER!

AS THE FLEET-FOOTED AMAZON RACES INTO THE BANK--

WE'VE SUMMONED THE SAFE COMPANY! BUT MR. TIGHE WILL DIE OF LACK OF OXYGEN LONG BEFORE ANYONE CAN COME HERE!
THEN I CANNOT WAIT!
THOS. TIGH
BANK

BUT AS WONDER WOMAN IS ABOUT TO SEIZE THE HANDLE OF THE VAULT--

LOOK OUT! THAT VAULT HAS SO BEEN CONSTRUCTED BY MR. TIGHE'S SPECIFICATIONS, THAT YOU WILL BE ELECTROCUTED IF YOU TOUCH THE DOOR DURING THE TIME THE LOCK IS ON!
BUT A DELAY MAY BE FATAL TO HIM!

WITHOUT HESITATION, THE INDOMITABLE AMAZON BEGINS HER RESCUE ATTEMPT. INSTANTLY, AS SHE HAD BEEN FOREWARNED, AN ELECTRIC CHARGE HURTLES THROUGH HER BODY!

WONDER WOMAN IS BEING ELECTROCUTED!
SHE'S LOSING HER LIFE TO SAVE A MAN WHO HATES WOMEN!
B-Z-Z
B-Z-Z-Z
B-Z-Z
B-Z-Z

BUT THE CRASHING BOLTS OF ELECTRICITY WHICH WOULD BE FATAL TO AN ORDINARY HUMAN, ONLY EXHILARATE THE AMAZING WONDER WOMAN!
SAVED BY A WOMAN! BLAZES!
THAT ELECTRIC CHARGE ONLY MAKES MY BODY TINGLE!
B-Z-Z-Z-
B-Z-Z-Z
B-Z-Z-Z
B-Z-Z-

DON'T THINK I'M GOING TO THANK YOU FOR SAVING MY LIFE, WONDER WOMAN! I WOULD, IF YOU WERE A MAN--BUT A WOMAN--NEVER!
I DIDN'T RESCUE YOU TO RECEIVE YOUR THANKS, MR. TIGHE. IT IS THE AMAZON'S CODE TO HELP ANYONE IN NEED, EVEN A WOMAN HATER!

THAT WAS A SENSATIONAL STUNT WONDER WOMAN PERFORMED TO SAVE YOUR LIFE, MR. TIGHE! YOU ARE GOING TO REWARD HER, OF COURSE! AFTER ALL, YOU'RE A MILLIONAIRE! MONEY DOESN'T MEAN A THING TO YOU!
YOU REPORTERS OUGHT TO KNOW BETTER THAN THAT! AN AMAZON CANNOT ACCEPT ANY REWARD FOR HER AID!
YES, YES, YOU WOULDN'T WANT WONDER WOMAN TO BREAK ANY RULES, WOULD YOU?

BUT IRONICAL FATE HAS A WAY OF STEPPING IN AND--
I'VE GOT A TERRIFIC IDEA! WONDER WOMAN IS PERSONALLY INTERESTED IN HOLLIDAY COLLEGE. THE SCHOOL NEEDS MONEY BADLY! MR. TIGHE CAN REWARD WONDER WOMAN BY GRANTING HOLLIDAY THE MONEY TO PAY ITS DEBTS!
WHAT A STORY!
GREAT PUBLICITY!
5

ALL MY LIFE--I'VE BEEN A WOMAN HATER! NOW I'VE BEEN SAVED BY A WOMAN! AND NOT ONLY THAT--UNLESS I GRANT A WOMEN'S COLLEGE MONEY TO PAY ITS DEBTS--THE PRESS WILL GIVE ME SUCH UNFAVORABLE PUBLICITY--THAT IT MIGHT AFFECT MY BUSINESS INTERESTS!

I'LL FIND A WAY TO HAVE THE LAST LAUGH ON WONDER WOMAN AND THE HOLLIDAY GIRLS SO THAT THEY'LL NEVER BE ABLE TO COLLECT THE MONEY!
OF COURSE I'LL BE HAPPY TO HELP HOLLIDAY OUT!
THANK YOU, MR. TIGHE! YOU'RE VERY KIND! YOU'LL FIND THAT THERE IS GREAT HAPPINESS IN HELPING OTHERS!

THAT SAME DAY, THE FINANCIER HAS A SECRET CONFERENCE WITH HIS AIDES--
BZZZ--BZ--BZZZ-ZZ!
SOON, HE RECEIVES MANY REPORTS--
EXCELLENT! NOW I'M READY TO GRANT HOLLIDAY A MILLION DOLLARS--IF THOSE WOMEN ARE ABLE TO COLLECT IT! HA, HA!

SHORTLY, AN AMAZON PLANE FLIES OVER THE HOLLIDAY CAMPUS AND--
WOO WOO! LOOK, DEAN MERRILY! HERE COMES WONDER WOMAN! I TOLD YOU SHE'D COME AS SOON AS I MENTAL-RADIOED HER!
GOOD! NOW WE CAN START--JUST AS MR. TIGHE REQUESTED!

IN DEAN MERRILY'S OFFICE--
....AND SO I, THOMAS TIGHE, IN EVERLASTING GRATITUDE TO WONDER WOMAN FOR SAVING MY LIFE, DO HEREBY GRANT TO HOLLIDAY COLLEGE, FIVE SCHOLARSHIPS VALUED AT $200,000 EACH...
A MILLION DOLLARS! THAT'S VERY GENEROUS OF YOU, MR. TIGHE!
HOLLIDAY IS SAVED!
HURRAY FOR MR. TIGHE!

SUDDENLY, THE FINANCIER'S DIABOLICAL PLAN BECOMES APPARENT WHEN--
WAIT A MOMENT! THERE'S A PARAGRAPH IN SMALL PRINT AT THE BOTTOM OF THE PAGE IT'S TOO SMALL FOR ME TO READ!
I'LL READ IT, DEAN MERRILY!
6

"IN ORDER TO FULFILL THE REQUIREMENTS OF THE SCHOLARSHIPS, THE GIRLS WHO WIN THEM MUST NOT ONLY DISPLAY GREAT MENTAL BUT ALSO *ATHLETIC* SKILL, BY SUCCEEDING AT THE FOLLOWING TASKS WHERE MEN HAVE FAILED--OR THE SCHOLARSHIPS WILL EXPIRE WITHIN 24 HOURS AFTER THEY HAVE BEEN MADE KNOWN! THE TASKS ARE TO: CAPTURE CAPT. RAB'S *WHITE DEMON*, CUT DOWN MR. MAGNUS' ROJO TREES, GUIDE THE DEAN EXPEDITION TO THE TOP OF *ROCKY CRAG* PEAK..."

YOU'VE GOT 24 HOURS TO COLLECT THE MILLION DOLLARS--BUT YOU'LL NEVER BE ABLE TO DO IT! AND YOU CAN EVEN HAVE **WONDER WOMAN** HELP YOU--BECAUSE SHE CERTAINLY CAN'T BE IN FIVE DIFFERENT PLACES AT ONCE! HA, HA! GOODBY, LADIES!

WE AREN'T BEATEN YET!
WE WON'T LET HOLLI-DAY DOWN!
WONDER WOMAN HAS SHOWN US NOTHING IS IMPOSSIBLE--IF ONE NEVER ACKNOWLEDGES FAILURE!
SPOKEN LIKE TRUE AMAZONS.
YOUR LOYALTY--MAKES ME--VERY HAPPY--

THE TOP-RANKING ATHLETES OF HOLLIDAY ARE SUMMONED TO THE STUDY HALL WHERE--
ALL RIGHT, GIRLS! TIME'S UP FOR THE COMPETITIVE EXAMINATIONS TO DEMONSTRATE YOUR MENTAL FITNESS FOR THE SCHOLARSHIPS!
HERE'S MY PAPER!
I'M FINISHED!

WITH AMAZON FLEETNESS, **WONDER WOMAN** CORRECTS THE TEST PAPERS IN A MATTER OF SECONDS, TO CHOOSE THE FIVE HIGHEST MARKS--
AS I CALL YOUR NAMES, PLEASE STEP FORWARD! RUTH RORICK··· MARY LANE··· JEAN TOWNSEND··· JANET FOSTER··· AND···

ONLY ONE MORE GIRL CAN WIN! IT'S GOT TO BE ME! I TRIED SO HARD--I CAN'T FAIL! THIS IS MY BIG CHANCE TO HELP HOLLIDAY AND SHOW **WONDER WOMAN** HOW WELL I'VE LEARNED THE AMAZON CODE OF HELPING OTHERS!

···THE FIFTH AND LAST GIRL IS····ETTA CANDY!
WOO WOO! HERE I COME!
Etta Candy

CALLING HER AMAZON PLANE, WONDER WOMAN SWIFTLY DEPARTS WITH THE FIVE CONTESTANTS--
THE FATE OF HOLLIDAY COLLEGE IS NOW IN YOUR HANDS!

INSIDE THE PLANE, A STRANGE LOTTERY TAKES PLACE--

WE HAVEN'T A MOMENT TO LOSE, GIRLS! WHILE I FLY TO THE FIRST OF THE TASKS SELECTED BY MR. TIGHE, PICK ONE FROM THE HAT! THAT WILL LEAVE THE ONE EACH OF YOU GETS ENTIRELY TO CHANCE! I'LL DROP YOU OF AT THE APPOINTED PLACES! GOOD LUCK!
THANKS!
LOOK WHAT I'VE DRAWN!

AND SO FIVE HOLLIDAY GIRLS DARE TASKS WHICH HAVE ALREADY THWARTED STRONG, EXPERIERCED MEN! WHAT WILL BE THEIR FATE?

UNABLE TO RAISE A CREW TO MAN HIS SHIP, CAPT. RAB, ACCOMPANIED ONLY BY RUTH RORICK, SETS OUT BY MOTOR-BOAT TO TRAIL A KILLER WHALE!

KEEP YOUR EYE PEELED FOR THE WHITE DEMON, LASS! IF WE DON'T SEE IT IN TIME FOR ME TO SINK A HARPOON INTO IT, WE'LL BE LOST!

AYE, AYE, CAPTAIN! BUT I WISH YOU WOULDN'T USE THAT HARPOON! IF WONDER WOMAN WERE HERE, SHE'D FIND A WAY OF CAPTURING THE KILLER WHALE WITHOUT HARMING IT!

SUDDENLY, THE MIGHTY LEVIATHAN OF THE DEEP APPEARS AND--

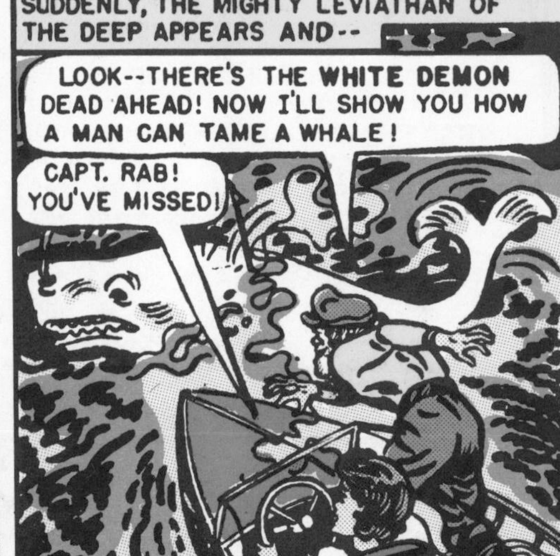

LOOK--THERE'S THE WHITE DEMON DEAD AHEAD! NOW I'LL SHOW YOU HOW A MAN CAN TAME A WHALE!
CAPT. RAB! YOU'VE MISSED!

THE INFURIATED SEA BEAST DIVES, AND EMERGES DIRECTLY UNDER THE FRAIL CRAFT--
THE DEMON'S LIFTING US INTO THE AIR! IT'S GOING TO SMASH US WITH ITS TAIL!

BUT JUST THEN, RETURING FROM HER LAST DESTINATION, WONDER WOMAN SPOTS THE PLIGHT OF THE TWO AND SAVES THEM FROM THE MIGHTY LASHING OF THE WHALE'S TAIL!

WONDER WOMAN!

WE'RE LOST!

AMAZONS DON'T GIVE UP THAT EASILY!

LEAPING OFF THE WHALE WITH CAPT. RAB'S BOAT, THE DARING AMAZON LASSOES THE SEA GIANT AND HOLDS FAST AS IT PLUNGES AWAY IN A MAD EFFORT TO SHAKE HER HOLD LOOSE!
A WOMAN DRIVING A KILLER WHALE AS IF IT WERE A SEA HORSE! I'VE NEVER SEEN THE LIKES OF THIS IN THE SEVEN SEAS!
YOU'VE NEVER SEEN WONDER WOMAN IN ACTION BEFORE!

LEAVING THE UNHARMED WHALE SAFELY CAPTURED IN THE NEAREST PORT, WONDER WOMAN SUMMONS HER PLANE AND--
THE FIRST TASK IS DONE— FOUR MORE TO GO!

MEANWHILE, AS MARY LANE CUTS DOWN THE UPPER HALF OF A LOFTY ROJO TREE, SHE REALIZES WHY EXPERIENCED LUMBERJACKS HAVE QUAILED AT THIS TASK--
IT'S IMPOSSIBLE TO REMAIN TIED-- THE TREE IS SHAKING SO --IT'S WHIPPING ME OFF—HELP!
HELP!

SPEEDING ABOVE THE FOREST, THE ALERT AMAZON HEARS MARY'S CRY FOR HELP AND --
WONDER WOMAN! IF IT WEREN'T FOR YOU-- I'D HAVE BEEN—!
YOU'RE ALL RIGHT NOW, MARY!
9

NOW WE'VE GOT TO FULFILL THE CONDITIONS OF MR. TIGHE'S SECOND SCHOLARSHIP, MARY, BY CUTTING DOWN THOSE TREES! WE HAVEN'T TIME TO DO THEM ONE AT A TIME ANYMORE! HERE'S MY PLAN! WHILE YOU PILOT THE PLANE — I'LL--

DANGLING FROM HER PLANE, WHICH MARY GUIDES ABOVE THE FOREST, THE FEARLESS AMAZON MAID CUTS DOWN THE GIANT ROJO TREES WITH INCREDIBLE SPEED, WHILE SWINGING THROUGH THE AIR!

FASTER, MARY, FASTER!

MOMENTS LATER, THE SECOND TASK IS DONE, AND LEAVING MARY BEHIND HER TO RECEIVE THE THANKS OF MR. MAGNUS WHO IS NOW ABLE TO BUILD HOUSES FOR THE NEEDY, **WONDER WOMAN** SPEEDS OFF TO THE THIRD TASK--AT **ROCKY CRAG PEAK!**

THERE'S JEAN TOWNSEND--LEADING THE DEAN EXPEDITION UP THE PEAK! AND SUCCEEDING!

AT THAT MOMENT—HALFWAY UP THE PEAK--

BRACE YOURSELVES --EVERYONE!

HELP! I'M FALLING!

10

BUT THE WEIGHT OF THE FALLING MAN TAKES THE OTHERS BY SURPRISE AND--
DIG IN--DIG IN!
CAN'T GET A FOOTHOLD!
HELP!
WE'LL ALL GO OVER!
HELP!

BUT **WONDER WOMAN** HAS ALREADY SPOTTED THE PREDICAMENT OF THE CLIMBING PARTY, AND WITH ONE LEAP, HAS SEIZED HOLD OF THE END OF THE ROPE WHICH HOLDS ALL OF THE CLIMBERS TOGETHER!

WONDER WOMAN! YOU'VE CAUGHT US IN THE NICK OF TIME!

YES, JEAN! BUT STOPPING YOU FROM FALLING DOESN'T GET THE DEAN EXPEDITION TO THE TOP, TO FULFILL MR. TIGHE'S CONDITIONS!

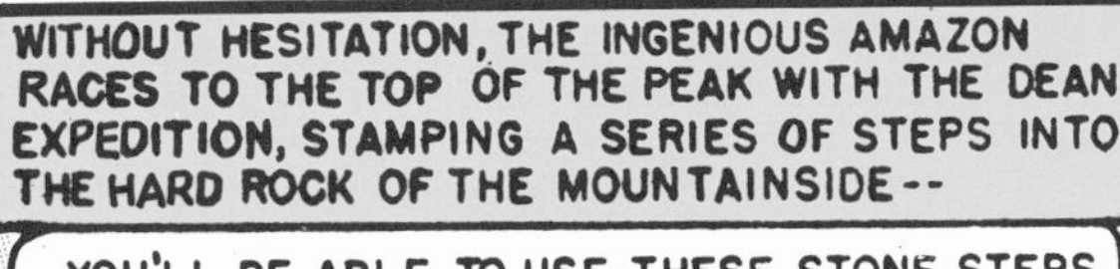

WITHOUT HESITATION, THE INGENIOUS AMAZON RACES TO THE TOP OF THE PEAK WITH THE DEAN EXPEDITION, STAMPING A SERIES OF STEPS INTO THE HARD ROCK OF THE MOUNTAINSIDE--

YOU'LL BE ABLE TO USE THESE STONE STEPS TO DESCEND THE MOUNTAIN WITH SAFETY!
WE'RE MAKING RECORD TIME, THANKS TO YOU, WONDER WOMAN!
AMAZING!

MEANWHILE, JANET FOSTER HAS PREVAILED UPON THE CAPTAIN OF THE **NEPTUNE SALVAGE COMPANY** TO ALLOW HER TO DIVE AFTER THE SUNKEN RADIUM AND--

I'VE GOT THE RADIUM! AND I HAVEN'T SEEN A THING TO ALARM ME! I WONDER WHAT HAPPENED TO THE OTHER DIVERS?

SUDDENLY--

WHATEVER IT IS--I GUESS IT'S GONE! AND--OHH--A GIANT CLAM! IT MUST HAVE COME OUT OF AN UNDERSEA CAVE! IT'S--IT'S COMING AT ME! HELP! HELP!
HELP!

CIRCLING OVER THE AREA, **WONDER WOMAN** OVERHEARS JANET'S CALL FOR HELP COMING OVER THE DIVING COMMUNICATIONS, AND INSTANTLY DIVES INTO THE MURKY WATERS IN SEARCH OF THE HOLLIDAY GIRL--

A GIANT CLAM! THIS WILL DISCOURAGE IT!
YOU CAN DEPEND ON WONDER WOMAN TO HELP WHEN ALL LOOKS LOST!
POW!

WHAT IS HAPPENING TO ETTA ON THE FIFTH TASK? IF SHE FAILS--ALL OF **WONDER WOMAN'S** AMAZING FEATS ARE OF NO AVAIL!

AT GIANT'S HOLLOW PASS, ETTA IS FARING NO BETTER THAN HER PREDECESSORS, AS SHE TOO SEEMS DOOMED TO CRASH--
CALLING WONDER WOMAN! HURRY! AM GOING TO CRASH!

ANSWERING ETTA'S DESPERATE MENTAL RADIO MESSAGE, **WONDER WOMAN** FLASHES TO THE PASS AND INSTANTLY PERCEIVES THE CAUSE OF THE MYSTERIOUS PLANE CRASHES--

A DOWNDRAFT, CREATED BY A HUGE OPENING IN THE GROUND AT THE BOTTOM OF THE PASS, PULLS THE PLANES DOWN LIKE AN AERIAL WHIRLPOOL! THERE'S ONLY ONE CHANCE!

LASSOING THE TOPS OF THE PASS TOGETHER, THE QUICK-THINKING AMAZON RACES TO THE BOTTOM, AND FORCES THE ROCKY WALLS OVER THE HUGE OPENING IN THE GROUND, IMMEDIATELY STIFLING THE DOWNDRAFT, AND SAVING ETTA.

THE OPENING IS CLOSED FOREVER! ETTA IS FLYING THROUGH THE PASS, LEADING THE WAY FOR OTHER PLANES TO FOLLOW, AND BRING PROGRESS TO THE PEOPLE IN THE VALLEY BEYOND!

LATER, AT HOLLIDAY COLLEGE--
YOUR TIME IS UP, DEAN MERRILY! TOO BAD YOU'VE FAILED! HA, HA!
12

SUDDENLY--

WAIT! IT STILL LACKS ONE SECOND TO THE END OF THE 24TH HOUR AND--AND--THERE IS **WONDER WOMAN** AND THE GIRLS!

INCREDIBLE! **WONDER WOMAN** HAS SUCCEEDED WHERE EVERY MAN HAS FAILED!

YOU WIN, **WONDER WOMAN**! AND I MUST CONFESS, THAT YOU AND THE GIRLS HAVE MADE ME CHANGE MY MIND ABOUT WOMEN! I'M NO LONGER A WOMAN-HATER!

THEN **YOU'RE** THE REAL WINNER, MR. TIGHE! BECAUSE WHEN ONE CEASES TO HATE, HE BECOMES STRONGER!

ROMANCE

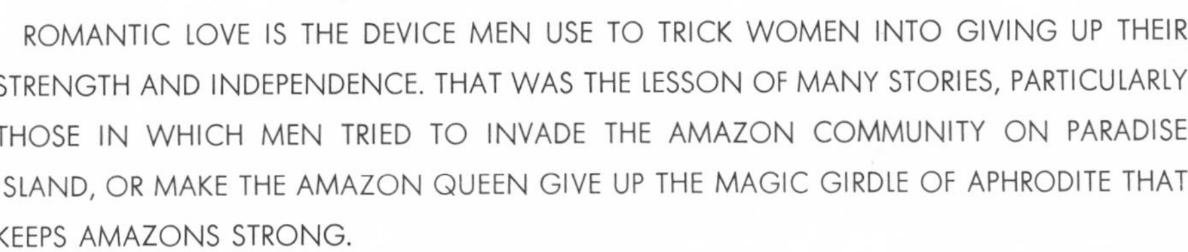

ROMANTIC LOVE IS THE DEVICE MEN USE TO TRICK WOMEN INTO GIVING UP THEIR STRENGTH AND INDEPENDENCE. THAT WAS THE LESSON OF MANY STORIES, PARTICULARLY THOSE IN WHICH MEN TRIED TO INVADE THE AMAZON COMMUNITY ON PARADISE ISLAND, OR MAKE THE AMAZON QUEEN GIVE UP THE MAGIC GIRDLE OF APHRODITE THAT KEEPS AMAZONS STRONG.

ROMANTIC LOVE, ON THE OTHER HAND, LURED WONDER WOMAN AWAY FROM PARADISE ISLAND, AND KEPT HER CONCERNED WITH THE WELFARE OF THE RATHER BORING CAPTAIN STEVE TREVOR IN STORY AFTER STORY. IT EVEN MADE HER ODDLY JEALOUS FROM TIME TO TIME.

TO MAKE MATTERS MORE CONFUSING, LOVE WAS SUPPOSED TO BE THE SOURCE OF AMAZON STRENGTH: IT TEMPERED VIOLENCE AND MADE THEIR SOCIETY MORE PEACEFUL AND SUPERIOR TO THAT OF MEN.

WONDER WOMAN HINTED AT AN ANSWER WHEN SHE ALTERNATELY ADMIRED STRENGTH IN STEVE, AND SAID SHE COULD NOT LOVE A MAN WHO DOMINATED HER. APPARENTLY, SHE COULD ONLY LOVE AN EQUAL. HER CONSTANT MESSAGE TO SOCIETY IN GENERAL WAS LOVE, EQUALITY, AND JUSTICE. WHEN THAT LESSON IS LEARNED BY THE PATRIARCHAL SOCIETIES OF THE WORLD, WILL PARADISE ISLAND NO LONGER NEED TO EXIST? WILL LOVE BE POSSIBLE AT LAST?

WE'LL NEED MANY MORE ADVENTURES OF WONDER WOMAN TO FIND OUT.

Wonder Woman
By CHARLES MOULTON
AN ENEMY'S SUBTLE PLOT GIVES STEVE HERCULEAN STRENGTH- CAN WONDER WOMAN RESIST HIM? DOES AN AMAZON - OR ANY OTHER GIRL FOR THAT MATTER - FALL IRRESISTIBLY FOR A MAN OF COLOSSAL POWER? IN THIS STRANGE CHAPTER OF THE BEAUTIFUL PRINCESS' CAREER, THE GIRL FROM PARADISE ISLE FINDS HERSELF CONFRONTED WITH THE NEW SCIENCE OF ELECTRONICS WHICH COOKS AN ENTIRE MEAL - OR A HUMAN BEING - IN ONE MINUTE!
ONLY WONDER WOMAN, BEAUTIFUL AS APHRODITE, WISE AS ATHENA, STRONGER THAN HERCULES, AND SWIFTER THAN MERCURY, DARES FACE WITHOUT FLINCHING, THE AMAZING MENACE OF
"THE LAWBREAKERS' LEAGUE."
HG PETER
1
STEVE AND DIANA (WONDER WOMAN) PRINCE APPROACH NEW YORK ON THE 20TH CENTURY LIMITED FROM CHICAGO.
WE'RE ON TIME TO THE MINUTE.

BUT OUR TRAIN'S SLOWING DOWN — IT'S ALMOST STOPPED.
MMHM — WE'RE IN THE BRONX. THE 20TH CENTURY ALWAYS SLOWS DOWN HERE TO LET A LOCAL WESTCHESTER TRAIN PASS IT ENTERING GRAND CENTRAL STATION.

SLOWLY THE LOCAL TRAIN OVERTAKES THE CRACK CHICAGO EXPRESS — WESTCHESTER COMMUTERS STARE CURIOUSLY AS THEY CREEP PAST THE WINDOWS OF THE DELUXE PULLMANS.

DIANA, SEATED BACKWARD, RECOGNIZES A SINISTER FACE AT THE APPROACHING TRAIN WINDOW.
GREAT HERA! THERE'S "SURE-SHOT" HOGAN ON THAT TRAIN —
WHAT?

AS HOGAN'S WINDOW DRAWS OPPOSITE STEVE'S —
BLAZES! IF THIS WINDOW'D ONLY OPEN, I COULD GRAB THAT MUG —

LOOK OUT, STEVE!
UG-ULP- STOP PULLING ME —
2

IF I STOP PULLING, YOU'LL STOP BULLETS!
BANG!
YE GODS — YOU SAVED MY LIFE, DIANA!

QUICKER THAN THE EYE CAN FOLLOW, DIANA RACES INTO THE CAR VESTIBULE AND TRANSFORMS HERSELF TO WONDER WOMAN.
SHOOTING STEVE FROM THAT PASSING TRAIN WAS DELIBERATELY PLANNED! I MUST GET HOGAN AND QUESTION HIM.

AS THE LOCAL TRAIN PASSES, WONDER WOMAN LEAPS LIGHTLY TO ITS ROOF.

I SHOULD BE ABLE TO SURPRISE HOGAN— I DOUBT THAT HE'S EXPECTING ME!

BUT WONDER WOMAN RECKONS WITHOUT THE GANGSTER'S CLEVER GIRL COMPANION.
THERE SHE IS— I TOLD YOU WONDER WOMAN'D BE AROUND TREVOR!
I'LL SHOOT HER, TOO—

YOU FOOL - BULLETS WON'T HARM WONDER WOMAN! DON'T LET HER CATCH YOU - JUMP—
STOP, HOGAN - YOU'LL BE KILLED—

HE IS A FOOL— NOTHING CAN SAVE HIM NOW. THAT GIRL IS DELIBERATELY MURDERING HIM!

IT'S NO USE - HOGAN'S BEEN SWEPT AWAY IN THIS TERRIFIC CURRENT. I'D BETTER GET BACK BEFORE STEVE BROADCASTS DIANA'S DISAPPEARANCE!

WONDER WOMAN OVERTAKES HER TRAIN IN THE PARK AVE. TUNNEL.
20th Century

CHANGING SWIFTLY TO DIANA -
WHERE IN BLAZES HAVE YOU BEEN? I SEARCHED THE TRAIN-
I-ER-HAD TO FIX MY DRESS AFTER SUCH STRENUOUS EXERTION -

THIS ATTEMPT TO MURDER YOU, STEVE, WAS CLEVERLY PLANNED - PROBABLY BY SPIES YOU'RE TRAILING WHO ARE DESPERATELY AFRAID YOU'RE ABOUT TO CATCH THEM.
NOT BY THE SPIES THEMSELVES, BUT BY THE LAWBREAKERS' PROTECTIVE LEAGUE, WHICH IS HIDING THEM.

THIS "LAWBREAKERS' LEAGUE" HAS GROWN VERY POWERFUL. IT HIDES ANY CRIMINAL WHO'LL SPLIT HIS BOODLE WITH THEM AND BOASTS THAT NO CROOK PROTECTED BY THE LEAGUE WAS EVER CAUGHT. YESTERDAY I RECEIVED A LETTER -

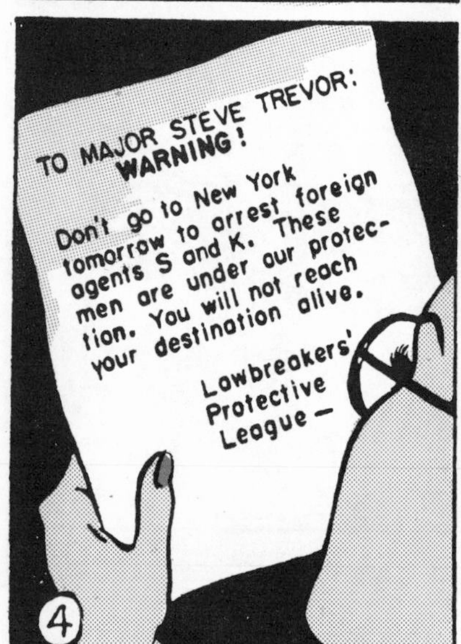
TO MAJOR STEVE TREVOR:
WARNING!
Don't go to New York tomorrow to arrest foreign agents S and K. These men are under our protection. You will not reach your destination alive.
Lawbreakers' Protective League -

MEANWHILE, THE LATE HOGAN'S GIRL COMPANION, ENTERING HER SWANKY APARTMENT IN NEW YORK, FINDS RODRIGUEZ CABALLOS, INVENTOR OF RADIO DEVICES, AWAITING HER.
WELL, FERVA?
WONDER WOMAN SPOILED OUR PLAN - PLAGUE TAKE THAT AMAZON!

SAPRISTA! IF HOGAN'S CAUGHT HE'LL SING —
DON'T WORRY- HOGAN'S SO DEEP IN THE EAST RIVER HE'LL NEVER GURGLE. TREVOR ESCAPED, BUT HE'LL NEVER FIND THE SPIES **WE'RE** HIDING!

BUT TREVOR'S DANGEROUS—
NO, NO, ROD- **WONDER WOMAN'S** OUR REAL MENACE. NOBODY CAN KILL THAT WENCH, BUT TREVOR CAN SUBDUE HER! ONCE SHE MARRIES **HIM** THE MIGHTY AMAZON'LL BECOME A MEEK HOUSEWIFE WHO WILL NEVER BOTHER US!

IF TREVOR BECOMES **STRONGER THAN WONDER WOMAN**, SHE'LL GO GA-GA OVER HIM! SHE'LL MARRY HIM AND STAY AT HOME AS HE COMMANDS. LISTEN, RODRIGUEZ, I HAVE A PLAN —
IT BETTER BE GOOD- OR **ELSE!**

LATER - STEVE IS CHANGING FOR DINNER AT HIS HOTEL WHEN —
TELEGRAM FOR MAJOR TREVOR!
OKAY - COME IN.

GOOD EVENING, MAJOR, PLEASE RAISE YOUR HANDS- **STAND WHERE YOU ARE!**
HUH? WHO IN BLAZES ARE YOU?

SIT DOWN, MAJOR TREVOR, **AND KEEP YOUR HANDS ABOVE THE TABLE!**
WHAT IS THIS ALL ABOUT?

BELIEVE ME, MAJOR, I'M YOUR FRIEND. I'VE COME TO DO YOU A **TREMENDOUS** FAVOR- I'LL SHOW YOU HOW TO WIN **WONDER WOMAN!**
WIN-ER-UH-**WHAT?**
THIS GAL'S A SCREWBALL- I'D BETTER HUMOR HER.

5

I LIKE YOU, STEVE TREVOR- YOU BIG HANDSOME HUNK OF MAN! I THINK THAT AMAZON GIRL TREATS YOU SHAMEFULLY- I WANT TO SEE YOU MAKE HER MARRY YOU!
GREAT IDEA - HEY! CAREFUL WITH THOSE GUNS!

IF YOU WERE STRONGER THAN WONDER WOMAN, SHE'D HAVE MARRIED YOU LONG AGO. GIRLS WANT SUPERIOR MEN TO BOSS THEM AROUND. YOU'RE STRONG, STEVE, BUT YOU MUST BECOME STRONGER- STRONGER THAN THE AMAZON!!

OH PHOOEY! THAT'S ENOUGH NONSENSE-
OH NO YOU DON'T, BIG BOY! SIT BACK THERE AND RELAX. I'M GOING TO MAKE YOU STRONGER THAN WONDER WOMAN!

PUT YOUR HANDS BEHIND YOU - IF YOU WON'T COOPERATE I'LL HAVE TO TIE YOU UP.
SHE'S GOT AN ITCHY TRIGGER FINGER - I'D BETTER LET HER PLAY COPS AND ROBBERS WITH ME!

I'M BINDING YOU WITH ROPE, ADHESIVE TAPE, AND WIRE. EVEN WONDER WOMAN WOULD FIND THOSE BONDS SNUG. BUT WITH YOUR NEW POWER YOU'LL BREAK THEM LIKE COTTON THREAD!
CERTAINLY- NOTHING TO IT!

I'M USING WONDER WOMAN'S OWN METHOD TO GIVE YOU SUPERSTRENGTH! AMAZONS CAN RELEASE BRAIN ENERGY INTO THEIR MUSCLES AT WILL- I'VE BROUGHT AN ELECTRONIC GLOBE WHICH WILL GIVE YOU THE SAME POWER!
6

GAZE AT THIS ELECTRONIC GLOBE AND TREMENDOUS NERVE ENERGY WILL BE RELEASED. YOUR SUPERSTRENGTH WILL LAST ONLY 30 MINUTES, SO KEEP THE GLOBE ALWAYS WITH YOU-
SHEER NONSENSE- BUT- BUT I AM GETTING A STRONG FEELING AT THAT-!

DIANA, RETURNING TO HER OWN ROOM, SEES THE GIRL LEAVING TREVOR'S.
HM - A WOMAN VISITING STEVE! THAT RED HAIR LOOKS FAMILIAR- I'D BETTER SEE WHAT MISCHIEF SHE'S BEEN UP TO!

SHADES OF PLUTO! THAT REDHEAD'S TRUSSED YOU UP LIKE A BUNDLE OF CORN! I'LL NEED WIRECUTTERS TO FREE YOU—
NO YOU WON'T, DIANA—

WHY - WHY STEVE - THAT'S IMPOSSIBLE! I'M SEEING DOUBLE -
HO HO — IT'S EASY TO BREAK THESE FLIMSY BONDS!

OH, STEVE - YOU ARE WONDERFUL - MAGNIFICENT! WHY, YOU'RE ALMOST AS STRONG AS WONDER WOMAN!
I AM STRONGER THAN SHE- WAIT TILL I SHOW HER!

I'LL CALL WONDER WOMAN- SHE'S IN MY ROOM —
CONGRATULATIONS, STEVE! I HEAR YOU'RE STRONGER THAN I AM!
7.

THAT'S RIGHT, BEAUTIFUL - NOW I CAN BOSS YOU AROUND- HA HA!!
NO MAN CAN BOSS AN AMAZON.
BUT STEVE'S NEW STRENGTH IS THRILLING!

AN ELECTRONIC GLOBE- HOW INTERESTING! THIS IS LIT BY A RADIO BEAM. I'D LIKE TO KNOW WHERE THAT BEAM COMES FROM. DID A RED-HAIRED GIRL GIVE YOU THIS, STEVE?
YES- HOW'D YOU KNOW?

I SAW HER - SHE BELONGS TO THE "LAWBREAKERS' LEAGUE" GANG. BY FOLLOWING THE ELECTRONIC BEAM, WHICH LIGHTS THIS GLOBE, WITH MY MENTAL RADIO I MAY DISCOVER THEIR HEADQUARTERS!
YOU'RE MISTAKEN- THAT GIRL'S MY FRIEND!

SO SHE'S YOUR "FRIEND" - WELL, WELL! LET GO MY WRIST!
GIVE ME MY GLOBE!

GREAT HERA! YOU- YOU ARE STRONGER THAN I AM, STEVE!
8.

WHENEVER I ASKED YOU TO MARRY ME, YOU'VE ALWAYS BRUSHED ME OFF. THIS TIME I'LL MAKE YOU LISTEN!
SO THIS IS WHAT IT FEELS LIKE TO BE BOSSED BY A STRONG MAN!

SOME GIRLS LOVE TO HAVE A MAN STRONGER THAN THEY ARE MAKE THEM DO THINGS. DO I LIKE IT? I DON'T KNOW- IT'S SORT OF THRILLING. BUT- ISN'T IT MORE FUN TO MAKE THE MAN OBEY?

SUDDENLY, THE AMAZON MAID FREES HERSELF.
UNF- COME BACK HERE, BEAUTIFUL, OR I'LL -
NO YOU WON'T - I CAN STILL RUN FASTER THAN YOU AND I'M NOT SUBDUED - YET!

WITH HER MENTAL RADIO, WONDER WOMAN CROUCHES OUTSIDE STEVE'S WINDOW.
STEVE CAN KEEP HIS GLOBE - I'LL TRACE THE RADIO BEAM THAT LIGHTS IT JUST THE SAME!
B-ZZZ
B-ZZ

FOLLOWING THE RADIO PATH, WONDER WOMAN RACES ACROSS NEW YORK ROOFTOPS.
THE ELECTRONIC BEAM SEEMS TO COME FROM THAT DANCING SCHOOL- CAN THE REDHEAD BE FERVA SHAYNE?
BZZZ
B-ZZZ-ZZ
FERVA SHAYNE DANCING

IF THE REDHEAD'S IN THERE, SHE'LL RECOGNIZE ME AND WARN THE GANG. LUCKY THE HOLLIDAY BAND IS IN NEW YORK - I'LL CALL ETTA ON THE MENTAL RADIO.
GO TO SHAYNE'S DANCING CONSERVATORY ----

ANSWERING WONDER WOMAN'S CALL, THE GIRLS HURRY TO FERVA'S DANCING SCHOOL.
THE TERMS ARE $10 A LESSON - THESE ARE THE DANCING INSTRUCTORS.
WOO WOO - LET US AT 'EM - WE'LL TAKE THE WHOLE COURSE!

THROUGH A SECRET PANEL IN FERVA'S OFFICE, RODRIGUEZ CABALLOS WATCHES THE DANCE FLOOR.
CARAMBA! THAT FAT RUNT IS ETTA CANDY, A WONDER WOMAN SPY!
9

IS THIS YOUR "PLAN", FERVA, DOUBLE-CROSSING ME? WONDER WOMAN'S GIRLS ARE OUT THERE CASING THIS JOINT- I'LL FIX THEIR BOOK AND THEN I'LL ATTEND TO YOU!
WAIT, RODRIGUEZ, I'M NOT DOUBLE-CROSSING YOU-
FERVA SHAYNE

CABALLOS, HURRYING TO HIS RADIO CONTROL ROOM, CALLS THE "DANCE INSTRUCTORS" ON AN ULTRA-SHORT WAVE.
SOME GIRLS JUST ARRIVED! LEAD 'EM TO SPOT 43 — FOLLOW PLAN 19 —

SAY, PAL, WHAT'S THAT THING IN YOUR EAR?
OH- THAT? IT'S-ER- AN EARPHONE. I'M A LITTLE DEAF. BUT I CAN HEAR EVERYTHING YOUR SWEET VOICE SAYS!
PLAN-19

LET'S DANCE BEHIND THIS SCREEN, LOVELY ONE, WHERE WE'LL BE ALONE TOGETHER!
OKAY, HANDSOME -OH! EE-EEK-WOO WOO!

ONE BY ONE THE GIRLS FALL THROUGH A TRAP DOOR BEHIND THE SCREEN AND ARE SEIZED BY ROUGH HANDS.
E-EE-K! WOO! WOO!

THE PRISONERS ARE LED BEFORE A RADIO SPEAKER.
WELCOME, GIRLS, TO THE INNER SANCTUM OF THE LAWBREAKERS' LEAGUE! OUR MEMBERS LIKE TO MEET ALL SPIES SO WE'LL INVITE YOU TO ATTEND OUR HEADQUARTERS LINE-UP!

LAWBREAKERS, WEARING MASKS, INSPECT THE PRISONERS, AS THOUGH IT WERE A POLICE LINE-UP.
YOU'RE WONDER WOMAN'S SPIES FROM HOLLIDAY COLLEGE, AREN'T YOU?
WE'LL SAY NOTHING!
HO HO! PUT 'EM ON THE ELECTRONIC GRID!
10

ETTA DECIDES IT'S TIME TO SEND A MENTAL RADIO MESSAGE!
WONDER WOMAN-HELP! THE "LAWBREAKERS" HAVE GOT US - THEY'RE PUTTIN' US ON A GRIDDLE - COME QUICK!!

WONDER WOMAN, WAITING ON THE ROOF, CATCHES ETTA'S CALL FOR HELP ON HER MENTAL RADIO AND LEAPS THROUGH THE SKY-LIGHT.
BZ-Z-Z-Z-Z-Z

THE PRISONERS ARE PLACED ON AN ELECTRONIC GRID HEATED BY RADIO BEAM.
EVERY QUESTION ON THIS WAVE LENGTH HEATS THE GRID - TO TURN IT OFF YOU MUST ANSWER FULLY. WHERE IS WONDER WOMAN?
WE'LL NEVER TELL! OUCH! OW-W-W! WOO WOO!

AT THIS MOMENT, WONDER WOMAN, FOLLOWING THE RADIO BEAM, CRASHES CABALLOS' CONTROL ROOM.
STOP, WONDER WOMAN, OR YOUR GIRLS WILL BURN!

SEEING THE PRISONERS THROUGH A WALL PANEL, WONDER WOMAN SURRENDERS.
I'LL GRILL YOU NOW - THIS METAL STRIP IS HEATED ELECTRONICALLY BY RADIO QUESTIONS.

MEANWHILE FERVA, FEARING RODRIGUEZ' THREATENED VENGEANCE, TELEPHONES STEVE AND -
HERE'S EVERY CROOK WE'VE BEEN HUNTING FOR YEARS - MOW 'EM DOWN BOYS!
11

SEIZING THE MASSIVE ELECTRONIC GRILL WITH HERCULEAN STRENGTH, STEVE ASSEMBLES THE "LAWBREAKERS' LEAGUE."
I'LL GET THESE LADS TOGETHER FOR A MEETING - IN ALCATRAZ!

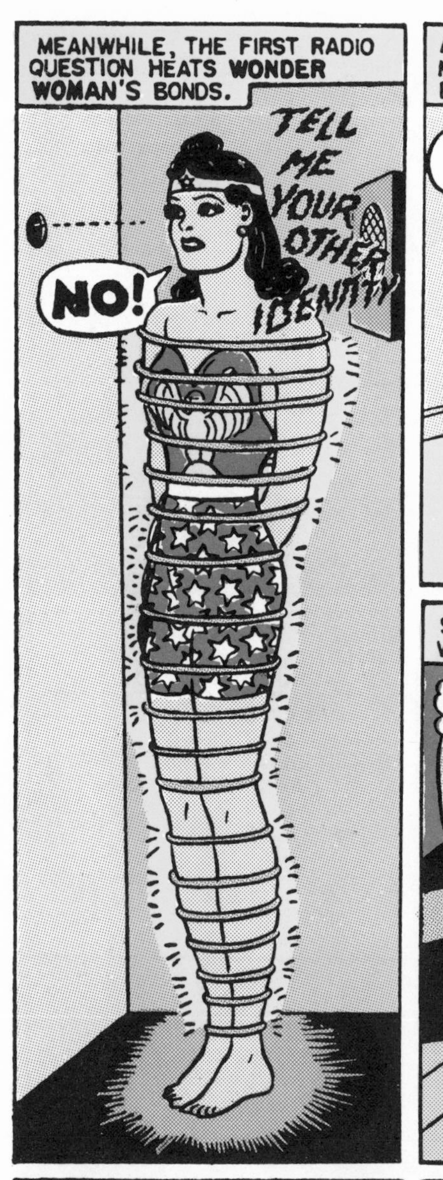
MEANWHILE, THE FIRST RADIO QUESTION HEATS WONDER WOMAN'S BONDS.
TELL ME YOUR OTHER IDENTITY
NO!

AS WONDER WOMAN, THROUGH THE PANEL, SEES STEVE AND HIS MEN APPEAR, SHE WHIRLS LIKE A RELEASED THUNDERBOLT, BURSTING HER BONDS.
YOUR CLEVER ELECTRONIC BONDS WARMED ME UP NICELY FOR ACTION!
UG! ULP!

STEVE'S COLOSSAL STRENGTH WEAKENS SUDDENLY.
OH-H- THIS'LL CRUSH ME - I CAN'T MOVE IT!

OH, STEVE- WHAT HAPPENED? ARE YOU HURT?
NO, ANGEL, YOU ARRIVED JUST IN TIME! MY SUPER-STRENGTH QUIT BECAUSE I HAVE NOT LOOKED AT THE ELECTRONIC GLOBE FOR HALF AN HOUR.

I'LL RELEASE MORE BRAIN ENERGY INTO MY MUSCLES- THEN YOU'LL MARRY ME—
NO, I WON'T, STEVE- I'VE DISCOVERED THAT I CAN NEVER LOVE A DOMINANT MAN WHO'S STRONGER THAN I AM!
12

IF YOU PREFER ME WEAKER THAN YOU, TO HECK WITH THIS GADGET!
YOU FOOL- THAT CAN'T BE REPLACED!
OH, STEVE! I DO L-L-LIKE YOU- JUST AS YOU ARE NOW!
SMASH
MORE ADVENTURES OF WONDER WOMAN IN EVERY ISSUE OF SENSATION COMICS!

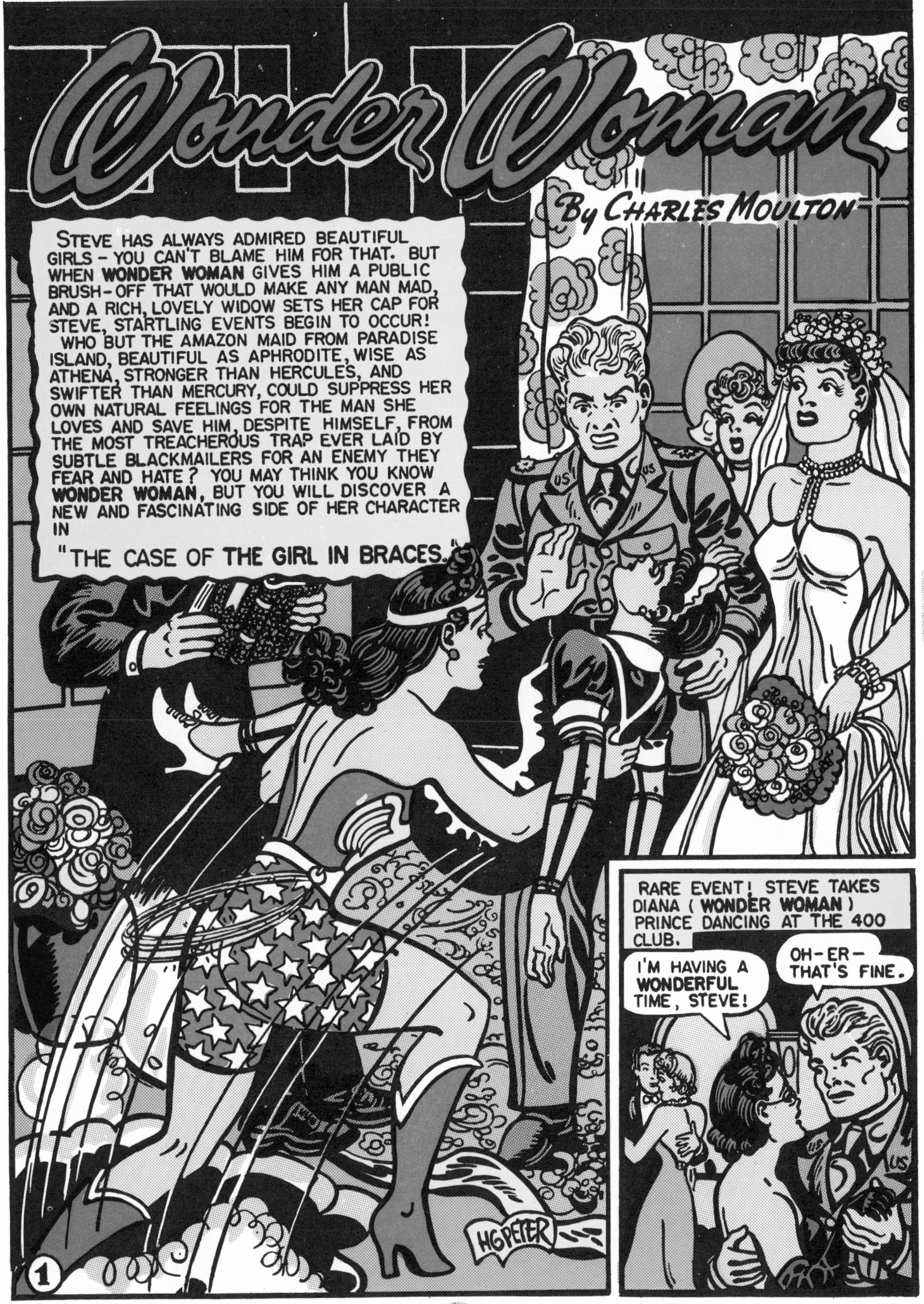
Wonder Woman
By Charles Moulton
STEVE HAS ALWAYS ADMIRED BEAUTIFUL GIRLS - YOU CAN'T BLAME HIM FOR THAT. BUT WHEN WONDER WOMAN GIVES HIM A PUBLIC BRUSH-OFF THAT WOULD MAKE ANY MAN MAD, AND A RICH, LOVELY WIDOW SETS HER CAP FOR STEVE, STARTLING EVENTS BEGIN TO OCCUR!
WHO BUT THE AMAZON MAID FROM PARADISE ISLAND, BEAUTIFUL AS APHRODITE, WISE AS ATHENA, STRONGER THAN HERCULES, AND SWIFTER THAN MERCURY, COULD SUPPRESS HER OWN NATURAL FEELINGS FOR THE MAN SHE LOVES AND SAVE HIM, DESPITE HIMSELF, FROM THE MOST TREACHEROUS TRAP EVER LAID BY SUBTLE BLACKMAILERS FOR AN ENEMY THEY FEAR AND HATE? YOU MAY THINK YOU KNOW WONDER WOMAN, BUT YOU WILL DISCOVER A NEW AND FASCINATING SIDE OF HER CHARACTER IN
"THE CASE OF THE GIRL IN BRACES."
HG PETER
1
RARE EVENT! STEVE TAKES DIANA (WONDER WOMAN) PRINCE DANCING AT THE 400 CLUB.
I'M HAVING A WONDERFUL TIME, STEVE!
OH-ER- THAT'S FINE.

COME NOW, STEVE, TELL ME - WHAT'S THE REAL REASON YOU BROUGHT ME HERE TONIGHT?
WHY - AH - REAL REASON? TO DANCE, OF COURSE!
WATCH THAT ORDNANCE OFFICER, THAT'S CAPT. BLANK - HE'S THE LAD I WANTED YOU TO GET A LINE ON — -
HA HA! THIS IS WHY STEVE BROUGHT ME - I KNEW IT! IT'S BUSINESS AS USUAL!! WHAT'S THAT BEAUTIFUL GIRL SAYING TO THE CAPTAIN?
DIANA'S KEEN AMAZON EARS OVERHEAR THE CONVERSATION—
I DID LET THE INFORMATION SLIP, MARGO. ARMY INTELLIGENCE KNOWS I'M THE ONLY ONE WHO COULD BE RESPONSIBLE FOR THE LEAK—
SILLY BOY- SO WHAT? IT WASN'T IMPORTANT INFORMATION—
NOT TO FOREIGN SPIES. BUT AMERICAN GUN MANUFACTURERS'LL PROFIT- I'M RUINED!
BUT NOBODY KNOWS YOU LET THE SECRET OUT—
THEY WILL KNOW! A BLACKMAIL GANG CALLED "FELLOCK'S INVESTIGATORS" ARE BEHIND THIS. UNLESS I GIVE THEM $10,000, THEY'LL INFORM ARMY INTELLIGENCE. I WON'T PAY! I'D RATHER COMMIT - - -
GREAT MINERVA! DID YOU HEAR WHAT CAPT. BLANK SAID? HE'S GONE! I MUST FIND HIM-
HEAR WHAT BLANK SAID - ARE YOU WACKY, DI? NOBODY COULD HEAR AT THIS DISTANCE — COME BACK!
BUT EVEN AS DIANA SEEKS CAPT. BLANK IN THE CROWDED LOUNGE, A SHOT RINGS OUT—
BANG!
GREAT APHRODITE - I'M TOO LATE!
EEK!
EEK!

LIKE A FLASH OF LIGHT, DIANA DISAPPEARS BEHIND A DIVAN TO APPEAR AGAIN INSTANTLY AS WONDER WOMAN.
IF ONLY I'D BEEN QUICKER –

ARE YOU SURE HE'S DEAD, DOCTOR?
ABSOLUTELY – BULLET WENT CLEAR THROUGH HIS HEAD – KILLED HIM INSTANTLY!

BUT I STILL MAY BE ABLE TO SAVE THE CAPTAIN'S LIFE –
SAVE A DEAD MAN'S LIFE? DON'T BE RIDICULOUS!

WHAT'RE YOU DOING? COME BACK HERE -- STOP HER!
THAT'S WONDER WOMAN, DOC, SHE KNOWS WHAT SHE'S DOING. I'LL BE RESPONSIBLE.

IN PAULA'S SECRET LABORATORY CAPT. BLANK IS TREATED WITH WONDER WOMAN'S PURPLE RAY, WHICH ONCE SAVED TREVOR'S LIFE.
YOU GOT HIM HERE IN TIME, PRINCESS – HIS HEART BEATS AGAIN!
GOOD!

WON'T PAY – GIRL GOT SECRET – MY CAREER RUINED –
HE'S BABBLING INCOHERENTLY. HE WON'T BE ABLE TO TELL ME ABOUT THIS BLACKMAIL RACKET UNTIL HIS BRAIN WOUND HEALS. I'LL HAVE TO INVESTIGATE THESE RACKETEERS SOME OTHER WAY.

RETURNING TO THE 400 CLUB, WONDER WOMAN FINDS STEVE WITH FRIENDS.
BEAUTIFUL! I WAS HOPING YOU'D COME BACK. LET ME PRESENT MRS. MARGO VANDERGILT AND MY BEST FRIEND, COL. JACK HARVEY.
HOLA!

CAPT. BLANK'S RECOVERING - WHAT'S THIS BLACKMAIL RACKET, STEVE?
IT'S RUN BY A SLIMY CHARACTER CALLED "EARS" FELLOCK. HIS GIRLS VAMP IMPORTANT OFFICIALS INTO TALKING TOO MUCH- THEN HE THREATENS TO EXPOSE THEM FOR GIVING AWAY GOVERNMENT SECRETS.

BUT LISTEN, ANGEL, YOU'VE DONE ENOUGH GOOD WORK TONIGHT, BRINGING BLANK BACK TO LIFE — FORGET RACKETS AND LET'S DANCE!
WHY, STEVE — YOU'RE FORGETTING POOR DIANA!

DI LEFT ME — YOU'RE THE GIRL I WANT, BEAUTIFUL - UNF!!
YOU'LL NEVER GET AN AMAZON THAT WAY - TRY YOUR CAVE MAN STYLE ON MAN'S WORLD GIRLS!

4

WONDER WOMAN, MEANWHILE, FLASHING BEHIND A SERVICE SCREEN, RETURNS AS DIANA.
I CERTAINLY APOLOGIZE —
NO, NO, MAJOR TREVOR - IT'S WONDER WOMAN WHO SHOULD APOLOGIZE!
I'M SORRY I - ER - THAT IS, I'M SORRY WONDER WOMAN GOT SO ROUGH!

WHILE MARGO VISITS THE POWDER ROOM TO REPAIR DAMAGES, COL. HARVEY ADVISES HIS OLD FRIEND.
STEVE, WHY LET **WONDER WOMAN** MAKE A FOOL OF YOU? YOU'RE WASTING YOUR TIME AND MAKING YOURSELF UNHAPPY!

WHY NOT MARRY SOME NICE, SWEET AMERICAN GIRL WHO'LL APPRECIATE YOU – LIKE MARGO VANDERGILT, FOR INSTANCE? SHE'S BEAUTIFUL, POPULAR, SOCIALLY PROMINENT, AND HER LATE HUSBAND LEFT HER A MILLION!
OH, **NO**, COLONEL! **MARGO** COULDN'T MAKE STEVE HAPPY!

BUT STEVE DOESN'T SEEM TO AGREE WITH DIANA–
YOU'RE A WONDERFUL DANCER, MRS. VANDERGILT –
CALL ME MARGO, **STEVE**!

WHAT A HANDSOME COUPLE THEY MAKE DANCING TOGETHER!
I CAN'T BEAR TO LOOK! MAYBE I'M JEALOUS, BUT I DON'T TRUST THAT WOMAN. CAPT. BLANK CONFIDED IN HER – I WONDER IF THERE'S ANY EVIDENCE – HM! WHAT'S THAT STICKING OUT OF HER HANDBAG –?

I SHOULDN'T READ THE LADY'S PRIVATE CORRESPONDENCE. BUT THIS CHEAP ENVELOPE WITH A HAND-PRINTED ADDRESS LOOKS QUEER IN A WEALTHY WOMAN'S HANDBAG.

WE'LL MEET YOU AT YOUR HOUSE TO-NIGHT AS PLANNED

GREAT HERA! A NOTE FROM "EARS" FELLOCK TO MRS. VANDERGILT – OLD PALS, EH? THEY'RE TO MEET "AS PLANNED" – WELL, WELL! I THINK **WONDER WOMAN** HAD BETTER ATTEND THAT MEETING.

MEANWHILE STEVE'S ACQUAINTANCE WITH MARGO PROGRESSES.
OH, STEVE, HOW FAST TIME FLIES WHEN I DANCE WITH YOU! COL. HARVEY AND MISS PRINCE HAVE LEFT - I MUST GO HOME —
I'LL DRIVE YOU.

AT THE VANDERGILT MANSION —
NO, NO, STEVE - YOU MUST NOT COME INTO MY HOUSE! THE MEN I'M MEETING ARE DANGEROUS —
WHAT! IF YOU'RE IN DANGER, I'LL PROTECT YOU —

SUDDENLY THEY ARE SURROUNDED BY HEAVILY ARMED GANGSTERS IN DRESS SUITS.
HANDS UP, YOU!
WE'RE YOUR GUESTS, MRS. SLICKCHICK — LET'S GO INTO YOUR HOUSE AND HAVE A CHAT.

BUT AS THE GANGSTER "FRISKS" STEVE FOR WEAPONS —

OOF - UGH!
SWISH!

.......FROM THE REAR A TREACHEROUS BLOW DESCENDS.
BRING HIM INTO THE HOUSE QUICK, BOYS, BEFORE SOME FLATFOOT SPOTS US - YOU CAN TIE HIM UP INSIDE.

STEVE, RECOVERING CONSCIOUSNESS, FINDS HIMSELF HELPLESS IN MARGO'S SITTING ROOM.
W-WHY ARE YOU DOING THIS TO ME? I-I SAID I'D PAY–
YEAH– AND THEN YOU BRING THIS ARMY INTELLIGENCE MUG TO TRAP US!

OKAY, SLICKCHICK– IT'S YOUR FAULT WE HAVE TO MARK THIS NUMBER OFF!

OH, NO–NO! PLEASE DON'T KILL STEVE. I'LL PAY YOU DOUBLE–TRIPLE–

I'LL PAY THIS CREDITOR FOR YOU!
AWK! OW-WW!
BANG!

NOW, MY FRIEND, YOU AND I'LL MAKE A TRIP TO THE POLICE STATION!
7

LEAVE THE BOSS GO OR I'LL FILL YER BOYFRIEND'S BRAINBOX WIT' LEAD!

OKAY, MY FRIENDS– GOODBYE NOW– BUT I'LL BE SEEING YOU, AND SOON!
IT WON'T BE US YOU'LL BE LOOKING FOR –HA-HAHA!

AS WONDER WOMAN FREES THE PRISONERS, MARGO RUSHES INTO STEVE'S ARMS.
OH, STEVE, I'M SO FRIGHTENED – I NEED YOUR PROTECTION!
YOU'LL BE SAFE, DEAR.
WELL – WELL!

SORRY TO INTERRUPT THE TOUCHING LOVE SCENE, BUT WHAT'S THIS ALL ABOUT?
NOW, ANGEL, GO EASY ON POOR MARGO. SHE'S HAD AN AWFUL SHOCK –
I SHALL TELL THE WHOLE STORY.

IT STARTED WHILE MY LATE HUSBAND, NAUTILUS VANDERGILT, WAS ALIVE AND HEAD OF THE U.S. FINANCIAL BOARD. FELLOCK'S GANG STOLE SECRET INFORMATION AND THREATENED TO BLAME MY HUSBAND. HE'D HAVE BEEN RUINED! SO HE PAID THEM BLACKMAIL.

WHAT'S THAT GOT TO DO WITH YOU?
I DEARLY LOVED MY HUSBAND, SO WHEN THIS GANG THREATENED TO AIR THE OLD SCANDAL AGAINST HIM I AGREED TO PAY THEM $10,000 TO PROTECT HIS MEMORY!

I APPRECIATE YOUR HELP, WONDER WOMAN, BUT I'D RATHER HAVE STEVE HANDLE THIS CASE. IT'S A MAN'S JOB!
YOU SEE HOW IT IS –
I WISH STEVE LUCK WITH THE JOB – AND WITH YOU!

A FEW DAYS LATER –
WELL, GENERAL, I'VE DONE IT – I'M ENGAGED TO MARGO VANDERGILT!
CONGRATULATIONS! MARGO'S A LOVELY GIRL.
I WOULDN'T HAVE BELIEVED IT OF STEVE! BUT I SUPPOSE IT'S MY OWN FAULT –
8

CONGRATULATIONS, STEVE! MRS. VANDERGILT CERTAINLY IS PRETTY. SHE'S REMARKABLY YOUNG LOOKING FOR HER AGE!
NOW, DI, DON'T BE CATTY – MARGO'S ONLY 30.

I MUST FIND OUT WHAT BEAUTY PARLOR MARGO USES. SHE SIMPLY CAN'T BE 30! BUT STEVE IS RIGHT, SHE IS – HER LIFE HISTORY'S IN OUR BLACKMAIL CASE FILE. HM, I WONDER!

BY THE WAY, STEVE, DID YOU TAKE THE BLACKMAIL CASE FOLDER OUT OF THIS FILE?
WHY-ER-YES, I DID. AND I REGRET TO SAY IT'S LOST.
BUT, STEVE, THAT FOLDER CONTAINED ALL OUR EVIDENCE AGAINST "EARS" FELLOCK AND HIS GANG!
YES, I KNOW. MARGO OFFERED TO HELP ME CHECK THE EVIDENCE, SO I TOOK IT TO HER HOUSE.
WHILE WE WERE-ER-TALKING, SOMEONE, PROBABLY "EARS'" AGENT, PINCHED THE FOLDER. BUT DON'T WORRY-MARGO'LL HELP ME CONVICT THE GANG AFTER WE'RE MARRIED. I'LL SHOW WONDER WOMAN I'M NOT TIED TO HER APRON STRINGS!
COMES THE FATEFUL DAY OF STEVE'S WEDDING, AND WONDER WOMAN, URGENTLY INVITED, PREPARES TO ATTEND.
I DISTRUST THAT SLY, "SLICK PRETTY" STEVE IS MARRYING!
I SUPPOSE I'M JEALOUS-I MUST CONTROL MYSELF! IF, ACCORDING TO AMAZON LAW, I CAN'T MARRY STEVE, I'VE NO RIGHT TO STAND IN ANOTHER WOMAN'S WAY-OH-OH! THERE'S PAULA ON THE MENTAL RADIO
CALLING WONDER WOMAN!
CAPT. BLANK, THE SUICIDE YOU BROUGHT BACK TO LIFE HAS RECOVERED FULL CONSCIOUSNESS. HE HAS IMPORTANT INFORMATION —
I'D BETTER SEE HIM — IF I HURRY, I CAN STILL MAKE THE WEDDING.
FLASHING AT TERRIFIC SPEED, THE AMAZON MAID QUICKLY REACHES PAULA'S SECRET LABORATORY.
HOLA, PRINCESS! YOUR PATIENT IS READY TO TALK.
IT WAS MARGO WHO WORMED THE SECRET INFORMATION OUT OF ME - SHE MUST HAVE TOLD FELLOCK - SHE MUST BELONG TO HIS GANG -
GREAT MINERVA! IF I'D ONLY KNOWN THIS BEFORE! NOW IT'S PROBABLY TOO LATE.
9

SECONDS LATER THE WEDDING GUESTS IN THE VANDERGILT MANSION ARE ASTOUNDED TO SEE WONDER WOMAN LEAP OVER THEM UP THE STAIRS.
BRIDE'S STILL DRESSING — I'LL CATCH HER IN HER ROOM —

THAT'S MRS. VANDERGILT'S PRIVATE ROOM — NOBODY CAN GO IN THERE—
THANKS FOR THE TIP, BUDDY — HOW EXTRAORDINARY TO HAVE A BANK VAULT DOOR ON A BEDROOM!

THE BRIDE, ATTENDED BY A STRANGELY CRIPPLED MAID, SURVEYS HER COSTUME.
YOUR BRACES WILL REMAIN LOCKED UNTIL - HUH? WHAT'S THIS?

SORRY TO INTRUDE AT SUCH AN EXCITING MOMENT, MARGO, BUT YOUR GAME'S UP! YOU'RE A MEMBER OF "EARS" FELLOCK'S GANG — YOU PUT ON AN ACT PRETENDING TO BE BLACKMAILED TO FOOL TREVOR, BUT NOW YOU'RE THROUGH!

DON'T BE ABSURD! I LOVE STEVE — I —
YOU'RE MARRYING MAJOR TREVOR TO USE HIM! ALREADY YOU'VE STOLEN THE EVIDENCE AGAINST YOUR GANG, AND YOU HOPE TO GET MORE INFORMATION FROM STEVE TO BLACKMAIL OTHER VICTIMS!

YOU'RE CLEVER, MY DEAR! LET'S DISCUSS THIS IN A FRIENDLY WAY — HAVE A CIGARET?
NO, THANKS. DON'T SMOKE. NOW LISTEN—

PRESSING A SECRET CATCH, MARGO SHOOTS THE "CIGARET" INTO WONDER WOMAN'S FACE.
YOU MAY NOT SMOKE, DARLING, BUT YOU MUST INHALE MY LITTLE GAS BOMB. HA HA!
POUFF!

WONDER WOMAN WAKES IN STRANGE COMPANY.
DON'T MOVE OR YOU'LL BLOW US BOTH TO BITS! WE'RE BOOBY-TRAPPED!
UH! WHAT!

BUT - BUT YOU ARE MARGO!
I'M THE REAL MRS. VANDERGILT. THE FELLOCK GANG KIDNAPPED ME. THEIR MOLL, CORINE, IS MY DOUBLE. I'VE BEEN KEPT PRISONER IN THESE BRACES TO SIGN CHECKS AND LEGAL PAPERS WHICH CORINE COULDN'T DO, OF COURSE!
GREAT HERA! STEVE IS BEING MARRIED TO CORINE THIS VERY MINUTE! I CAN'T RISK POOR MARGO'S LIFE BY BREAKING MY BONDS— APHRODITE, HELP ME!--- I'LL RADIO THE HOLLIDAY GIRLS—

BY GOOD LUCK ETTA GETS WONDER WOMAN'S MESSAGE PROMPTLY.
WOO WOO! THE CHIEF'S IN HOT WATER AGAIN AN' CALLIN' HER TRUSTY COHORTS! COME, KIDS- WE GOT WORK TO DO!

RUSHING TO THE VANDERGILT HOUSE, THE HOLLIDAY GANG GO TO WORK ON THE ELECTRIC SUPPLY CABLE.
I DON'T KNOW WHY WONDER WOMAN WANTS THE WIRE CUT, BUT THAR SHE BLOWS!
SNIPP!

WONDER WOMAN, MEANWHILE, LYING MOTIONLESS, WATCHES THE ELECTRIC LIGHT.
WHEN THAT LIGHT GOES OUT, IT'LL MEAN THE CURRENT'S CUT AND THE BOMB CAN'T EXPLODE - THEN I'LL BREAK MY BONDS!

BUT THE MIGHTY AMAZON, MOVING FASTER THAN LIGHT, FREES HERSELF A SPLIT SECOND TOO SOON - A TINY FUSE SPARK CREEPS TO THE HIGH EXPLOSIVE.

AS THE BOMB EXPLODES, WONDER WOMAN SEIZES THE HELPLESS MARGO IN HER ARMS AND LEAPS STRAIGHT UP THROUGH THE CEILING.
BOOM

BY ODD COINCIDENCE, WONDER WOMAN'S LEAP CARRIES HER INTO THE MIDST OF THE MARRIAGE CEREMONY.
DO YOU TAKE THIS WOMAN TO BE YOUR WIFE?
I—
DON'T!

IF YOU STILL WANT TO MARRY MARGO VANDERGILT, STEVE — HERE SHE IS!
I DON'T - SHE DOES - WE'RE NOT - OH BLAZES! WHAT'S THE USE? I'VE MADE A COMPLETE FOOL OF MYSELF!

OUTSIDE, MEANWHILE, THE HOLLIDAY GIRLS CAPTURE "EARS" AND HIS GANG ATTEMPTING ESCAPE.
12

HONEST, BEAUTIFUL, I NEVER REALLY LOVED THAT WITCH, CORINE - I ONLY WANTED TO SHOW YOU -
YOU DID SHOW ME, STEVE - THAT I SHOULD NEVER LEAVE YOU ALONE WITH A PRETTY GIRL!
MORE ADVENTURES OF WONDER WOMAN IN EVERY ISSUE OF SENSATION COMICS.

Wonder Woman
By CHARLES MOULTON
A VICIOUS GANG OF COUNTERFEITERS THREATEN THE SECURITY OF THE UNITED STATES MONETARY SYSTEM. MILLIONS OF PEOPLE WILL BE RUINED, OUR WHOLE COUNTRY POVERTY STRICKEN IF THESE CULPRITS ARE NOT STOPPED!
YOU'LL CHEER LOUDER THAN EVER FOR THE ALLURING AMAZON PRINCESS, BEAUTIFUL AS APHRODITE, WISE AS ATHENA, SWIFTER THAN MERCURY, AND STRONGER THAN HERCULES, WHEN SHE UNCOVERS....
"THE CRIME OF BOSS BREKEL!"
1
ETTA CANDY BURSTS INTO DIANA (WONDER WOMAN) PRINCE'S APARTMENT—
WHEE! I SOLD ALL MY TICKETS FOR OUR CHARITY BALL. LOOK—I MADE $100!
BUT, ETTA, THAT'S A COUNTERFEIT BILL!

WHERE DID YOU GET IT?
SOME MAN SAID HE'D BUY MY LAST TWO TICKETS. HE HAD ONLY A $100 BILL, SO I GAVE HIM $95 IN SMALL BILLS FOR CHANGE.
100

OH WOE! ARE YOU SURE IT'S COUNTERFEIT, DI?
ABSOLUTE-LY. THIS ISN'T GOVERNMENT PAPER. IN ALL REGULAR GOVERNMENT BILLS YOU CAN ALWAYS SPOT TINY RED AND BLUE SILKEN THREADS. THERE AREN'T ANY IN THIS BILL.

SAY, I THOUGHT YOUR EYESIGHT WAS BAD. WHY YOU'D HAVE T'HAVE WONDER WOMAN'S EYES TO NOTICE THAT SO FAST AND—
ER— DON'T BE SILLY, ETTA! IT'S JUST THAT I'VE MADE A DE-TAILED STUDY OF COUN-TERFEIT MON-EY.
100

THIS IS AWFUL! I'M GONNA CALL THE SECRET SERVICE—

BUT SUDDENLY A BULLET WHIZZES THROUGH THE OPEN WINDOW MARKING ETTA FOR CERTAIN DEATH—
GREAT HERA! WONDER WOMAN HAD BETTER GO INTO ACTION!
ZING

PING
ZING
2

WOO! WOO! WONDER WOMAN, THAT WAS A CLOSE SHAVE. HEY, WHERE IS DI?
SHE WENT AFT-ER THE GUNNER. I'LL TAKE A SHORTCUT—

OOOF!

DO YOU SHOOT PEOPLE FOR A HOBBY OR ARE YOU LOOKING OUT FOR THE INTERESTS OF YOUR COUNTERFEITING GANG?
HOLD ON, WONDER WOMAN— I'M SPEED FERRETT, SECRET AGENT. HERE'S MY IDENTIFICATION.

THERE'S YOUR KILLER. HE'S LOUIE, THE LUG, GUNMAN FOR THE COUNTERFEITING GANG. I SHADOWED HIM HERE—
OH— MY MISTAKE— I WAS SHADOWING HIS BULLET.

YOUR SECRET SERVICE CHIEF WARNED ARMY INTELLIGENCE THAT COUNTERFEIT BILLS ARE IN CIRCULATION— I'M WONDER WOMAN AND—
OF COURSE— EVERYBODY KNOWS WONDER WOMAN! YOU'LL BE A GREAT HELP TO ME— A VERY GREAT HELP—

I FOUND A PAPER IN LOUIE'S POCKET GIVING THE HEADQUARTERS OF THE DISTRIBUTERS OF THE COUNTERFEIT MONEY. WITH YOUR HELP WE CAN NAB THE GANG SINGLE-HANDED.

LET'S GO!

JUST A SEC, WONDER WOMAN. I'D BETTER NOTIFY THE COPS TO PICK UP LOUIE'S REMAINS.
AND I'D BETTER SEND A MENTAL RADIO MESSAGE TO ETTA—

WONDER WOMAN AND SPEED FERRETT CAUTIOUSLY APPROACH THE COUNTERFEIT MONEY DISTRIBUTERS' HIDEOUT—
THERE'S THE WAREHOUSE—

I HEAR MEN'S VOICES—
GOOD—WE'LL GIVE THEM A LITTLE SURPRISE PARTY—

4.

I HATE TO DO THIS, BUT IT'S NECESSARY—

LOOK OUT BEHIND YOU, WONDER WOMAN!

WHY YOU DIRTY, DOUBLE----
UGHHHHH!
BANG

SPEED, YOU SAVED MY LIFE! I'M VERY GRATEFUL-
YOU'RE VERY BEAUTIFUL, WONDER WOMAN, AND -ER- IMPORTANT. NOTHING MUST HAPPEN TO YOU!

I'VE NEVER MET ANY WOMAN AS WONDERFUL AS YOU -
YOU'RE VERY SWEET, SPEED, BUT REMEMBER- WE STILL HAVE TO CATCH THE COUNTERFEITERS.
WELL!
HA HA! WHATTA YUH KNOW!

OH-ER-HELLO--STEVE AND--ER-GIRLS--ER-UH, SPEED, I MENTAL RADIOED ETTA WHILE YOU WERE TELEPHONING THE POLICE AND TOLD HER WE WERE COMING HERE-
5

YEAH- THEN ETTA CALLED ME- TOLD ME YOU WERE IN DANGER- THAT YOU MIGHT NEED HELP- BUT IT LOOKS LIKE YOU HAD PLENTY OF HELP. SPEED CERTAINLY LIVES UP TO HIS NAME!

STOP BEING THE JEALOUS MALE, STEVE. SPEED FERRETT IS A SECRET SERVICE AGENT. AND WHAT'S MORE HE JUST SAVED MY LIFE—
THAT'S FINE! I'M GLAD I'M LEAVING YOU IN CAPABLE HANDS.

CONGRATULATIONS, FERRETT! YOU SHOULD BE PUT ON EXHIBITION AS THE ONE EXCEPTION TO AMAZON LAW! GOOD-BYE!
STEVE, WAIT-
LET HIM GO. REMEMBER, WE HAVE A JOB TO FINISH.
WOO! WOO! I'M GONNA KEEP MY AFFECTIONS CENTERED ON CANDY. YUH CAN'T HAVE A LOVERS' QUARREL WITH CANDY!
NO, BUT YOU CAN GET AWFUL STOMACH ACHES!

THE THUGS WHO "PASS THE QUEER" ESCAPED AND THEY'RE SURE TO TIP OFF THE BIG BOSS AND THE ENGRAVERS THAT WE'RE HOT ON THEIR TRAIL—

ON THESE SHEETS OF PAPER ARE DESCRIPTIONS OF THE MEN SUSPECTED OF BEING IN THE COUNTERFEIT RACKET AND THEIR FAVORITE HANGOUTS—

EACH OF YOU SHADOW ONE MAN AND SEE HOW MUCH INFORMATION YOU CAN GET—
WOO WOO! GET YOUR MAN, GIRLS!
WE'LL MEET LATER AT DI'S APARTMENT.
6.

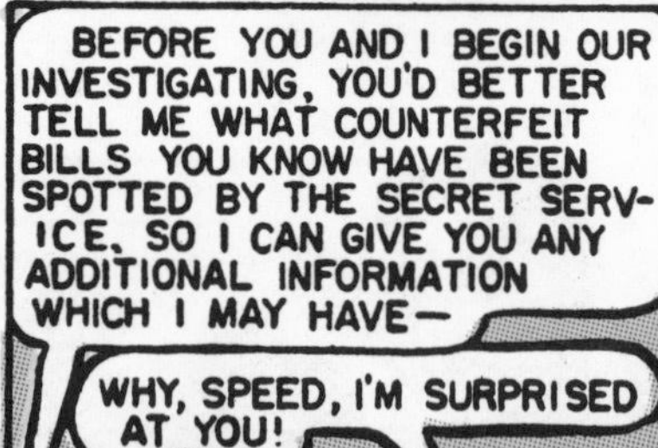
BEFORE YOU AND I BEGIN OUR INVESTIGATING, YOU'D BETTER TELL ME WHAT COUNTERFEIT BILLS YOU KNOW HAVE BEEN SPOTTED BY THE SECRET SERVICE, SO I CAN GIVE YOU ANY ADDITIONAL INFORMATION WHICH I MAY HAVE—

WHY, SPEED, I'M SURPRISED AT YOU!

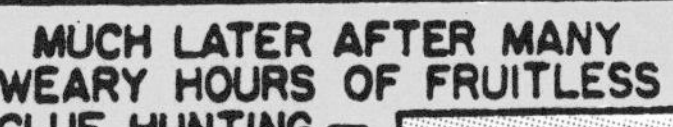
WONDER WOMAN

YOU KNOW WE'RE FORBIDDEN TO REPEAT THAT INFORMATION—
OH-ER-YES -OF COURSE. YOU **ARE** EXTRAORDINARY! A WOMAN WHO CAN ACTUALLY KEEP A SECRET!

MUCH LATER AFTER MANY WEARY HOURS OF FRUITLESS CLUE HUNTING—
THE GIRLS ARE LATE—HOPE NOTHING'S HAPPENED TO THEM. THERE'S THE PHONE—
RRRINNNNG!

WONDER WOMAN, ALL US GIRLS HAVE BEEN CAPTURED BY THE COUNTERFEIT GANG, THEY SAY THEY'LL KILL US IF YOU DON'T SURRENDER TO THEM AT THE FORK IN THE OLD MILL ROAD—BUT DON'T DO IT—

WHAT'S WRONG? NOT BAD NEWS I HOPE—
THE COUNTERFEITERS HAVE CAPTURED THE HOLLIDAY GIRLS. I HAVE TO SURRENDER TO THEM OR THE GIRLS WILL BE KILLED!

NO! I WON'T LET YOU DO IT. THEY WILL KILL YOU **AND** THE GIRLS!
I'LL HAVE TO TAKE THAT CHANCE. IF I DON'T SURRENDER, THE GANGSTERS CAN EASILY KILL THE GIRLS BEFORE I FIND THEM—

YOU ARE BRAVE—BUT DON'T WORRY, DEAREST, I'LL SEE TO IT THAT NEITHER YOU NOR THE GIRLS'LL BE HARMED!
I KNOW I CAN DEPEND ON YOU TO DO ALL YOU CAN FOR US, SPEED. BUT I'D BETTER GO!
7

AT THE DESIGNATED SPOT, THE LOVELY AMAZON PRINCESS HAS ONLY A SHORT TIME TO WAIT FOR HER CAPTORS—
YOUSE DIDN'T WASTE NO TIME! WE'RE GONTA BLINDFOLD YOUSE AND TIE YOUSE UP WID YER MAGIC LASSO—BOSS' ORDERS!

MEANWHILE AT INTELLIGENCE HEADQUARTERS—
BLAZES! WHY DID I LOSE MY HEAD AND ACT LIKE A JEALOUS FOOL? AND WHY HAVEN'T I HEARD SOMETHING FROM WONDER WOMAN AND THE GIRLS? MAYBE THEY'RE IN DANGER—

THOSE COUNTERFEITERS ARE SLICK MUGS—THEY MAY HAVE SET A TRAP—I'M GOING TO CALL SECRET SERVICE HEADQUARTERS AND CHECK UP ON A FEW THINGS—

MEANTIME, WONDER WOMAN IS DRIVEN TO AN ISOLATED, BUT CHARMING SUMMER COTTAGE ALONG THE RIVER'S EDGE—
SPUD, YOUSE LUG TH' DAME INTO DE CELLAR—
OKAY—CARRYIN' DIS EYEFUL AROUND AIN'T HARD TA TAKE!

WHERE ARE YOU TAKING ME?
INTO DE MOST PROSPEROUS CELLARS IN DE COUNTRY--- WHERE WE TOIN OUT THOUSANDS OF DOLLARS!

I GOT WONDER WOMAN, BOSS. WHAT'LL I DO WID HER?
TAKE THE BLINDFOLD OFF AND CARRY HER INTO THE SHOP.
8

THE COUNTERFEITERS' CHIEF SPEAKS FROM BEHIND A SCREEN.
YOU SEEM AMAZED AND RIGHTLY SO. ON THOSE PRESSES WE TURN OUT EVERY DENOMINATION OF PAPER MONEY SO PERFECTLY ONLY THE MOST EXPERIENCED EYE CAN DETECT IT IS COUNTERFEIT.

WHERE ARE THE HOLLIDAY GIRLS? WHAT'VE YOU DONE TO THEM?

THEY'RE SAFE AND WILL REMAIN SO - IF YOU COOPERATE! TELL ME WHICH OF OUR COUNTERFEIT BILLS HAVE BEEN SPOTTED BY THE SECRET SERVICE AND WHAT WERE THE DEFECTS IN THE BILLS!

I'LL NEVER TELL. IF YOU COUNTERFEITERS ARE PERMITTED TO GET AWAY WITH YOUR VICIOUS RACKET, THE WHOLE. U.S. MONETARY SYSTEM WILL BE RUINED!

WHEN YOU WATCH YOUR GIRLFRIENDS ABOUT TO PLUNGE TO THEIR DEATH IN A MOST UNFORTUNATE ACCIDENT, YOU MAY FEEL MORE TALKATIVE, **WONDER WOMAN**. TAKE HER OUTSIDE, SPUD!

MEANWHILE—
I HOPE THE SECRET SERVICE WAS RIGHT ABOUT BOSS BREKEL'S HIDEOUT— AND THAT WE'RE IN TIME!
THEY WOULDN'T HAVE ASKED ARMY INTELLIGENCE TO HELP UNLESS THEY KNEW THE SITUATION WAS DESPERATE—

AND AT THIS MOMENT, **WONDER WOMAN** LEARNS THE COUNTERFEITERS' FIENDISH PLAN TO COLD-BLOODEDLY MURDER THE HOLLIDAY GIRLS.
YOUR PALS IS IN DAT CAR— BOUND HAND AND FOOT! AN' WHATTA YUH KNOW— DE BRIDGE IS MOVIN'—
9

WHEN DE CAR NEARS DE END OF DE BRIDGE, OUR MEN'LL JUMP OUT AND YER FRIENDS'LL BE DROWNED!

BUT ONE OF OUR MEN IS OPERATIN' DE BRIDGE SO IF YOUSE GIVES OUT WID DE INFORMATION, WE'LL TELEPHONE HIM TA STOP TOININ' DE BRIDGE!

MERCIFUL MINERVA! THE GIRLS ARE TIED UP IN THAT CAR —! — OH APHRODITE, HELP ME!

WONDER WOMAN'S PRAYER IS ANSWERED — THE ARMY INTELLIGENCE AND SECRET SERVICE MEN REACH THE COTTAGE —

THANK APHRODITE YOU'VE COME! UNTIE ME QUICKLY, STEVE!

BLAZES BUT I WORRIED ABOUT YOU, ANGEL—
I'M ALL RIGHT, BUT ETTA AND THE HOLLIDAY GIRLS WON'T BE. OH HURRY, STEVE!
10.

FREED FROM HER BONDS, WONDER WOMAN LASSOS THE BRIDGE WITH AMAZON SUPER-ACCURACY.

AS THE CAR HURTLES OFF THE BRIDGE, THE GANGSTERS JUMP TO SAFETY—

THE COURAGEOUS AMAZON MAID MAKES A DEATH-DEFYING DIVE OFF THE BRIDGE—
TOMATOES
11.

AND PLUNGES TO THE BOTTOM OF THE RIVER.

SPRINGING UPWARD FROM THE RIVER BOTTOM TO THE SURFACE, THE AMAZING PRINCESS CATCHES THE FALLING CAR AND—

EASILY HOLDING TONS OF STEEL WITH ONE HAND, THE HERCULEAN AMAZON ATHLETE SWIMS ACROSS THE RIVER WITH LIGHTNING SWIFTNESS.

GAILY WE SING OF THE PRINCESS SO BRAVE, WHO SAVED ALL US GIRLS FROM A WATERY GRAVE! RAH! RAH! WONDER WOMAN!

WONDER WOMAN SETS DOWN THE CAR AND—

YOUR GREAT LOVER IS BOSS BREKEL, BRAINS OF THE COUNTERFEITERS. HE SHOT AT ETTA, KILLED THE REAL SPEED FERRETT, TOOK HIS PAPERS, AND CONVINCED YOU OF HIS FALSE IDENTITY. LATER HE KILLED A MEMBER OF HIS GANG SO YOU'D THINK HE SAVED YOUR LIFE.
PLUTO TAKE ME FOR A FOOL—FOR TRUSTING A MAN!
12

WHEN I CALLED SECRET SERVICE, ANGEL, THEY RECOGNIZED YOUR "SPEED FERRETT"—
NOT MY SPEED, STEVE—WHEN HE GRABBED ME I FOUND HIS ARMS WEREN'T HALF AS STRONG AS YOURS—

OH! YOU'RE EVEN STRONGER THAN I REMEMBERED—
MORE ADVENTURES OF WONDER WOMAN IN EVERY ISSUE OF SENSATION COMICS!

BIBLIOGRAPHY

ANCIENT GREEK AND ROMAN SOURCES

The following is a selected list of Greek and Roman writers—poets, historians, geographers, philosophers—who have contributed to our knowledge of Amazons. The dates that accompany each represent the period of greatest productivity.

Aeschylus, 480 B.C.
Apollodorus, 150 B.C.
Apollodorus, 100 A.D. (?)
Apollonious Rhodius, 265 B.C.
Appianus, 105 A.D. (?)
Arctinus of Miletus, 650 B.C. (?)
Diodorus Siculus, 20 B.C.
Dionysius Scythobrachian, 30 B.C.
Ephorus, 350 B.C.
Eusebius, 320 A.D.
Hellanicos, 460 B.C.
Herodotus, 440 B.C.
Hesiod, 720 B.C. (?)
Hippocrates, 420 B.C.
Homer, 820 B.C. (?)
Isocrates, 400 B.C.
Megasthenes, 300 B.C.
Pausanias, 140 A.D.
Pherecydes, 460 B.C.
Philostrates, 210 A.D.
Plato, 390 B.C.
Pliny the Elder, 20 A.D.
Plutarch, 80 A.D.
Pompeius Trogus, 20 B.C.
Polybius, 160 B.C.
Sappho, 612 B.C.
Strabo, 20 B.C.
Tacitus, 100 A.D.
Thucydides, 430 B.C.
Virgil, 40 B.C.
Quintus Smyrnus, 350 A.D.
Xenophon, 400 B.C.

EUROPEAN SOURCES: SIXTEENTH, SEVENTEENTH, AND EIGHTEENTH CENTURY

From the time of the Roman Empire, but especially during the sixteenth and seventeenth centuries, European explorers, soldiers, travelers, chroniclers, and priests wrote about female warriors, chiefs, queens, and priestesses encountered in the European Caucasus and the Middle East, in India, Africa, and the Americas. These travelers also documented the almost universal native (i.e., non-European) belief in the existence of a legendary Amazon tribe or state. Among them:

SIXTEENTH CENTURY

Father Francisco Alvarez, Abyssinia
Father Christobal D'Acuña, Brazil
Father Jao Bermudez, Abyssinia
Francisco de Carbajal, Peru and Brazil
Juan de la Cosa, Orinoco River
Nuno de Gusman, Brazil
Francisco de Orellana, Brazil
Antonio Pigafetta, Congo
Sir Walter Ralegh, Guiana
Father Jaos dos Santos, Abyssinia
Lopez Vaz, Peru and Brazil
Garcilaso (el Inca) de la Vega, Peru and Brazil

SEVENTEENTH CENTURY

Sir John Cartwright, European Caucasus
Father Giovanni Antonio Cavazzi, Ethiopia
Sir John Chardin, European Caucasus
Father Gili, Guiana
Anthony Knivet, Brazil
Father Angelo Lamberti, European Caucasus
Hernando de Ribera, Peru

EIGHTEENTH CENTURY

Gilbert Charles le Gendre, European Caucasus
Charles Marie de La Condamine, Peru and Brazil
Joseph François Lafitau, North America
Jacob Reineggs, European Caucasus

EUROPEAN AND AMERICAN SOURCES: NINETEENTH AND TWENTIETH CENTURY

Bachofen, J. J. *Myth, Religion, and Mother-Right*. Bollingen Series, vol. LXXIV. Princeton, N.J.: Princeton University Press, 1967. (First published in three volumes in Switzerland in the nineteenth century.)

Briffault, Robert. *The Mothers*. New York: Grosset and Dunlap, Universal Library, 1963. (First published in 1927.)

Burton, Sir Richard. *A Mission to Gelele, King of Dahome*. New York: Praeger Publishers, 1966. (First published in 1864.)

Clarke, John H. *The Black Woman: A Figure in World History*. Unpublished ms., 1972.

Curtis, Edmund. *A History of Ireland*. London: Methuen, 1950.

Davis, Elizabeth Gould. *The First Sex*. New York: G. P. Putnam, 1971.

Dillon, Myles and Chadwick, Nora. *The Celtic Realms*. New York: New American Library 1967.

Diner, Helen. *Mothers and Amazons: The First Feminine History of Culture*. New York: The Julian Press, 1965. (First published in Austria in the 1930's.)

Evans, Sir Arthur. *The Earliest Religions of Greece in the Light of Cretan Discoveries*. The Frazer Lecture. London, 1931.

________. *The Palace of Minos at Knossos*. London, 1921.

Forsdyke, Sir John. *Greece Before Homer: Ancient Chronology and Mythology*. New York: W. W. Norton, 1964.

Gibbon, Edward. *The Decline and Fall of the Roman Empire*. New York: W. W. Norton, 1967. (First published in several volumes between 1776 and 1788.)

Graves, Robert. *The White Goddess: A Historical Grammar of Poetic Myth*. New York: Farrar, Straus and Giroux, 1970. (First published in 1948.)

________. *The Greek Myths*. New York: Penguin Books, 1964.

Harrison, Jane E. *Prolegomena to the Study of Greek Religion*. New Hyde Park, N.Y.: University Books, 1962. (First published in 1922.)

Hergeon, Jacques. *Daily Life of the Etruscans*. New York: Macmillan, 1964.

Jung, C. G. and Kerenyi, C. *Essays on a Science of Mythology. The Myth of the Divine Child and the Mysteries of Eleusis*. Bollingen Series, vol. XXII. Princeton, N.J.: Princeton University Press, 1971.

Kantor, Emanuel. *The Amazons: A Marxian Study*. Chicago, Ill.: Charles H. Kerr, 1926.

Kerenyi, C. *Eleusis: Archetypal Image of Mother and Daughter*. Translated by Ralph Manheim. Bollingen Series, vol. LXV, No. 4. New York: Pantheon Books, 1967.

MacManus, Sheumas. *The Story of the Irish Race*. Old Greenwich, Conn.: Devin-Adair, 1944.

Morgan, Henry Lewis. *Ancient Society*. London, 1877.

Murray, Margaret A. *The Splendor That Was Egypt*. New York: Hawthorn Books, 1963.

Pankhurst, Sylvia. *Ethiopia: A Cultural History*. Woodford Green, Essex: Lalibela House, 1959.

Payne, Elizabeth. *The Pharaohs of Ancient Egypt*. New York: Random House, 1964.

Neumann, Erich. *The Great Mother: An Analysis of the Archetype*. Bollingen Series, vol. XLVII. New York: Pantheon Books, 1955.

Reeves, Nancy. *Womankind: Beyond the Stereotypes*. Chicago-New York: Aldine-Atherton Press, 1971.

Rothery, Guy Cadogan. *The Amazons in Antiquity and Modern Times*. London: Francis Griffiths, 1910.

Slater, Philip E. *The Glory of Hera: Greek Mythology and the Greek Family*. Boston: Beacon Press, 1971.

Von Puttkamer, Jescoe and Sales, Altair. *Time*, December 27, 1971.

Wells, Evelyn. *Hatshepsut*. New York: Doubleday, 1969.

Wittig, Monique. *Les Guerilleres*. New York: Viking Press, 1969.